5-
r

THE
BISHOPS'
PROGRESS

Smithsonian Series in Ethnographic Inquiry
William L. Merrill and Ivan Karp, Series Editors

Enthnography as fieldwork, analysis, and literary form is the distinguishing feature of modern anthropology. Guided by the assumption that anthropological theory and ethnography are inextricably linked, this series is devoted to exploring the ethnographic enterprise.

ADVISORY BOARD

THE BISHOPS' PROGRESS

A
Historical Ethnography
of
Catholic Missionary Experience
on
the Sepik Frontier
by
Mary Taylor Huber

SMITHSONIAN INSTITUTION PRESS
WASHINGTON AND LONDON

This book was edited by Carol Clark and designed by Linda McKnight.

Library of Congress Cataloging-in-Publication Data

Huber, Mary Taylor, 1944–
   The bishops' progress.

   Bibliography: p.
   1. Society of the Divine Word—Missions—Papua
New Guinea—East Sepik Province.   2. Catholic
Church—Missions—Papua New Guinea—East Sepik
Province.   3. Missions—Anthropological aspects.   I.
Title.
BV3680.N5H8   1988   266′.2953   87-23562
ISBN 0-87474-544-6

British Library Cataloging-in-Publication Data is
available.

⊗ The Paper used in this publication meets the minimum
requirements of the American National Standard for
Permanence of Paper for Printed Library Materials
Z39.48-1984.

Contents

Preface

It is a fact proven to me many times over, that an anthropologist who claims to be studying missionaries will likely be misunderstood.

Let me make clear from the start, then, that this book is less about the changes to which missionaries have contributed in the Sepik region of Papua New Guinea, than about how missionaries' experience of living and working there changed the mission project itself. *The Bishops' Progress* is about how, through missionaries' accommodations to frontier conditions, the Catholic church in the Sepik acquired some of its locally specific forms.

Unlike Bunyan's allegorical Christian, whose story the title of this book recalls, real missionaries must respond to local conditions to be effective, often at the cost of departing from other goals. This dilemma gives missionary experience an ironic dimension that I explore in this book. The title, in fact, refers not only to what was "going forward" in different periods of mission history, but also to some of the rhetorical means by which missionaries managed the inevitable contradictions between local imperatives and metropolitan ideals.

My thinking about missionaries has been affected most deeply by T. O. Beidelman, whose theoretically developed treatment of the ambiguities of colonial evangelism inspired this book. I am also indebted to Paul Fussell's elegant study, *The Great War and Modern Memory* (1975), for insight into "the simultaneous and reciprocal process by which life feeds materials to literature while literature returns the favor by conferring forms upon life" (1975:ix).

It is a pleasure to have the opportunity to thank in print a number of scholars who have provided advice, criticism, and encouragement over the years. Ivan Karp has read and critiqued my work on missionaries in all stages of preparation; without his initiative, theoretical insight, and support, this book would not have been written. Carl Thune, Ivan Karp, Richard Scaglion, and Linda Layne have been demanding critics and patient friends. T. O. Beidelman's comments on an early draft of the manuscript were invaluable for the task of revision, as were those of William Burrows, who read the manuscript from a theologian's and former missionary's point of view. Paul Roscoe and Father John Tschauder, SVD, provided special help on the fine points of Sepik and mission history. I would also like to thank John Barker, Kenelm Burridge, James Fernandez, Hildred Geertz, and Richard Huntington who read earlier papers I had written on missionaries and whose comments encouraged me to persevere.

The Bishops' Progress is a revision of my doctoral dissertation, and I owe a special debt of gratitude to professors Alexander Spoehr, Keith Brown, and Richard Scaglion, who served successively as chair of my dissertation committee at the University of Pittsburgh. I also am grateful to the Wenner-Gren Foundation for the opportunity to present my work to colleagues at a stimulating conference, "Sepik Research Today," in Basel, Switzerland, in 1984. *The American Ethnologist* gave me the opportunity to rewrite that paper for publication, and to receive helpful criticism from two anonymous reviewers just as I was preparing the manuscript for this book. I thank Daniel Goodwin at the Smithsonian Institution Press for his care and attention to my manuscript, and Carol Clark for her sensitive editorial work.

My fieldwork in Wewak, Papua New Guinea, was conducted from 1976 to 1977, and was funded by a research grant from the National Science Foundation (BNS-15269), a Mellon predoctoral fellowship from the University of Pittsburgh, my family's own resources, and by my mother, Rachel N. Taylor, who also accompanied us in the field. Peter Huber's anthropological imagination and companionship contributed greatly to this field experience. Our sons, Birkett and Benjamin, probably cannot remember when their mother was not either planning fieldwork, doing it, or writing the results.

Finally, I would like to thank the people of Koil Island who hosted our large household at their settlement in Wewak, the many other friends we made in Papua New Guinea and, especially, the Catholic missionaries whose project is the subject of this book.

CHAPTER I

Introduction
Ethnography in the Ironic Mode

The singularity of a "vocation" is never better displayed than when it is contradicted—but not denied, far from it—by a prosaic incarnation: this is an old trick of all hagiography.

—ROLAND BARTHES

So far, no saints have emerged in the history of Catholic missionization of Papua New Guinea. Yet, there have been persons about whom tales, if not legends, have been spun. If you talk to Catholic missionaries along the north coast region of Papua New Guinea, where the Society of the Divine Word has been working since 1896, you will no doubt hear about the frontier pilot, Leo Arkfeld, who presided over the Diocese of Wewak as "the flying bishop" from the late 1940s to the late 1970s, and who is still flying as the Archbishop of Madang today. If you have an interest in the history of the region and read memoirs from the 1920s and 1930s, you will come across Joseph Loerks, the boat captain, who was known as "the fighting bishop" in the Sepik region during the interwar years. If you go back a bit further, you will come across stories of the mission's first leader, Eberhard Limbrock, who became known as "the man of Providence," after his controversial system of mission plantations and industries enabled the missionaries to continue their work in the region when they were cut off from Europe during World War I.

This book is about Catholic missionaries of the Society of the Divine Word in the Sepik region of Papua New Guinea, about some of the

The epigraph at the head of this chapter is from
Roland Barthes's *Mythologies* (New York: Hill and
Wang, 1972), 31.

I

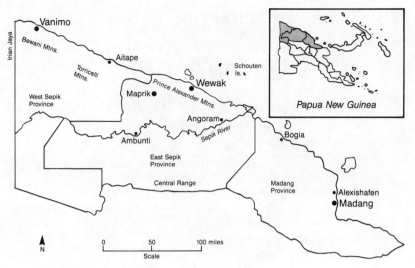

Figure 1. The East Sepik Province and Its Neighbors.

directions their work has taken, and about some of the images in which they have represented their work over a period of eighty years. This study focuses on aspects of mission practice that have emerged in response to the locale, and on "prosaic" images, like those above, in which missionaries have reconciled locally effective practice with ecclesiastical ideals. Like other anthropologists who have studied missions, I examine ironies in the missionary situation. Yet, I am particularly interested in how missionaries themselves have used such gaps and incongruities to define the special character of their project and of their particular mission field.

ANTHROPOLOGISTS AND MISSIONARIES

Missionaries are portrayed as veritable tricksters in anthropologists' field lore. On the one hand, missionary stories frequently portray their protagonists as ineffectual or unenlightened; on the other hand, missionaries are often singled out as having effected change on a grand, or even cosmic, scale. Of course, human activity often leads to unexpected consequences, and people are often unable to live up to their ideals. Many poignant records of both the comic and the tragic aspects of the human condition are contained in the literature—oral and written, fact and fiction—of European colonialism. Yet, of all the parties to the imperial enterprise, missionaries seem to have been the most vulnerable, at least among anthropologists, to ironic interpretation. This is probably not because missionaries have acted less honorably or with less wisdom than other figures on the colonial scene, but because missionaries have proclaimed loftier ideals and more inclusive ends. Like bureaucrats who are burdened with an ideal of rational efficiency and cannot help but bungle, missionaries are burdened by their own benevolence and cannot help but fail.

Missionary Stories

Anthropologists are not the only ones who tell missionary stories, but they seem to take them more seriously than others, and have been known to exchange evidence among themselves showing how precipitously missionaries can fall. Their testimony has frequently been offered with some emotion—incredulity about missionaries' lack of sociological competence in the field, hostility towards their unappreciative views on native culture, anger at their insensitive interventions in native life, and satisfaction at signs of native resistance to missionaries' intrusions into their autonomy and self-respect. Because of missionaries' moral stance towards others, stories about missionaries' drunkenness, sexual peccadilloes, and other personal idiosyncrasies elicit easy laughs. Should the people in anthropologists' field communities evince such attitudes towards *their* neighbors, anthropologists would no doubt find it worthy of explanation, but they have seldom seen fit to do so in regard to themselves (Burridge 1978:9). Besides, as Beidelman has observed, anthropologists' vision has often dimmed "with the colour line" when contemplating their experience in the field (1974:235).

This picture of anthropologists' attitudes towards missionaries is perhaps somewhat dated, but it was only as anthropologists grew more reflective about their own project in the early to mid-1970s, that they began to submit their attitudes towards missionaries to more than passing concern.

Certainly no one who has recently turned attention to the matter has been content to suggest that anthropologists' distaste for missionaries has been merely a special case of their traditional distaste for other outsiders on the colonial (or postcolonial) scene.[1] Most commentators have insisted that anthropologists' attitudes towards missionaries have been colored by more subtle tensions, not least because of the close historical connection between the missionary enterprise and ethnology itself. As Kenelm Burridge has noted, "In the suggestion that there were oedipal overtones to Malinowski's attitudes toward missionaries is the implication that the relations between missionaries and anthropologists have in them something profound and elusive" (1978:7).

Certainly, most work on the subject of anthropologist–missionary relations identifies competition vis-à-vis "the people" as *the* significant factor in comprehending the hostility that anthropologists so frequently evince towards missionary "Fathers" in the field. Many manifestations of this conflict have been surveyed: different attitudes towards change; different roles taken by the anthropologist and missionary in native communities; and, different assessments of native religion, culture, and society (Salamone 1977; Stipe 1980). Perhaps what has most distinguished missionaries from other outsiders in the anthropological bestiary, however, is missionaries' claim of moral right to question the morality of another people's way of life—to minister to another people's "soul."[2]

While Burridge has argued that moral critique of *any* established order (including our own) is essential in Christianity (1978:16, 18–19), many anthropologists have taken offense at what often seems an uninformed a priori condemnation of indigenous ways of life. Indeed, even Burridge felt obliged to admit that "there is something about the moral stance of missionaries of whatever denomination, which is totally exasperating" (1978:10). If missionaries style themselves after the biblical shepherd, few anthropologists have cared to have indigenous people styled as sheep. To cross beyond informed exasperation to ethnographic study, however, is a step anthropologists have only begun to take.

The Ethnography of Missionaries

In a 1980 article in *Current anthropology,* George Marcus suggested the need for studying ethnography as a mode of discourse with its own conventions and range of styles, proposing as a model Hayden White's analysis of historiography, *Metahistory: The Historical Imagination in Nineteenth Century Europe* (1973). White's analytical strategy for distinguishing between different styles of historical writing employs the four principal tropes of "traditional poetics and modern language theory . . . Metaphor, Metonymy, Synecdoche, and Irony" (1973:31). These tropes are then used to characterize the ways in which historians have "prefigured" historical fields prior to constructing their narrative accounts. According to White, these means of prefiguration affect not only the initial conception that historians make of their material, but also their final accounts. "In the poetic act which precedes the formal analysis of the field, the historian both creates his object of analysis and predetermines the modality of the conceptual strategies he will use to explain it" (1973:31).

Since Marcus published his article, a whole literature has begun to emerge on the subject of the style and structure of ethnographic texts (Clifford and Marcus 1986; Marcus and Fischer 1986). This is not the place to review this literature, but I do wish to suggest that anthropologists' preanalytical way of "figuring" missionaries, discussed above, has been reflected in the ethnographies about missionaries that anthropologists have begun to produce. Anthropoligists, I would argue, have approached the study of missionaries from a critical stance seldom adopted in their approach to the study of native peoples; thus, unlike most con-

4

ventional ethnographies in anthropology, their accounts tend to be cast in the ironic mode.

The principal characteristic of this literature is a skepticism about the hopes and aspirations on which mission work is founded and about the very nature of the mission project itself. The mission enterprise, it should be noted, is based on a view of history in which transcendence over the usual limits of the social world is not only possible, but enjoined. Although anthropologists have seldom addressed themselves explicitly to this point, their analyses tend to be based on a presumption of the ultimate inadequacy of this vision, especially when encountered among other outsiders on the colonial or postcolonial scene. In more familiar styles of ethnographic writing, we expect (among other things), a sympathetic treatment of the native situation and the native world view. When anthropologists apprehend their subject ironically, however, the native (missionary) view is made problematic, shown as misguided, inadequate, or simply false. As Geertz has noted, "irony rests on a perception of the way in which reality derides merely human views of it, reduces grand attitudes and large hopes to self-mockery" (1968:147).

Consider, for example, Fernandez's early article on the quintessential missionary, Albert Schweitzer (1964), whose highly publicized ideals of service once inspired a huge public in Europe and elsewhere. By 1964, when the "postcolonial" age in Africa had begun, Schweitzer's image had tarnished. However, in 1958, when Fernandez left America to do fieldwork in Gabon, the country in which the Swiss doctor's hospital had been located for nearly fifty years, "Schweitzer was still charisma itself" (1964:538). Fernandez's story, framed as a reflection on his brief stay as a patient in Schweitzer's hospital at Lambarene, is about the "irony of colonialism" (p. 553), as reflected in the contrast between the doctor's humanitarian ideals and the "unalterably colonial" regime at his hospital. "In Schweitzer, Fernandez says, "we see the whole contradiction of colonization: the sacrifice of the natives for a greater good" (p. 556).

Schweitzer, of course, was a special case. Yet, "since he saw clearly but planned and performed inadequately he is, though the man of another era, still relevant" (p. 561). In his writings, he rejected the casual denunciations that his contemporaries so often made of Africans—that they were lazy, exceptionally disputatious, immoral, incapable of rational thought. However, the one charge that Schweitzer could not reject was that Africans were undisciplined and inefficient. Schweitzer, according to Fernandez, had specifically come to Africa to escape the pressures of working for an organization at home, but had carried with him a "commitment to organization," to providing Africans efficient, orderly, medical care. His sympathy for Africans could not extend to tolerating characteristics that interfered with this mission, and he resolved the problem through social distance between himself and the Africans round him, maintaining an organization in which whites were in firm control.

"Schweitzer, like all colonials, whatever humanitarian motives inspired him, imposed a system upon a people according to which, in the end, he judged that people's behavior and in whose name he justified impersonal treatment however mild" (p. 557).

Another analysis of missionaries, focused on a similar difficulty, can be found in Tonkinson's ethnography, *The Jigalong Mob: Aboriginal Victors of the Desert Crusade* (1974). Here was a group of missionaries who maintained maximum social distance from the people they had ostensibly come to "save," and whose treatment of the people was any-thing but mild. Given an organization in the field that supported the missionaries in the most severe judgments on all aspects of aboriginal character, it is not surprising that the aborigines never recognized the moral authority the missionaries presumed. Yet, while Tonkinson points to many smaller ironies in this situation, "one of the most ironic aspects . . . is the fact that the mission, unwittingly and indirectly, has facilitated the [Aborigines'] retention of the Law and its focal manifestation, the religious life" (p. 135). The mission at Jigalong, Tonkinson notes, has even been referred to as " 'the mission that fostered tribal custom' " (p. 135)—a classic example of the ironic pattern of "the cure which perpetu-ates the disease."

Perhaps no anthropologist has approached the study of missionaries with as acute an eye for irony as Beidelman, in his series of articles and books about the Church Missionary Society in Ukaguru, Tanzania (1971:117–127, 1974, 1981, 1982a, 1982b, n.d). Yet Beidelman's real con-tribution to the ethnography of missionaries lies less in his ironic insight than in his theoretical development of this theme. To Beidelman, mis-sions are preeminent examples of "colonial organization," displaying many of the same qualities of modern, complex organizations that We-berian theory has helped us to understand (1982a:3–5). In Beidelman's hands, ethnography in the ironic mode passes from the short reflection to sustained sociological analysis with a distinctive "Weberian thrust" (Karp 1984:215).

The key to this characterization lies in a particular reading of Weber-ian sociology as distinctively concerned with actors' aims and goals, as expressed in the notion of the "ideal type," and with historical processes, such as "the routinization of charisma," that confound the actors' at-tempts to realize their goals in practice (Karp 1984:215). According to Falding:

> Weber appreciated that when a group decides that something is worth accomplishing, a whole set of activities has to be started in order to accomplish it. These diverse activities have to elbow their way in, competing with other things for time and support, and so on. They therefore may or may not come to their full unfolding. Whether they do will depend on a variety of things: the strength of

*dedication of the people concerned, the strength of their competing
aims, their knowledge, their resources, any outside opposition to
what they are trying to do . . . [1968:26].*

For Beidelman, the "fact" that missionaries may fail to achieve their goals
is less significant than how they respond to it. As Karp notes,
Beidelman's missionary studies stem from a perspective in which "much
of social and symbolic action is spent in negotiating the space between
our ideal strivings and the forms in which we enact them" (1984:215).

Even in its theoretically developed form, ethnography in the ironic
mode strikes a jarring note to some anthropologists, conveying an attitude at odds with conventional anthropological relativism. In a session
on the anthropology of missionaries at the 1979 meetings of the American
Anthropological Association, for example, one member of the audience
objected to T.O. Beidelman's graphic presentation of the many practical
dilemmas that faced evangelical missionaries when they had to lead caravans across eastern Africa in the late nineteenth century (Beidelman 1981;
1982a:63–65; 1982b). It sounded, the speaker said with dismay, as though
Beidelman was laughing at "his people," and this was hardly a "professional attitude."

Of course, it is true that Beidelman focused his analysis on an area in
which the behavior required for success in the African milieu contradicted some of these missionaries' most cherished ideals. Yet there is
nothing inherently derogatory in noting that people who embrace "anti-
materialism" might face special problems when they had to organize
hundreds of carriers for a caravan. Nor is there anything inherently
antirelativistic in asking what happens when circumstances require behavior that contradicts people's ideals. The problem appears to be that
anthropologists, like many others, tend to use and interpret irony as an
oppositional stance, and it is this stance towards the subject of analysis,
rather than the ironic insight itself, that is offensive.

Anthropological Irony

Certainly there is historical justification for taking irony as a sign of
critical intent. As Kenneth Burke has noted, "romantic irony" arose "as
an aesthetic opposition to cultural philistinism . . . in which the artist
considered himself *outside of* and *superior to* the role he was rejecting.
. . ." (1969:514). Yet there is another alternative equally rooted in the
history of western rhetorical styles. "Classic" irony is "humble" by comparison. In Burke's formulation, the attitude of classic irony is "not
superior . . . [but] is based upon a sense of fundamental kinship with the
enemy, as one *needs* him, is *indebted,* is not merely outside him as an
observer but contains him *within,* being consubstantial with him"

(1969:514). The point, of course, is that while ethnography in the ironic mode may originate in a critical attitude, it need not be smug.

Indeed, while most anthropologists writing about the ironies of evangelical work maintain a certain distance between themselves and their subjects, it is not always an unsympathetic distance. The sense of kinship that underlies this sympathy may, as with Beidelman, be cast in a vision of the essentially tragic nature of the human condition or, as with Fernandez, in terms of the difficulties that attend anyone's attempts to help others:

> The tensions [Schweitzer] faced in the act of benevolence remain
> relevant to us today—for those at least, like Schweitzer, to whom aid
> to the less fortunate is not simply a technical and self-interested task
> but a moral responsibility . . . the lesson is inescapable . . . the
> situations in which well-intentioned men place themselves may yet
> separate them from their most serious convictions. By becoming
> aware of the contradictions involved in our sincerities we can per-
> haps avoid being taken in by them [1964:562].

Burridge comes closest to approaching the "classic" attitude, however, for he considers his profession, anthropology (and indeed, the whole western intellectual tradition) indebted to Christianity, and he views both missionaries and anthropologists as outsiders in an alien world, equally committed to "universal" goals (1978:11).

Following through on Burridge's insight, one might suggest a connection between anthropologists' ironic construction of the missionary situation and the more general "crisis of representation" that anthropology, along with other human sciences, has recently undergone. As Marcus and Fischer have proposed, "periods of heightened irony in the means of representing social reality seem to go with heightened perceptions throughout society of living through historic moments of profound change" (1986:15). Indeed, at the same time that anthropologists began to turn serious attention to the ambiguities and contradictions of missionary work, many of anthropology's own "sincerities," to borrow Fernandez's term, were coming under scrutiny as well (Hymes 1969; Asad 1973; Clifford and Marcus 1986; Marcus and Fischer 1986). As anthropology's relation to colonialism and to the intellectual and literary traditions of the west were explored, it became increasingly evident that anthropological practice itself—fieldwork and ethnographic writing—could be characterized ironically.[3]

Thus, it is especially significant to note that in an early contribution to this literature, Geertz used the term "anthropological irony" to capture some of the ethical ambiguities of the fieldwork experience in "the new states" (1968:147). At issue for Geertz was how the relation between anthropologist and informant was maintained in a situation that con-

8

stantly threatened to expose their contrasting motives for collaboration—the investigator "believes in cross-cultural communion (he calls it 'rapport') as his subjects believe in tomorrow" (1968:151). Geertz suggests that the presumption that anthropologist and observer form part of a "single moral community" is a mutually arranged "fiction, not falsehood—that lies at the heart of successful anthropological field research; and, because it is never completely convincing for any of the participants, it renders such research, considered as a form of conduct, continuously ironic" (1968:154).

Perhaps it is not a coincidence that James Clifford, one of the more active contributors to the literature on fieldwork and ethnographic writing, began his work with a study of Maurice Leenhardt, who was a missionary in New Caledonia before taking up the chair at L'Ecole des Hautes Etudes that had previously been occupied by Marcel Mauss and was later occupied by Claude Levi-Strauss (Clifford 1982). With the possible exception of Clifford, who, at any rate, identifies himself as an historian of anthropology rather than as an anthropologist per se, ethnographic studies of missionaries have seldom been undertaken by anthropologists for purposes of self-reflection. Nor have I done so here. I have, however, tried to keep in mind what we have learned about the ironies of anthropological practice in exploring the practice of missionaries in the pages that follow. Like anthropologists, missionaries work with "fictions" that make their practice possible, and although these fictions help to make missionary experience intelligible and attractive to missionaries themselves and to supporters at home, they render that experience ironic at the same time.

THE STORY OF THIS WORK

My first introduction to missionaries came as it comes to most anthropologists—inadvertently, while "in the field." At the time, from 1969 to 1971, I was assisting my husband in his ethnographic work among the Anggor–speaking people of Wamu village in the West Sepik Province of Papua New Guinea. The missionaries most active in that part of the country then were from the Summer Institute of Linguistics (SIL) and from Christian Missions in Many Lands (CMML). The SIL couple in our field area were on home leave when we were there—he, in fact, was studying linguistics at the University of Pennsylvania—but when in New Guinea, they normally lived in the neighboring village of Bibriari for six months each year, spending much of their time doing linguistic and ethnographic fieldwork similar to our own. The grammatical notes these missionaries had assembled on the Anggor language were of great value to us, and they had established a model, quite congenial to us, for what villagers in this area might expect of European guests.

The CMML establishment, based at Amanab, the nearest administrative post, was more typical of mission stations in this country. Although the missionary in charge took occasional trips through villages in the area, he and his wife spent most of their time at Amanab, where they ran a Bible School for native mission workers, managed a small trade store, and did some rather impressive carpentry and landscaping to improve the station's buildings and grounds. They were gracious hosts when we were in Amanab, and saw to any cargo of ours that came in on the mission plane. None of these missionaries, however, was particularly active in our own field village, and like most anthropologists, I left the country with only fleeting images of the missionaries I had met, and a most cursory understanding of the work they were trying to do.

I also came away with a small repertoire of missionary stories, most of which I heard from Europeans in casual conversations about life in New Guinea. Some derived from our own experience, however, and we polished them up to tell. My favorite was one that ultimately came from the villagers with whom we had lived. Among the people of Wamu, the local CMML missionary was less renowned for impressive feats of carpentry at Amanab station, than for his impressive treks through the village at breakneck speed. Indeed, he was so fond of beating his previous track time that he occasionally took the wrong path, obliging villagers along the way to send some youngster to lead him back safely from the bush. The villagers found this story very amusing, probably as an illustration of white men's foibles (Basso 1979). I liked it because of its subtle twist on who was saving whom.

Research in Wewak

This anecdote, an example of the type anthropologists tell more often at parties than in print, was probably the closest my first research situation allowed me to come to the topic of missionary-villager relations in Papua New Guinea. Nor was I alone. Christian missionaries have had a great deal of success in Papua New Guinea over the years. Yet, while mission churches were among the most conspicuous institutions introduced by westerners in Papua New Guinea when I first visited the country in the period from 1969 to 1971, very little ethnographic work on them had been done. Thus, when I returned to Papua New Guinea from 1976 to 1977 to do my own dissertation research, it was to study one of the churches in the area of the country I knew best. I selected Catholic missionaries because of their long history in the Sepik, and I selected the town of Wewak because it was the center for a region in which this church had traditionally been strong.

The port town of Wewak—capital of the East Sepik Province since the mid-1930s and seat of the Catholic Bishop of Wewak since the late 1940s—was the fifth largest town in Papua New Guinea, with a population estimated at 19,000 for 1976 (Bureau of the Census, 1976). I had visited Wewak several times during my first trip to New Guinea, and even then had been impressed by the size of the Catholic mission headquarters, as well as by its central location in the town (Figure 2). From census reports, I knew that much of the town's population came from nearby districts, and that a large proportion of people in the town claimed to be Catholic.[4]

To facilitate studying relations between the mission and people living in Wewak, I decided to live in a migrant settlement so that I could ground my inquires among other townspeople in a situation that I could come to know reasonably well. My chief requirements were that the people in the settlement be willing to have me (and my household of husband, two children, and mother), that it be reasonably attractive, not too far from the mission headquarters, and that the people be from a Catholic home area.

Given the nature of the town, these requirements were not very restrictive, and my choice had a random element built in. In brief, I met a well-known Canadian artifact buyer at the Windjammer Motel during my first week in Wewak; he introduced me to some friends at a settlement of Koil Islanders at Kreer Beach (Figure 2); through Sara (one of these friends), I met Tony, the "big man" of the settlement, who agreed that I could build a house there. Through Tony, I met Kumun, of Kreer Village, who owned the settlement's land, and who also had no objections to my plans. Thus, within only a couple of weeks, my field situation was set, although it took another month before the new house was ready for me to move in. Language was no problem, for I was already fluent in New Guinea Pidgin, the regional lingua franca that is almost universally spoken by Sepik people when in town. In addition, I soon realized that Koil Island lies next door to Vokeo Island, studied by Ian Hogbin during the 1930s and again briefly from December 1974 to January 1975 (Hogbin 1978). As Koil and Vokeo were quite similar in language and culture, I would, therefore, not be completely on my own in gaining an understanding of the context from which those islanders living in Wewak had come.

My research routine was quite simple. I gathered as much material as I could from the Koil Islanders with whom I lived about all aspects of their experience in the town, and I periodically visited informants from other settlements and other sectors of Wewak society for additional perspectives on the mission and urban life. I also visited the mission several times a week to talk with missionaries, and to attend church services, meetings, and public events. I have presented some of the material I gathered on migrants' experience in the town, and on mission-town relations elsewhere (Huber 1979a; 1979b; 1983; 1984). This book, however, is primarily concerned with the historical development of the missionaries' project, and it is to its conception that I now turn.

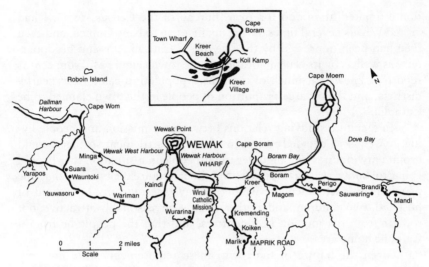

Figure 2. The Wewak Area. Inset: Settlements near Kreer Beach, Wewak, 1976–1977.

Research at the Mission

In 1976 and 1977, the Catholic mission in Wewak was one of the largest "expatriate" communities in town. As headquarters for a diocese nearly coterminous with the East Sepik Province itself, the Wewak station was home base for approximately 227 missionaries—priests, brothers, sisters, and overseas lay personnel—of whom all but thirty-eight were from abroad (Chapter 7). Of course, many of these missionaries, along with a large but unspecified number of Papua New Guinean catechists and school teachers, served at mission stations scattered throughout the diocese. Yet, nearly 100 were stationed in or near Wewak—at Wirui, the central station; at St. Benedict's Teacher's Training College at Kaindi in Wewak; and at Yarapos, just outside of town, at the mission's high school for girls. There was also much coming and going from the mission in Wewak, as missionaries from the outstations came into town for a rest, a meeting, or supplies.

My fieldwork at the mission was certainly influenced by the fact that I was an anthropologist living in a native settlement, and not a participant-observer living and working within the missionary community itself. The missionaries I met were without exception cooperative and forthcoming, but I do not believe that any grasped the fact that I was interested in the mission as a community, and not simply in their work with people in their station-areas (in the case of missionaries visiting Wewak from outlying posts) or in the town.

Of course, they had good reason to expect anthropologists to be interested primarily in native people. The Society of the Divine Word has been a pioneer in applying anthropology to mission work, and has long sponsored anthropological studies by its own members, and supported anthropological research through the journal *Anthropos,* which was founded in 1906 by one of its most distinguished ethnologists, Father Wilhelm Schmidt (Chapter 4). It is also worth noting that the Sepik has had its share of anthropologists passing through, many of whom have worked in areas served by Catholic mission stations. Virtually all of these encounters with anthropology and anthropologists, however, have involved the study of native cultures and peoples, not the study of missionaries or other expatriates as foci for communities themselves.

I would also like to note that my own religious background is not Roman Catholic but "generalized American mainstream Protestant," as I think I accurately, if inelegantly, described it to those few who asked. This fact appeared not to disturb the missionaries at all, although I suspect that I missed many nuances that an anthropologist of Catholic upbringing might have seen. My visits to the mission put me in touch with a large number of missionaries, mostly priests, but some brothers, sisters, and lay workers, as well. The missionaries I came to know best were those at posts in Wewak itself, and there were several I eventually felt I could visit frequently, completely unannounced. Although I imagine I became a somewhat too familiar figure for some, I never really crossed the line separating those outside the community from those who were "in." One problem that resulted from this situation was that I had to introduce myself and explain my project over and over again, to each new person I met. Clearly, my project and I were not sufficiently interesting to become items of news or gossip that might travel through the community's networks. This was an unusual and, indeed, uncomfortable situation, differing considerably from my experience in native villages and urban settlements. Perhaps this is a normal part of "studying up." I just wanted to sit and talk. The missionaries, however, had "real" work to do, in the same way that most of us do in our organizations at home.

The range of the work these missionaries did, in fact, was the single thing that most impressed me about them. There were mission personnel who farmed, who designed and constructed buildings, captained boats, flew planes, taught school, published a newspaper, ran a printing press, fixed cars, did plumbing, made furniture, cooked food, ran a laundry, operated radio communications, managed stores, showed movies, kept the grounds, and myriad other things, in addition to the "preaching and teaching" that usually define a missionary in western eyes. One reason this caught my attention was that so many other people remarked on it as well. The mission was an important institution in the region, and political discourse in Wewak included interpretations of missionary work. Native and expatriate commentators alike voiced opinions about what were and were not, legitimate missionary activities, and even a cursory acquaintance with the literature about cargo cults in the region (Burridge 1960; Lawrence 1964) and with published memoirs from earlier periods in Sepik history (Marshall 1938, McCarthy 1963, Townsend 1968) indicated that this had long been so.

It was in contemplating this issue that my interest in looking at mission practice from the missionaries' point of view began to take hold. The work they did had a place in the lives of others, but deciding what kinds of work needed doing, and attempting to control its interpretation, was of special importance to the missionaries themselves. I had, of course, spent much time talking with missionaries about the various projects in which they were involved. I had also heard a great many stories from missionaries, more or less in passing, about their "flying bishop," Leo Arkfeld, which clearly connected mission aviation—an apparently secular function—with the mission's most obvious religious and ecclesiastical goals.

After I returned from New Guinea and began to explore the historical literature more carefully, I noted that the mission's previous bishop and its founding leader had both been represented in a similar way. Eberhard Limbrock, who led the pioneer mission from 1896 to 1913, had been renowned as the designer of the mission's plantation system, while Joseph Loerks, bishop from 1928 to 1943, had been renowned as a boat captain and equestrian. The questions that this observation raised concerning the external, public function of such imagery were soon complemented by questions concerning its role within the mission. For as I continued to read about mission history, I became convinced that this episcopal imagery was related to internal controversies and problems within the mission community itself.

Historical Research

The historical material that I have used to explore this hypothesis was obtained primarily from published work. The only documentary sources that I have used were those available to me in the field. Government documents included the patrol reports and court records to which I had access in Wewak. Mission documents were scarce, but included several newsletters from the 1950s and, more important, a long letter home from an American missionary who had been posted to the region in 1935. As one missionary explained to me, the files in the mission headquarters at Wewak were thin because most early records had been destroyed during World War II, and because the postwar bishop had been, and still was, intent on the future, not the past. He seldom even had carbons made of his correspondence, much less wasted time worrying about their preservation. This fact leads to an important observation about this missionary group. The creeping bureaucratization that anthropologists have noted among other mission bodies (Beidelman 1982a; Burridge 1978) was, by the standard of recordkeeping, at any rate, not very far advanced.

This does not mean, of course, that there were no official records for this mission, or that there are not, somewhere, caches of letters home from the missionaries who have worked there over the years. I have not, however, had the opportunity to explore the libraries in the United States and Europe where such documents might be found, nor was the new library planned for such things in the archdiocese of Madang open when I was in the field. Fortunately, the published work already available has proved sufficient to enable me to explore my hypothesis in some depth. The particular sources that I have used are described in the body of the text. Translations from German are my own.

EFFECTIVE PRACTICE AND AUTHENTIC IDEALS

As H. C. Brookfield has defined it, " 'colonialism' is a thoroughgoing, comprehensive and deliberate penetration of a local or 'residentiary' system by agents of an external system, who aim to restructure the patterns of organization, resource use, circulation and outlook so as to bring these into a linked relationship with their own system" (1972:1–2). This study has more to do with the effects that work in a particular region of the world (a particular "residentiary system") has had on a specific colonial project, rather than the other way around. However, I have tried to keep in touch with the spirit of Brookfield's definition by focusing on the organizational (that is, ecclesiastical) aims of that project rather than on missionaries' other ideals or beliefs. Catholics, of course, have traditionally viewed the Church as central to salvation, and—with some differences in emphasis—Catholic missiologists have generally viewed "planting the church" as a central missionary task.

Although this focus may be especially apt for a study of Catholic missionaries, it should be recognized that "fellowship structures" are critically important to most Christian denominations. Indeed, they are frequently used to distinguish one group from another, and to identify a religious community as authentically this or that kind of Christian community. No matter how much emphasis a missionary group places on conversion, or on the individual's relation to God, most begin their work with the idea of bringing people in the mission field into a "linked relationship" with their own religious community, and aim eventually to reproduce a specific type of church polity, or fellowship structure in the mission field. It follows that the problems they encounter in the process and the ways they manage these problems will be not only a function of the "residentiary systems" they encounter, but also of the very structure they are trying to reproduce.

C. D. Rowley has noted in regard to the various mission groups that began work early in the colonial period in Papua and New Guinea:

> *Each of these bodies had and has maintained its own individuality, its own policy and its own faith: within a broad but suggestive similarity of technique largely made inevitable by the nature of the tasks, there were differences so striking that each had its very special history; and each is a worthy subject for detailed research which has not yet been made (1965:138).*

Although a number of historians have since filled some of these gaps, the tendency increasingly has been to identify the "residentiary system" as the source of a mission's "special history." This is a commendable alternative to conventional mission historiography, which in Melanesia as in Africa tended to focus on "European strategies for the planting of Christianity . . . and on heroic missionary efforts to implement these plans. . . . seldom examin[ing] the theme of encounter at all" (Strayer 1978:1). Yet, recent work by anthropologists on structure and history, especially that of Sahlins (1981; 1983; 1985), should make us wary of neglecting the value of conventional mission historiography as data about the missionaries themselves. Like the Hawaiians, Tongans, and Maori discussed by Sahlins, missionaries make their own history, and this history is constituted in part by the way in which they organize their efforts, and these efforts in turn are related to the structure of the community that they hope to establish in the mission field.

Missionaries of most denominations stand somewhat outside and apart from ordinary church authorities, and the mission churches that they first establish also stand apart from the "mature" form of the church as it is found at home. The briefest glance at an "official" mission history is usually sufficient to establish that sociological and geographical distance from church centers have temporal correlates as well. A close connection is almost inevitably drawn between time and the organization of a church, for movements in time are marked by changes in the position of the missionaries and by change in ecclesiastical form. The story missionary historians usually tell is one of progress, and the temporal flow is inflected, if not precisely defined, by the promotion of a mission through varying stages of maturity until it achieves the status of a church.

Consider the following ritual performed in the 1950s by Lutherans in an eastern province of Papua New Guinea to celebrate the occasion of the mission's elevation to the status of church. Though well prepared in advance, the actual adoption of the order to create the Evangelical Lutheran Church of New Guinea (ELCONG) from two previously separate Lutheran missions was delayed until the year of the seventieth anniversary of Lutheran mission activity in New Guinea. The site of the ceremony was Simbang village where the first Lutheran missionary had begun work. The ceremony itself was in the form of a synod meeting with representatives from "every district of the new church," and included important witnesses from the Lutheran World Federation, the American Lutheran Church, and from Neuendettelsau in Germany—headquarters of the society of missionaries to which the founder of Lutheran mission work in New Guinea had belonged. The event was further dramatized by two plays.

> One depicted the difficulties Senior Missionary Flierl encountered when he reached Simbang in 1886, and the other the advance of the gospel in New Guinea. A rope soaked with gasoline had been suspended on a line of posts. A flame kindled at one end travelled swiftly to the other [Frerichs 1957:102].

As it goes, this is a specifically Lutheran passage, straight and swift, from a single beleaguered missionary to a synod, from a single, isolated post to an acronymic organization representing all districts and recognized by witnesses from international Lutheranism. If written mission histories seem to suffer almost as much from restricted vision of the historical process, the stories they tell are still of value for the anthropology of missions because they vary according to different ideas about church polity and different ideals of ecclesiastical form.

The particular way in which organization is conceived is a critical factor in directing the efforts of missionaries and, indeed, in placing them within the history of their project—the emergent church. The aims and, thus, the situation of missionaries from the Christian Missions in Many Lands (CMML) can be taken as an instructive contrast to the Lutherans, as discussed above. Although their histories tell a similar story in a similar way, they appear to be traveling in different directions on the same road. The Lutheran church, ELCONG, is marked by the joining of different mission churches, but the mature form of the church of the Brethren (for whom the CMML is the missionary arm) is marked by their separation, instead.

The Brethren conceive of a mature church as a collection of independent congregations ("assemblies"), the cooperation of which in common ventures is purely voluntary and without ecclesiastical significance. The aim of the Brethren missionaries is to recreate in their mission fields the same kind of independent congregations as at home. Yet, like most missionaries, they start in the wilderness from its conceptual opposite to develop the conditions in which the mature form can thrive. In short, the Brethren's mission work is conducted in the context of a centralized organization—the CMML—which coordinates their work, mediates affairs with secular authorities, provides support services, and enables the group collectively to benefit from certain economies of scale. To the outsider, the little groups of adherents in the villages surrounding a CMML station may appear as satellites to the mission post. To the missionaries, however, whose vision of the present is inflected by their future aims, these village congregations are, in fact, incipient assemblies and the missionaries point proudly to the growing number of these congregations as evidence of a mission on the road to success. The missionaries place themselves "outside" these little groups, and work to develop them, so that ultimately the central organization can be dismantled and the missionaries can go home, leaving a large number of autonomous, but "mechanically" solidary, congregations, each replicating the other, to occupy the field (Smart 1967:153–154).

Roman Catholics situate a mission quite differently in history than the CMML. Instead of standing on the outside of the developing local church, Catholic missionaries form its "shadow" center, approximating ever more closely in recruitment and organization the model of the clergy and staff of a mature church.The leader of the mission is given the office of leader of the church; as time progresses, his status is raised from prefect, to vicar, to bishop as the church he leads matures. With this movement in the status of the leader, characterized in canon law as one of progressively greater independence of tenure, it is expected that he will come to rely less on missionaries of the religious society originally entrusted with the territory, and develop a staff of his own, not bound by vows to their Society, but to the leader (bishop), himself. In the territories entrusted to the Society of the Divine Word (SVD) in New Guinea, bishops have always been chosen from within the Society's ranks, and thus mediate both the past and present status of their project as a mission, and its future as a mature church.

The history of this mission differs from the Lutheran and CMML models presented above, for instead of proceeding from one point to another on a continuum of organizational types, the Catholics tend to view progress as the gradual elaboration of an originally primitive whole. Thus, a newly created mission territory may cover a huge area, and gradually be split into smaller territories, each with its own leader as a prefect or vicar. The church itself is not fully constituted, however, until these parts articulate in an ecclesiastical organization for the whole. The formula that this conception provides for synopsis is well illustrated by the following summary of Catholic mission history in Melanesia (first) and New Guinea (second):

> In the original Melanesia-Micronesia area there are today 22 ecclesiastical districts: 4 archdioceses, 17 dioceses, 1 vicariate apostolic [Wiltgen 1969b].

> What was once the Prefecture Apostolic of Wilhelmsland without a single Catholic is today a full-fledged ecclesiastical province with an

established hierarchy, containing one archdiocese at Madang and six
suffragen sees [Wiltgen 1969b:24].

Unlike Lutheran mission history that merges the separate parts of its
original mission field, Catholic mission history—stripped to its
essentials—differentiates parts that were once merged. In contrast to the
CMML, however, which anticipates the future autonomy of village assemblies by refusing to consider them part of the mission organization at
all, the temporal horizon for a Catholic mission involves the establishment of hierarchy and the formal subordination of the part to the whole.
It is interesting to note that like the Lutherans, the Catholic mission's
seventieth anniversary in mainland New Guinea was made the occasion
for the formal creation of the church. In this case, however, what was
celebrated was the establishment of the hierarchy by the authority of the
Vatican in Rome.

I do not know how this event was marked locally in New Guinea,
but a contrast with the Lutheran ceremony is available in an article in the
Society of the Divine Word's publication, *The Word in the World*. Entitled "A Fitting Anniversary," the article elaborates on the meaning of the
consecration of John Cohill, SVD, in Newark, New Jersey, as bishop of
the diocese of Goroka—one of the ecclesiastical districts in the highlands
of New Guinea carved from the original Prefecture Apostolic of
Wilhelmsland, mentioned above:

> There could not have been a more fitting and satisfying manner in
> which to mark the Seventieth Anniversary of a mission. The conse-
> crating Bishop extended his hands and let them rest firmly on the
> head of the tanned, broad-shouldered missionary kneeling before
> him. Thus the fourth Divine Word Missionary Bishop took his place
> among the ranks of the newly established Hierarchy of New Guinea.
>
> The scene was the Sacred Heart Cathedral of Newark, New
> Jersey, March 11, 1967. A crowded congregation of laity, diocesan
> and religious clergy and some 20 prelates were witnessing Father
> John Cohill, SVD, born in nearby Elizabeth, New Jersey 60 years
> previously, assume the fullness of the priesthood.
>
> He was to carry this fullness back to his mountain diocese of
> Goroka, New Guinea where he would work alongside the other
> three Divine Word Missionaries named to the New Guinea Hierar-
> chy: Archbishop Noser in Madang, Bishop Arkfeld in Wewak and
> Bishop Bernarding in Mount Hagen. Of the seven bishops named to
> the Ecclesiastical Province of Madang by the Vatican on December 3,
> four are SVDs.
>
> It was no mere coincidence that this special recognition of the
> SVD's efforts on the New Guinea front coincided with the Society's
> Seventieth Anniversary on the island. As Cardinal Agagianian wrote
> in his official letter of notification to Superior General Father John

Schuette, 'I would like to express my own and the Propaganda's [the Vatican office in charge of missions] congratulations for this proof of confidence which the Vicar of Christ has shown your missionaries who have toiled so selflessly in the service of the Church in those parts, and will no doubt continue to do so in the future. The Propaganda rejoices with you that after years of hard labor, your Society can count among its sons the Metropolitan and three Bishops in the new ecclesiastical province [Pung 1968:177].*

Clearly, the fact that the Catholic missionaries I studied have represented themselves through images of their bishops is explicable because—as the passage just quoted illustrates—their bishop is the guarantor of their project's authenticity, and its most direct link to the authoritative center of the Roman Catholic Church. Yet, why have these bishops been represented through images stressing their apparently secular skills? To understand this, we must realize that the bishops have been responsible for the effectiveness of the missionary project as well. As I argue in the following chapters, however, the requirements for effective and authentic practice frequently have conflicted in the mission field. By representing their bishops through skills uniquely valuable in the New Guinea situation, the missionaries display a gap that has been central to their experience, but bring effective practice and authentic ideals together again.

Mission Frontiers

While I have so far discussed "ecclesiastical ideals" as though they applied only to a restricted domain, it is true that for most missionaries these ideals have amounted to principles and attitudes that encompass a great deal more than the organization of the church, per se. Borrowing a concept from Coser (1974:67–88), Beidelman suggests that "all missions might be described as 'greedy institutions,' demanding total control rather than compartmentalized conduct" (1982a:21). Indeed, ecclesiastical ideals may inform a whole "social teaching" and not just notions about how people should be organized for worship (Troeltsch 1981).

In turn, of course, missionaries' social teaching is unavoidably influenced by the customs of their time, national origins, and class. For the missionaries studied by Beidelman, for example, "evangelical" ideals went well beyond such matters as church government and ministry to "notions of comfort, style, security, self-esteem, honor, privacy, sexuality, age, and status" (1982a:9). For Catholic missionaries, as Beidelman has also noted, these matters are somewhat complicated by the religious orders to which the missionaries usually belong. Yet, as I shall explain in later chapters, Catholic religious orders each have their own rules, their own "spirit," and their own style. As one of the SVD missionaries in Wewak told me, there were few members of his (originally German)

Society from France, because no proper Frenchman could find it a congenial spiritual home.

Of course, there are many direct ways in which a group's ecclesiastical traditions shape the ways in which they organize themselves and their projects in a mission field. One may note, in particular, the critical question of the clergy: whether there is one, officially, or not; how its members are recruited and trained; whether they are married or celibate, and so forth. Such factors are likely to influence the way in which the project is controlled, how the missionaries are perceived by natives and by other expatriates in the field, the kinds of problems the missionaries will face (need they worry about the health and education of their own families?), as well as the status of the indigenous workers that the missionaries may recruit. Indeed, Strayer has argued that such questions may be critical in understanding the internal dynamics of mission expansion. In the early years of Church Missionary Society (CMS) work in East Africa, for example, lay missionaries soon realized that the quickest way to ordination and the benefits they could obtain therefrom, was to start a new station in an area where one was the only CMS missionary around (Strayer 1978:30–51).

Nonetheless, as Beidelman has so astutely demonstrated in his own studies of the CMS, the ecclesiastical ideals of a group shape not only traditions that enable and constrain patterns of mission activity, but also its contradictions. The missionary's dilemma is that responding effectively to local conditions often means compromising the project's ideals. It is probably true that the more broadly these ideals are spread among the many regions of life, the more deeply they are held; the more explicitly they are valued as criteria of success, the more vulnerable a project will be to upsets and detours along the way.

In this study, I have used the term "frontier" to refer to the space between effective practice and authentic ideals. Yet, if the frontier is an imaginative construct to the extent that it depends on ideals to define its presence, its contours, and its shades of freedom and constraint, this frontier presents itself to those who live and work within it as a natural phenomenon comprising elements quite separate in origin from themselves. Such elements might include whether or not there are roads, ships, and stores to support a project and its personnel; whether or not the social, linguistic, and cultural configurations within the field facilitate a project's work; and whether or not one has powerful competitors. Like the caravans in Africa, which, to be staged successfully, required a kind of worldly, and indeed, inhumane, behavior that violated CMS missionaries' evangelical ideals, the situations faced by missionaries may place them in ambiguous and awkward positions, indeed. The following chapters explore a particular set of frontiers that a very different group of missionaries has encountered in a very different part of the world.

Outline

Chapter 2 sets the scene by presenting a brief account of the economic and political situation along the north coast of New Guinea from the beginning of the colonial period in the 1880s to the beginning of World War II. Chapter 3 begins with a view of colonial society as it was recalled by memoirists who traveled and worked in the region, and then focuses more closely on the Catholic missionaries in the era of their first bishop, prior to World War I, who they were, and how they responded to the economic problems posed by mission work in the region. I discuss how the missionaries' response led to a number of reversals in some of their most characteristic ideals; in particular, in their division of material and spiritual work between missionary brothers and missionary priests.

I open Chapter 4 with a view of the mission community from the perspective of an official observer who toured the region with the Society's Superior General in 1922. From Father Hagspiel's perspective, we see less concern with the economic problems that preoccupied the mission's first leader, and more concern with the political problems of internal cohesion that faced the group as they attempted to evangelize a large region populated by natives who were divided amongst themselves, spoke many different languages, and among whom the missionaries found great differences in custom and behavior as well. This chapter then goes on to discuss ecclesiastical changes that split the mission territory into two parts by the early 1930s, and raised the status of their leaders from prefects to vicars. It later examines changes in the conception of mission community that were reflected in the image of the bishop in the Sepik territory prior to World War II.

Chapter 5 traverses some of the same historical ground, but this time with an eye on the "triangle" of relations among missionaries, government agents, and native people (Burridge 1960), and explores how the power relations implied by this triangle eventually changed, especially with the emergence of cargo cults in the 1930s, and the Japanese invasion of 1942. Chapter 6 takes up the period following World War II with a discussion of "The Flying Bishop," the imagery of aviation, and the changes this imagery articulated in the missionaries' perception of their task. I focus in particular on the conception and practice of ministry that emerged as the missionaries rebuilt the mission system in an era characterized by a new progress-minded government and by an indigenous populace more capable and determined than before to participate equitably in a new order of economic and moral affairs.

Chapter 7 focuses on the period from the late 1960s to the mid-1970s, which was marked for the country as a whole by preparations for independence, and for the Catholic mission by Vatican II, as well. There is a discussion of the ways in which the mission tried to bring native Catholics more closely into positions of responsibility in the church, the aging of the mission community, and the new set of ambiguities that the missionaries faced as they set about the task of localization, examining in particular the placement of the priest. In the conclusion, Chapter 8, the argument about principles and practice is summarized, and there is a return to the issue of irony. This time, however, there is less concern with the use of irony in writing about missionaries than on its use by missionaries themselves.

One final geographical note may be helpful before moving on. There is some ambiguity about use of the term "Sepik," made largely unavoidable by the fact that political and ecclesiastical boundaries have changed during the eighty years covered in this work. The geographical territory defined in Chapter 2 conforms closely to the area defined by the East and West Sepik provinces of today. In Chapter 3, I confine the travelers' tales to those concerning this same area, but because the mission's original territory included the entire north coast from the region around Alexishafen in the east to the Dutch border in the west, material inevitably is included on the mission from both the Sepik provinces and the Madang Province, as they are known today. This occurs again for the same reason in Chapter 4, until the 1930s, when the eastern and western parts of the mission territory were split.

Although the focus is on the Wewak area of the Sepik region in Chapter 5, it was necessary to go east once again for the discussion of cargo cults, using Father Höltker's study of the Mambu movement (1941). His is the only contemporary study of an early cult in the Catholic mission's area that includes enough detail to suggest the nature of the mission's involvement and response. Although there is material about Yali, a renowned cargo cult leader from the Madang Province in Chapter 6, there should be no serious geographical ambiguity here or in Chapter 7, because after World War II the territories now encompassed by the Diocese of Wewak and the East Sepik Province have coincided fairly closely—the old territory of the Catholic mission in what is now the West Sepik Province was taken over by a different Catholic missionary group. For most readers, I suspect, these problems will not be distracting, but those with a special interest in the history of this particular mission or in the history of the Sepik region itself should approach the following chapters forewarned. Several maps are provided to specify the areas discussed along the way.

CHAPTER 2

The Formation of
a Colonial Frontier

If one is to understand the experience of Catholic missionaries in the Sepik region of Papua New Guinea, it is necessary to realize that during the first half century of missionary work, the Sepik was a place few other Europeans cared to call "home." From the missionaries' arrival in 1896 until after World War II, the region was a colonial frontier, of value chiefly as a source of indigenous labor for plantations and gold fields in more prosperous districts to the east. Administrative and commercial development within the Sepik remained rudimentary and the European population remained very small. The Catholic mission was the only Christian mission to work west of the mouth of the Sepik River prior to World War II, and its missionaries probably constituted the region's largest group of "settled" European personnel.

Perhaps it is because the European colonial effort was so limited that colonial society in the Sepik remains a historiographical frontier even today. Historians concerned with the political and economic development of the country understandably focus on the centers of colonial activity, relegating backwaters like the Sepik to the margins of their accounts. Drawing on this work, however, it is possible to outline the historical circumstances in which colonial penetration of the Sepik took place and to examine some distinctive features of the colonial society that developed in the region in the years before World War II. This chapter

Figure 3. German New Guinea.

focuses on commerce and government because their relative weakness is key to understanding both the situation of the Catholic mission and the position of the Sepik as a colonial frontier.

MODELS OF COLONIAL DEVELOPMENT

The formation of the Sepik as a frontier was accomplished even before its first European settler arrived in 1895. By that time the success of traders and planters in the Bismarck Archipelago had already become evident, while attempts by the Neu Guinea Compagnie to develop the mainland— first as a colony of small-holder settlers, and then on a Dutch East Indies model of large tobacco, cacao, and cotton plantations—had failed. The Neu Guinea Compagnie had already turned its attention to the Bismarck Archipelago and to a Pacific model for colonial development based on trade and coconut plantations pioneered by earlier settlers in these islands. It was this model that was recommended to settlers en route to the Sepik during the mid-1890s. As colonial activity in the Sepik was in so many ways derivative from the experience, and dependent on the fortunes of colonists in other parts of the country, an account of their enterprise may serve both to introduce the principal actors who entered the Sepik during the 1890s, and to place the conditions they encountered within the context of the time (Figure 3).

26

The Pacific Model in the Bismarck Archipelago

The coconut trade in the Pacific was the key to Europeans' successful settlement in the Bismarck Archipelago in the 1870s. The region had attracted Sydney-based traders for tortoise shell before, but it had been exclusively a visiting trade made possible by the skills and contacts of natives on the Duke of York Islands who "set themselves up as intermediaries between the European traders and the natives of the neighboring parts of New Britain and New Ireland" (Sack 1973:64). It was not until the beginning of the 1870s, when Polynesians began asking higher prices for their coconuts, that the German firms then dominating Pacific trade found the resources of the northern Melanesian islands attractive enough to warrant settlement. Godeffroys attempted to settle agents on Matupi and the Gazelle Peninsula in 1873, but native hostility soon forced them to flee, so honors for becoming the first permanent white settler in the islands went to George Brown, a Methodist missionary who arrived in 1875. The German firms of Hernsheims and Godeffroys soon followed, and by 1877 the mission and the two companies were all preparing to expand their operations (Sack 1973:64,66). Although the two commercial firms began by "engaging in barter with the islanders for such items as copra, trepang, and shell," labor recruitment soon followed. The Deutsche Handels-und Plantagen-Gesellschaft der Sudseeinseln, corporate successor to Godeffroys, began "to enrol workers for its Samoa plantations . . . in the early eighties . . ." (Moses 1969:47).

From 1875 to 1884 the expatriate community in the islands was composed of a few Methodist missionaries (aided by a staff of Polynesian teachers and their families), a few Catholic priests who began work during the 1880s, some refugees from an unsuccessful French settlement scheme in New Ireland, and a shifting group of traders, acting either on their own or loosely under the control of the companies whose stations they maintained. The period was checkered with incidents of native resistance, and relations within the European community itself were punctuated by quarrels arising from their competition for native trade and from their relative isolation from the outside world.

By 1884, however, these Europeans had succeeded in working through native trade networks to create a viable political and economic base. They also had made the beginnings of a new economic order. Backed by a chain of trading posts, the first plantation had been cleared and something of a land grab in anticipation of new profits had ensued. Although many of these early settlers feared that disadvantageous changes would follow German annexation of the region in 1884, they were to enjoy another decade of grace from serious official interference. The Neu Guinea Compagnie, chartered by Bismarck to administer the new German colony, was initially uninterested in the islands, concerning itself instead with developing the hitherto neglected mainland. For this enterprise, the Company had elaborate plans.

The Neu Guinea Compagnie's Settlement Scheme

The interests of the Neu Guinea Compagnie in the mainland were at first connected with the colonial sentiments of many well-to-do and propertied Germans during the 1870s. Adolf von Hansemann, who put together a consortium of financial institutions to found the Neu Guinea Compagnie in 1879, had in fact belonged to the *Zentralverein für Handelsgeographie und Forderung deutscher Interessen in Ausland,* and to the *Deutscher Kolonialverein,* groups that urged imperial expansion to the German public, to legislators, and to Bismarck himself (Firth 1972:36). Although historians have offered various explanations for German expansionism at that time, many now point to the German depression of the 1870s, to fears among the German middle classes of working-class socialism, and, most significantly for New Guinea, to the "emigration question." One colonial ideologue, for example,

> *saw the acquisition of German colonies as 'crisis therapy'. . . . The therapy was twofold: to encourage mass immigration to overseas possessions within the Reich rather than to America or Australia where Germans were lost to the Fatherland; and to provide the workers with alternative attractions to those of socialism, 'counterutopias' in the form of new opportunities in the colonies and new hope of personal advancement [Firth 1977:240].*

By 1884, such pressures from home converged with vociferous demands for protection by German firms with interests abroad, and Bismarck finally permitted the establishment of German colonies in Africa and in the South Pacific. He attempted to reduce the costs to the new German state, however, by delegating administrative responsibilities to private firms.

Although it has been said that "the New Guinea enterprise was not the expression of [German] National enthusiasm but rather one of over optimistic capitalism" (Moses 1969:49), Adolf von Hansemann clearly embraced both in his plans. Quite apart from knowledge of conditions in New Guinea, Hansemann had determined that the mainland would make a fine colony for German settlers from Australia, who, he imagined, would arrive in great numbers to take up farming and raise livestock on small holdings of land under the German flag. The Company's role, as Hansemann first conceived it, was to explore the country, build stations, establish shipping connections, and acquire land to sell to the settlers (Firth 1972:362). Although it took five years for Hansemann, based in Berlin, to realize that conditions in New Guinea would not support such a scheme, bureaucratic ineptitude and wildly unrealistic expectations disabused his employees in New Guinea much sooner.

> *Two days after arriving in Finschhafen [the Company's first settlement] in January 1886 the Company doctor recorded in his diary that*

the Berlin office must imagine there were impenetrable forests of coconut palms in Kaiser Wilhelmsland, because it had already fixed the price of copra, whereas in fact few coconut palms were to be seen. Detailed company regulations covered everything down to the return of empty packing cases, and the men on the spot were instructed to proceed to the interior of the country as quickly as possible and mark out the Dutch border with black, red, and white stakes [Firth 1972:363].

The staff of the Neu Guinea Compagnie in Finschhafen appears to have experienced little but misery and frustration in its efforts to "precipitate a rush of settlers" (Firth 1972:362). The Company's insistence upon formalities and regulations hampered the capacity of its staff to act in light of local circumstances (Sack 1973:82); it lacked both the means and the will to form an effective administration for either native or European affairs (Firth 1972:363–364; Moses 1969:50); and it failed to secure cooperation from the natives by indifference to their trading skills and by exhibiting interest chiefly in their labor and their land. By 1889 the Neu Guinea Compagnie had succeeded in establishing only six small stations on the mainland, and the people responding to their advertisements in Australia were seeking employment with the Company rather than buying land (Firth 1972:364).

The Dutch East Indies Plan

The failure of the Neu Guinea Compagnie's settlement scheme was recognized by Hansemann in 1889. Still optimistic about the investment's future success, however, Hansemann arranged to relinquish the Company's administrative duties to the Imperial Government, scrapped the "Australian" settlement model, and looked instead to developing a profitable plantation economy like that of the Dutch East Indies (Sack 1973:83; Firth 1972:364). Recognizing that labor from the mainland of New Guinea would not be forthcoming, Hansemann stepped up recruitment in the Bismarck Archipelago and arranged to import laborers from Dutch and British territories in Asia. Subsidiary companies were established to grow tobacco, cacao, and coffee; plantation managers with experience in tropical agriculture were hired; and several high officials toured the East Indies before taking up new posts with the New Guinea Compagnie (Firth 1972:370).

Though better prepared than the earlier settlement scheme, the Dutch East Indies plan also failed. Company policies hardly changed: "The state of chronic inefficiency among the commercial personnel is illustrated by the fact that 600 officials came and went [between 1892 and 1895] and of these only one stayed with the Company" (Moses 1969:50). Problems multiplied when natives residing near Company plantations took offense at the pace of land acquisition and planting. Attacks on the Hatzfeldhafen tobacco plantation caused it to close in 1891, and in the same year villagers attacked Company employees in the Astrolabe Bay and at the Company's cacao plantation. The manager of the latter hastened its downfall by so mistreating his laborers that they escaped en masse to tell the tale. Finally forced by the new Imperial Judge to dismiss the manager, the Company abandoned cacao as well (Firth 1972:368).

Sickness among Europeans and among the Chinese and Malay laborers also contributed to the downfall of the Company's Dutch East Indies plan. In 1891, Finschhafen—the capital—was abandoned after forty percent of its population died in an epidemic (Sack 1973:84; Moses 1969:50). The tobacco plantations run by a Neu Guinea Compagnie subsidiary, were troubled by illness among the laborers, and during the mid-1890s reports showed that tobacco harvests were decreasing as labor problems mounted. Recruitment in the islands of the Bismarck Archipelago, though never very successful, became more difficult as the evil reputation of the mainland spread (Firth 1972:372–375).

Hoping to save costs and salvage its operations, the Company resumed administration of the colony in 1892. Although its new administrator "was as convinced that Neu Guinea was a potential Sumatra as his employers in Berlin," the evidence from successive annual reports from the period 1892 and 1893 to 1895 and 1896 shows a gradual abandonment of the Asian plantation model and a growing interest in coconuts and in the old Pacific model that was bringing profits to business in the Bismarck Archipelago (Sack 1973:85–87; Firth 1972:375). Indeed, by 1891 the Company had begun interplanting coconuts with cotton at Herbertshohe in the Islands, and during the next few years they began to import coconuts as seedlings for mainland plantations as well (Wiltgen 1969a:332). By 1895, the Company had again decided to devote itself purely to business and had entered the negotiations that finally led to the full assumption of colonial administration by the Imperial Government in 1899. Finally settled on the same footing as the more prosperous island firms, the Neu Guinea Compagnie continued to develop its coconut industry and moved on to a profitable basis in the early part of the twentieth century.

By the end of the period of Neu Guinea Compagnie rule, then, the dominance of the Bismarck Archipelago vis-à-vis the mainland in the European economy had been clearly established. European commerce was still centered in the islands, copra exports still brought in the largest revenues, and of these the largest share continued to come from coconuts obtained by trade with the indigenous people. The colony thus "retained the contrast between mainland and Archipelago which had marked it 14 years before" (Firth 1972:376). Yet, the Neu Guinea Compagnie's enterprise had creative as well as conservative effects. In particular, a new contrast had developed on the mainland itself, for there the concentration of European capital and effort had left the western portion of Kaiser

Wilhelmsland quite outside the effective range of European influence and control.

There were many areas of the mainland that Europeans had not yet colonized when, in the late 1890s, the German Imperial Government assumed responsibility for colonial rule. The heavily populated valleys of the central cordillera, for example, were not really explored until the 1930s when aviation was introduced into the territory, and even near areas of colonial settlement, the early colonists seldom ventured far inland from the coast. Of the areas more readily accessible to colonists of the nineteenth century, however, the Sepik—with a coastline stretching from the mouth of the Sepik River to the border of Dutch New Guinea, and with an inland waterway navigable for approximately 500 miles— was the most obvious frontier. The economics of European expansion into this region will occupy much of the rest of this chapter. Here, however, a brief review is needed of the geographical, demographic, and cultural configurations that affected colonial penetration.

Geographical Zones

Like most large areas of Papua New Guinea, the Sepik is composed of a wide range of geographical zones. For the purposes of this exposition, however, we can proceed with only four: the offshore islands and the mainland coastal region in the north, a riverine system in the south, and an area of mountains, hills, and plains in between. Each of these roughly defined zones has provided a different set of opportunities and constraints to its indigenous residents and, ipso facto, to colonists attempting to link these "residentiary systems" with their own (Brookfield 1972:1–2).

All four of these geographical zones have internal gradients. Following the description and analysis of the region made by the social geographer, David Lea (1972), I will begin in the northeast with the Schouten Island chain, stretching west from Karkar and Manam in the Madang and Bogia areas, respectively; to Bam, opposite the mouth of the Ramu River; to Kadovar and Blup Blup, opposite the mouth of the Sepik River; to Wei, Koil, and Vokeo, lying north of the Murik Lakes. Closer in to shore in the Wewak area are the large volcanic islands of Kairiru, Mushu, Walis, and Tarawai, as well as a number of smaller, coral reef islands. Farther to the west, off the Aitape coast, are the small, low-lying islands, which eventually became the sites of the earliest European settlements. The coast of the mainland begins in the east with the Murik Lakes, a swampy and frequently inundated region near the Sepik River delta. Farther west are miles of exposed beaches that are punctuated by occasional coral headlands and backed by a narrow, forested, alluvial plain that widens considerably near Vanimo—the only good, natural, year-round harbor west of Madang (Lea 1972:1031).

Behind the coastal area, and rising from it rather abruptly, are the northern slopes of the coastal mountain range. Rising farthest from the coast are the Bewani Mountains in the west that, like the Torricelli Mountains in the center, have peaks as high as 5,000 and 6,000 feet. To the east, the Prince Alexander Mountains reach their highest point at Mt. Turu (4,000 feet), but then ease down beyond the Wewak area in a series of rounded hills to Marienberg on the lower Sepik River. Most of this countryside is rugged and covered with rain forest; it is also a tectonically unstable area with "frequent tremors, earthquakes and landslips" (Lea 1972:1031). In contrast to the steeply ascending hills on the north side of the coastal range, the foothills to the south descend more gradually to the Sepik plains. Even here the countryside is not open, for "the natural transition between foothills and plain has been obscured by southbound streams carving the soft sediments of the upper plain into a jumble of low hills" (Tuzin 1976:5). East of the Prince Alexander Mountains, however, forest cover gives way to grassland, which leads, in turn, to the region's namesake, the Sepik River and the Sepik River plain.

Traveling in a general northeasterly direction for approximately 700 miles, the Sepik River "has always been . . . the dominant and unifying feature" of the region as a whole (Lea 1972:1031). Draining the northern slopes of the island's central cordillera as well as the southern slopes of the coastal range, the river widens and deepens as it continues its twisting and tumultuous journey to the sea. Narrow and less deep near its source in the central highlands, the river comes first to run "along the northern edge of the floodplain" and then moves to its center, carving out countless levees, which are backed by a plain with "swamps, minor levees, scrools, and ox-bow lakes" (Lea 1972:1031). The central and lower reaches of the Sepik are subjected annually to months of inundation, greatly influencing the architectural styles and subsistence strategies of the people living there. Indeed, to bring this brief description of regional geography "full circle," it can be noted that flotsam from the Sepik River spews out so far into the Pacific Ocean that it has sometimes provided the people living on the Schouten Islands with their largest house timbers.

Demographic and Cultural Configurations

Population in the area in the late nineteenth century was probably distributed in a pattern broadly similar to that found today, with concentrations on the offshore islands, in the foothills and plains south of the central and eastern mountains of the coastal range, and finally along the middle and lower courses of the Sepik River. More than 200 languages are spoken in the region, making it "one of the most linguistically complex in the world" (Laycock 1973:54).[1] The distribution of language phyla and families suggests to some scholars that the region was settled through a series of migrations from the west, followed by a relatively recent series of migrations to the north from the area of the middle Sepik River (Laycock 1973:55). In all, these various migrations appear to have created something of a west-to-east cultural gradient, overlaid by more palpable north-to-south distinctions as people adapted to local ecological and political configurations (Tiesler 1969:12–14).

With few exceptions, people in the Sepik live in small hamlets and villages, combining either hunting or fishing with gardening and sago cultivation, depending on local conditions. Along the Sepik River, settlements occasionally have numbered as many as 1,000 people (Tuzin 1976:315), and one Arapesh village in the Torricelli foothills attained a population of 1,500 in its efforts to stem "predatory expansion" by neighboring groups (Tuzin 1976:xxi–xxiii, 82). For the most part, however, settlements have remained small—seldom more than 300 to 400 persons (see Tuzin 1976:305)—and the ability of people to organize in large numbers was limited to special, usually ceremonial, events. Forms of dual organization are frequently found along the coast and in the central and eastern parts of the Sepik, but their integrative capacity both in ideology and practice appears to have been quite circumscribed. Villages tended towards moral isolation, with warfare and, frequently, sorcery threatening from the outside. Notions of tribe and chiefdom were foreign to the village societies of the Sepik, and trade and ceremony provided the principal channels for imagining and conducting peaceable relations between groups.

Despite linguistic and political fragmentation, cultural items—such as nuts, sago, fish, tobacco, pots, baskets, shells, and plumes, as well as ceremonial protocols and artistic motifs, news and interpretations of distant events—traveled widely from one hamlet or village to another, passing as gifts between friends or as commodities to be bought and sold. Melanesian islanders traveled long distances in their canoes to exchange such items with trading partners along the coast (Hogbin 1935; Tiesler 1969). These coastal traders, in turn, engaged in what was sometimes a secretive and fear-ridden trade with those living farther inland (Mead 1970; Allen 1976). Indigenous markets enabled people along the Sepik River and its tributaries to exchange fish for sago with people from inland villages to the north and south (Gewertz 1983). For many Sepik peoples, trade relationships provided resources (that is, objects of wealth) essential for social reproduction and, in some cases, for subsistence as well.[2]

In broad comparative terms, it is useful to characterize the traditional mode of production in Sepik societies as "domestic," with households forming the principle units of both production and consumption (Sahlins 1972). Access to critical resources typically derived from householders' membership in certain kinship groups (clans). In contrast to societies in which a "chiefly" clan or lineage is accorded special privileges and powers, however, village societies in the Sepik, in general, have been based on the assumption of equality among constituent groups. As Bryant Allen has noted, "exchanges between individuals within each group, and between the groups" were theoretically "equal and blanced, or if the relationship was inherently always one of imbalance, the superior-inferior positions should have regularly passed back and forth between the groups" (Allen 1984:4) Although competition for leadership and renown was keener in the central and eastern parts of the region than along its western fringe, considerable effort was everywhere expended to keep exchange between individuals and groups on a "balanced and equal" basis.

From the point of view of the Europeans who entered the Sepik in the late nineteenth century, many features of these village societies appeared as obstacles to their aims. It is conceivable that colonists interested primarily in trade would have found the predominant social and cultural configurations in the Sepik to be more congenial, but although it was trade for coconuts that eventually led to European settlement in the Sepik in the mid-1890s, the *idea* of trade had tarnished in the twenty years since Europeans had first settled in the Bismarck Archipelago. Most settlers had their eyes on the future success of the infant plantation industry; thus it was land and labor rather than access to native traders and their networks that dominated the colonists' concerns. Although the propensity of Sepik people to trade and "try out" novel products certainly facilitated European penetration of the region, the native propensity to value "balanced and equal exchange" brought grave problems. It was soon clear that Europeans would refuse to enter into such relationships with native people, "and instead maintained, commonly by force, a superior and dominating position" (Allen 1984:4).

THE COLONIAL ECONOMY BEFORE WORLD WAR II

The capacity of the European colonists to foster the conditions under which the natural and human resources of the Sepik could be advantageously linked to their own economic system was by no means unlimited in the years before World War II. Indeed, it took approximately forty years to establish even a semblance of control in the hills and plains between the coastal and riverine zones. The coast provided the only suitable area for the development of a plantation economy and the colonization of this zone became the principal achievement of the German administration before its demise during World War I.

The great resource of the Sepik in the larger colonial scheme, however, was not its land, but its people. The Germans were well aware that the large and numerous villages accessible to water transport on the Sepik river could ease the growing demand for labor by plantation interests in more prosperous parts of the colony. However, the extension of government control along the river was, of necessity, left to the Australian administration, and it was not until the early 1930s that the region emerged as the major labor reserve for the old plantations and for the newly discovered gold fields in districts far to the east. Predatory labor recruitment in the hills and plains occurred throughout the period under consideration. Yet, it was only when alluvial gold was discovered there in the mid-1930s that this zone also was placed on the official agenda for colonial expansion (Curtain 1980).

Preludes to Colonial Penetration

Prior to the arrival of Europeans, the Sepik region had probably been entered from the west by Chinese or Malay hunters seeking birds of paradise (Allen 1976:57). It is also possible that independent Chinese had been trading for copra and recruiting labor along the coast before 1900—the date cited by Rowley in noting an energetic Asian presence around Aitape (1958:74). However, neither Malays, Chinese, nor even the European voyagers who may have traveled in this vicinity during the 16th century appear to have left written descriptions of the land or its people. The anthropologist and agent for the Neu Guinea Compagnie, Otto Finsch, stated in 1885 that "of all the coasts of New Guinea there was none so little known as the northwestern . . ." (Tiesler 1969:5).

Finsch's trips along the north coast in search of sites suitable for the Neu Guinea Compagnie's settlement scheme produced the first records of the region available to Europeans and also placed several choice locations in the Company's hands. Among these records were elaborately worded deeds certifying Finsch's acquisition of "ownerless" land along the coast west of the mouth of the Sepik River, at Dallmannhafen near present-day Wewak, and at Angriffshafen (Vanimo) near the Dutch border (Sack 1973:122). Although Dalmannhafen was rejected as a site for the Company's first settlement on mainland New Guinea (Sack 1973:81), the Company sponsored further coastal exploration. Commissioned by Admiral Georg von Schleinitz, the first Company administrator, this exploration's "most notable achievement . . . was the navigation of the Sepik [River] for some 380 knots" (Moses 1969:49).

Soon, however, Schleinitz left, the settlement scheme was dropped, and the Dutch East Indies plan was begun. The Company became too embroiled in its problems to the east to follow through on its early leads to the coastal and riverine zones of the Sepik, and the area was officially ignored. It is not surprising to learn that in 1896, the Catholic missionaries of the Society of the Divine Word received instructions from their Superior General to found their first stations south and east of Friedrich Wilhelmshafen (Madang), and "in any event . . . not yet go north (Wiltgen 1969a:331). The principal source of information about the mainland at this time were the official progress reports published monthly by the Neu Guinea Compagnie itself. Although the Superior General may not have realized that Company officials habitually "dressed up" reports on their progress to the south and east of Madang, he apparently realized the significance of the Company's silence about the colony's western frontier.

It was, in fact, only at the time of the critical juncture between the Dutch East Indies plan and the Pacific plan for colonial development that the first European is reported to have settled in the Sepik. Ludwig Kärnbach, a former Company employee who had turned to independent trade, established a station on Seleo Island in 1894. Just across from Berlinhafen (Aitape), it was near one of the few areas on the entire north coast to boast sufficient numbers of coconuts to support a profitable trade. The Company itself provided the market: "in 1896 . . . [it] imported to Friedrich Wilhelmshafen and the Astrolabe Bay area 15,000 coconuts for planting that had been won by trade in Berlinhafen and the Bismarck Archipelago" (Wiltgen 1969a:332). The Berlinhafen area subsequently became the headquarters and staging point for more serious colonial efforts in the Sepik, beginning with the Catholic missionaries who settled on Tumleo Island at Kärnbach's suggestion in 1896, and the Company itself which took over Kärnbach's business after his death in the following year.

Politics and Plantations

If the pattern of European settlement in the Sepik, with an independent trader followed closely by a Christian mission and a commercial firm, is reminiscent of the pattern of European settlement in the Bismarck Archipelago some twenty years before, it must be argued that the similarities are only superficial. The absence of a body with governing powers in these islands, and the reliance of the colonists on trade for both profit and peace with the natives seem to have served as centrifugal forces, directing the colonists' efforts inward toward the islands themselves. When the Catholic mission and the Neu Guinea Compagnie came to the Sepik, however, land, not trade, was their key economic concern; access to land was controlled by governmental authority, directing the attention of missionaries and company officials away from the Sepik itself and towards the authorities in Friedrich Wilhelmshafen (Madang), Rabaul, and beyond.

The positions of the company and the mission placed them in competition from the start. The company still had its monopoly over the rights to obtain land in the mid-1890s and was technically the governing authority in the colony. Yet, negotiations were well underway for the company to relinquish its monopoly, along with the responsibilities for colonial administration, to the German Reich. Clearly, the company hoped to obtain title to as much land as possible before negotiations were concluded. Although the mission's business was not basically agricultural, the missionaries had understood that if they were to assure themselves of adequate means to support evangelism in New Guinea, they would have to own and manage coconut plantations, and thus would have to acquire land. The mission's Superior General had already obtained promises of land suitable for a mission plantation from the Company's headquarters in Berlin, but local officials in the protectorate demurred (Wiltgen 1969a:331).

Indeed, the Neu Guinea Compagnie not only refused the missionaries permission to acquire sufficient land for a plantation, but also refused to permit them to begin a mission station near the capital, as had originally been planned. Ludwig Kärnbach, the Sepik coconut trader, urged the missionaries to begin their work on an island in the Aitape harbor, hoping that the shipping firm of Norddeutscher Lloyd would thus be induced to include Aitape among its regular ports of call. The missionaries agreed to this change in their plans; yet, no sooner had they settled themselves on Tumleo Island than Kärnbach died, and the company took over his business, instead. The agent stationed in Aitape promptly blocked the mission's request for plantation land again, and during the next two years engaged in a land-buying spree along the entire northwest coast. Although many of this agent's acquisitions were later disallowed by the Imperial Government, it still took many years before the mission was able to acquire sufficient land for stations and coconut plantations along the Sepik coast.

If the early history of colonial activity in the Sepik differed from that of the Bismarck Archipelago because of the far greater power commanded by one of the competing parties, it was also notable for the lack of interest that other colonists displayed. The islands were soon buzzing with traders and settlers all plotting against each other and occasionally against the natives or against administrative interference later on. The only early settlers in the Sepik aside from Catholic missionaries and company employees appear to have been Chinese traders, though it is not known whether they came from China or Indonesia as businessmen or from the east as former plantation laborers. The only subsequent planters to arrive before World War I appear to have been those induced to begin plantations by the government's bird-of-paradise scheme. When bird-of-paradise plumes came into fashion in Europe, the colonial government (then firmly in the hands of the Reich) attempted to link settlement to the hunt in the Sepik, so that hunting would subsidize the first years of a plantation, replacing the older pattern in which planting was subsidized by trade (Sturgeon 1942:309). The settlers who arrived in this way are not storied in history, but it is likely that they were soon bound up in ties of credit and debt to the Neu Guinea Compagnie, Norddeutscher Lloyd, or one of the other large trading firms that dominated the colonial economy in the first decade of the twentieth century (Sack 1973:104).

If the plantation sector along the northwest coast never flourished as it had in more dynamic parts of the colony, the surge of capital investment that these other regions enjoyed in the second decade of the twentieth century, never materialized in the Sepik at all. The only whisper that I have found reported by historians was a plan, in which "Erzberger, who had been a leading anticolonial member of Parliament, applied, encouraged by the Divine Word Mission, in 1913 for 250,000 acres of land for a settlement scheme in the Torricelli Mountains, inland of Aitape" (Sack 1973:105). Perhaps it was the success of the botanist, Rudolf Schlechter, who succeeded in crossing the Torricelli divide in 1909, that lay behind this curious plan. Certainly no Europeans, including the missionaries, had succeeded in settling away from navigable waters this early in the colonial history of the Sepik. Indeed, in most parts of the coastal range, "Malays and Chinese were the first outsiders to come into contact with the northern villages" (Allen 1976:58).

Labor Recruitment and Government Control

As I have noted earlier, it was neither through land and plantations nor through an ability to attract new capital investment that the Sepik eventually obtained its place in the developing colonial economy. In the country's "rapid transformation from a trading frontier to a plantation colony" (Firth 1976:56), it was labor that the Sepik could most obviously provide. From the start, in fact, this was a minor theme of colonial enterprise: Ludwig Kärnbach himself had recruited labor along the coast before taking up his coconut trade (Tiesler 1969:116). Perhaps more significant than German entrepreneurs in this early period, however, were the Malays and Chinese who readily added recruiting to their bird-of-paradise trade, making effective use of the trade networks of their coastal partners to reach into the villages of the coastal range and beyond.

One result of such incursions in the area of the Torricelli Mountains "was a widespread upheaval of village life on a scale previously unknown" (Allen 1976:60). Villagers here remember the period of early recruitment for its violence and terror. Asian recruiters appear to have directed their native assistants from the coast to descend on inland villages in raids at dawn, and to capture young men and women, often by holding their elders hostage. The young women might be taken as wives by the recruiters themselves, and the younger men (perhaps two to four per raid) indentured as laborers. Ridiculed for their lack of clothing and backward ways by more experienced coastal villagers, the new recruits would then be sent off in ships over an ocean which they had never seen before. Exposed to new diseases, to unfamiliar routines, and to unfamiliar languages and people, Allen notes, many never returned. "Those who came back to Aitape after three years," however, "were men of wide experience in the white man's world, relative to their fellows who remained in the bush" (Allen 1976:60–61; quotation, p. 61).[3]

This style of recruitment was not peculiar to the Chinese, nor was recruitment in the Sepik during the period of German rule limited to the mountains and hills south of Aitape. Firth notes that it was, in fact, "common German practice" to take (that is, kidnap) "villagers to Kokopo or Madang to dispel ignorance about signing on . . ." (1976:57). As to geographical range, Firth also notes that recruiters for the New Guinea Compagnie were sent as far as 100 kilometers upstream on the Sepik River in 1908 (1982:84). The governor of the colony, Albert Hahl, cruised up the Sepik River in that same year, and a naval commander on board reported: "For the Governor the first consideration in the further opening of the river basin is whether natives from there can be recruited as manpower" (Firth 1976:56). They could: "Figures given in the 1910–11 Report show the growing importance of the large populations of the Sepik Valley," although as new recruits, these Sepik River workers were not yet counted as established members of the experienced labor force (Rowley 1958:110).

Although the Sepik region did not realize its full value as a labor reserve until the 1930s, the importance of labor recruitment to colonial history in the Sepik was manifest early on, not least as a factor in moving the colonial government to action. According to Stewart Firth, Albert Hahl "looked forward to making New Guinea a colony of Southeast Asian type, populated by tens of thousands of Chinese, Filipinos and Indians, and he tried hard to interest planters in indentured Asian laborers" (1976:61–62). Yet, the poor record of Asians in New Guinea, as well as changes in the political position of Germany itself, made foreign colonial governments reluctant to permit their subjects to be recruited in large numbers for the German colony. There were internal pressures to develop a local labor force as well. Asian labor was costly, and planters preferred to obtain their work force from the territory, itself. The effects were evident by 1914, for

> the foreign coloured population . . . had reached a mere 1,609 . . . and few of them had come as indentured labourers. What had oc-

curred was an influx of artisans and traders, mostly Chinese, who brought valuable skills and services to the colony but did not replace New Guineans in the plantation fields [Firth 1976:63].

Although Governor Hahl could not have known in the early years of his administration that his plan to import Asian labor would meet a fate similar to the Neu Guinea Compagnie's Dutch East Indies plan, he did realize that alternative methods to those used before would be necessary both to recruit any satisfactory number of natives to the labor force and to maintain the peaceful conditions required for plantation agriculture and commerce. In place of *laissez faire* in regard to native affairs, Hahl adopted a policy of direct rule that finally endowed colonial government in the territory with a sense of urgency and purpose. Under this plan, previously independent areas were "organized" by appointing *luluais* and *tultuls* (headmen and assistants) in the villages. These men were frequently subjected to severe pressure to encourage young men to sign on as contract laborers, and head taxes were instituted to further the same end. The government's "presence" was intensified in a few organized areas by "control,"—that is, the establishment of a government station, the building of roads, and so forth (Rowley 1958:37–38).

The establishment of government and the creation of a local labor force appear to have been inextricably linked throughout the German colony:

> . . . the lesson which [the incoming administration] drew from the [New Guinea] Company's failure was that New Guineans would have to be conquered it they were to be turned into a useful labour force. A general mobilization of the villagers in the service of the Germans would follow naturally from the spread of government. Visiting punitive expeditions, the Germans now realized, were not enough; permanent government stations were needed to protect European settlers, carry out peaceful patrols, appoint luluais, build roads and assist labour recruiters. . . . The first new government station, set up in 1900, was at Kavieng in northern New Ireland. . . . From 1906 the emphasis switched to the mainland coast and the Admiralty islands: Aitape (1906), Morobe (1909), Manus (1911), Angoram (1913) and Lae (1914) [Firth 1976:55].

Although the need for the government to control the activities of Europeans and to establish a proper role for itself vis-à-vis competing commercial and missionary interests should not be discounted in understanding Hahl's "native policy," it must be recalled that recruiting was a field in which the government could meet all these objectives simultaneously.

In the Sepik, the connection between government and recruiting is clear. The station at Angoram, mentioned above by Firth, was on the lower Sepik River, a "growth area" for labor recruitment at the time of its opening in 1913. Aitape, on the north coast, has already been introduced as the principal staging point for various European activities in the region. As a site in the government's strategy to extend control, however, Aitape was not a great success for the station supplied far fewer recruits than expected and the officers experienced numerous acts of native defiance:

> The Aitape district in western Kaiser Wilhelmsland . . . never realized what the Germans thought was its recruiting potential. When the area was first opened to large-scale recruiting by the coming of the government station in 1906 the Germans knew that the hinterland villages were populous. But they were unable to exploit them for labour. For long the coastal peoples had monopolized trade with the Europeans and they proceeded to monopolize dealings with recruiters. The villager in the mountains might go once to the plantations but he would not go again after having to hand over his three years' earnings to a coastal enemy in order to get home again. Governor Hahl asked the navy to show the flag at Aitape in 1908: the district officer's work in building roads and furthering recruitment, he explained, could at any moment suffer a reverse. In January 1909 Hahl concluded that the situation would have to stay as it was because of lack of finance, with control incomplete and recruitment therefore well below the level allowed by the size of the population. Naval visits, repeated along that coastline up to the war, did little to intimidate the New Guineans: on the coast west of Aitape villagers reworked dud German shells into favourite sago stompers. Aitape's quota of recruits remained almost stable from 1911 onwards [Firth 1976:60].

As for the interior region of the Sepik, little was known and less was accomplished during the period of German colonial rule. Tuzin has suggested that with the stations of Aitape on the coast and Angoram on the Sepik River, there was little need to penetrate the hills and plains in between, and that, in any case, access was difficult: "visiting this region involved trekking over the precipitous Prince Alexander and Torricelli mountains or, even less inviting, traversing the mosquito-rich swamps north of the Sepik River" (1976:28).

It is likely, however, that if German officials had fully realized that parts of this interior harbored large and relatively dense settlements, they would have made the attempt because the labor demands of the colonists in other regions of the country were becoming increasingly insistent and strong (Firth 1976:63–64). However, although exploration of the Sepik River had occurred early enough to confirm the presence of large numbers of potential recruits, exploration of the interior came too late. In 1913 the anthropologist Richard Thurnwald made his first expedition from the river to the coast following an eastern route, through more sparsely settled territory. Later that year, however, Thurnwald traveled further to the west, and in his report waxed "lyric in his appreciation of the rich artistic and ceremonial life he glimpsed, the towering spirit houses, and the enormous villages—sometimes reaching an estimated 800 to 1,000 inhabitants" (Tuzin 1976:26). Thurnwald recognized the practical import of this discovery, pointing out that "recruitment would be a primary consideration in this region" (1914:83, cited in Scaglion 1983:471). World politics, of course, prevented the German colony from following through.

The Australian Military Occupation

It is customary in historical accounts of New Guinea to take stock of colonial accomplishments in 1914, the year that Australians rather quietly displaced the Germans at the behest of the British government. The Australians themselves took stock at this time, for they aimed to maintain the economy of the colony in as firm a shape as possible—partly because of the requirements of international law and partly because they expected to inherit the colony if the allied forces proved victorious in World War I. Historians present the statistics from 1914 not only because they exist, however, but also because the state in which the Germans left New Guinea remained something of a high point in colonial development for many years to come. During the Australian military administration and for several years after the resumption of civil administration in 1921, the apparatus of German "control" was allowed to erode, with jungle literally growing over many of the roads.

By 1914, the mainland of New Guinea had been graced with only five important government stations: the old capital at Madang; the second-and third-class stations of Morobe and Lae to the east; and the second- and third-class stations of Aitape and Angoram on the Sepik frontier. The German government's growing confidence and hopes in regard to the recruitment of labor, however, were expressed in plans to upgrade Aitape into a first-class station, to establish two new posts in the Sepik at Vanimo and at Wewak, and to connect the river post of Angoram with new stations on the Markham and Ramu rivers to the east. With the coming of the war and the new administration, however, Vanimo and Wewak were not established as government stations until 1918 and 1920, respectively, and Angoram was not connected with other stations but abandoned temporarily, instead. Aitape gained in importance during the war, for its office "had a special function in preventing contacts by German settlers with the outside world through Dutch New Guinea" (Rowley 1958:42).

Despite the new stations on the north coast, the area under government control diminished during the first years of Australian administration, and the government was removed as a presence from regions that the Germans had only considered "organized." Recruiters appear to have taken advantage of the situation wherever possible, and provoked chaos by their excessive zeal. In the Sepik, a German was killed in retaliation by inland natives, who then suffered a punitive expedition in which whole villages were burned. When the victims subsequently made plans to kill all Europeans in the area, the Australian patrol that investigated the rumor ended by killing twelve of them. Another series of incidents involving recruitment on the Sepik River also led to retaliation by inexperienced Australian officers, and thence to native attacks on the mission station at Marienberg, on the lower Sepik River, in January 1920 and on the reestablished government station at Angoram in June of the same year (Rowley 1958:202–205).

The number of Europeans actually settled in the Sepik could not have been large when the Australian government arrived. Rowley notes that on 1 December 1914, there were only 1,150 Germans in the entire colony, "when most of the officials and their wives were apparently still there. . . . When the officials departed, with some others, the purely German element in the European population must have been something less than 1,000" (1958:56). By 1917 the total European population was only 910, and its "German element" had declined to 680, of which 221 were missionaries, 144 settlers and planters, and 315 others, who "must have been mainly businessmen and their dependents" (Rowley 1958:57). In the Sepik, Germans predominated, but would nonetheless have numbered only a very small fraction of those in the colony as a whole.

For these few missionaries, planters, and business people, the time was one of great insecurity. They were not only isolated at their scattered stations or posts, but they were also under the unpredictable rule of inexperienced officers who considered them "enemy aliens." Although the Australian government was formally committed to protect the conditions under which the remaining Germans pursued their business, incidents of deportation and internment demonstrated the apprehension and suspicion with which officers on the spot regarded German nationals. In 1916 for example, the administrator of the territory "had to reprove a zealous Officer for having removed all settlers between [Aitape] and the border" (Rowley 1958:42).

The experience of the predominantly German Catholic missionaries of the Society of the Divine Word contained elements that were probably common to other German nationals in the Sepik and in the colony at large. The interruption of communications with Europe, and the disruption of the sea routes that had previously served as the source of supply brought economic hardships, only somewhat relieved by their newly enforced reliance on markets and merchants in Australia. Some problems faced by the missionaries involved the disruption of their organizational support—new members could not be sent to relieve those who were old, tired, and sick. For all Germans in New Guinea, however, there was insecurity about the future. Australia vacillated over the issue whether German missionaries would be permitted to remain in the colony after the war. Ultimately, the missionaries were more fortunate than others, for they were permitted to remain. However, their countrymen in business and in the public service were returned to Germany, and their possessions were expropriated and sold to non-German, principally Australian, bidders (Townsend 1968:27–29).

Civil Administration Before World War II

By the end of the period of Australian military administration in 1921, the flourish of hope that had colored the final years of German rule had been effaced and the basic pattern was set for conducting colonial affairs until after World War II. The three successive administrators of New Guinea (now a League of Nations mandate), were all military veterans, honored—or saddled—with a territory that Australians at home knew and cared little about. With a far from adequate budget and a skeleton staff at their disposal, they could take little initiative to change conditions anywhere, and the Sepik region continued as a frontier in relation to the rest of the colony.

Historians of colonialism in New Guinea frequently dwell on the poverty of the official colonial effort in the interwar period. It is true that the Mandated Territory of New Guinea received more funds than the Australian colony of Papua to the south, but the means available were still not sufficient to foster the lofty ends of native welfare and self-rule that were incorporated into the terms of the League of Nations mandate. The administrative field staff in New Guinea increased to more than seventy officers during the 1930s. Although this was better than the situation in 1924, when approximately forty inexperienced men constituted the administration's field staff, there were still too few officers to effectively administer native affairs.[4] According to a review of the Australian administration conducted by Colonel John Ainsworth in 1924, some of the early Australian officers had to depend "to a considerable extent on a prison population to keep their stations in order" (Mair 1970:35; Townsend 1968:52–54). It must also be noted, however, that "owing to the greater importance of the commercial community," many of the later officers "had to give their entire time to dealing with questions affecting Europeans" (Mair 1970:35).

It may have been partly because of the poverty of the administration that commercial interests predominated in the colony during the years between the two world wars. The private sector saw to its own in the Bismarck Archipelago and in Morobe after the gold strikes that began in 1926, but colonists in the Sepik shared in none of these "boom" conditions and experienced little relief from their chronic problems of supply and communications. As we shall see in the next chapter, the first leader of the Catholic mission in the Sepik had been obliged to move his headquarters from Aitape to the Madang area in 1904 when Norddeutscher Lloyd discontinued its six-week shipping service between Singapore and Aitape. He reported that only a subsidy from the German colonial government made it possible for them to continue service to the capitals of Friedrich Wilhelmshafen, on the mainland, and Herbertshohe, in the Bismarck Archipelago (Wiltgen 1969a:347). Later residents in the Sepik also realized that commercial production was essential if they wished better conditions of service and supply. Yet, apart from the few plantations owned by the mission and the private planters, the Sepik had little besides contract labor to export. G.W.L. Townsend, posted to the area as a government officer for most of the interwar period, hoped heartily for the success of an oil search party and for the success of the gold prospectors who arrived in the early 1930s, but with little result (1968:195).

Nonetheless, the changing economic interests of colonists in the Sepik did foster major shifts within the region itself. The small plantation sector on the coast was soon superseded in importance by labor recruitment, and the Sepik River became the "glamour" spot in the 1920s and 1930s, as administrators concentrated on pacification and recruiters sent increasing numbers of laborers out to the plantations and mine fields of the east. By the mid-1930s overrecruitment on the river, and the discovery of alluvial gold to the north brought the region behind the coastal range into focus. Yet, for the "settled" colonists hoping to improve the economic performance of the Sepik in relation to the rest of the colony, the mining effort was as disappointing in the long run as the plantation sector had proved to be earlier. It never attained the large scale of the gold strike in the Morobe region to the east. Although both of these mining operations can be credited with opening their respective areas to other kinds of colonial enterprise, the Maprik region could not compete in the colonial imagination with the vast network of densely settled intermontane valleys of the New Guinea highlands, which commanded national, and even international, attention in the late 1930s.

Events in the Sepik during the interwar years appear to have had an exclusively local significance, even though mining and planting elsewhere in the territory came to depend increasingly on the Sepik for labor. If, as Mair has stated, there was in the territory at large "an atmosphere in which rapid commerical development was regarded as the most important aim" (1970:13), the Sepik's position as a backwater for European enterprise made it all but invisible to the eyes of the contemporary colonial public. Population figures are particularly revealing in this respect. If the Sepik River is not included, there were, according to Sturgeon, only about 66 Europeans "who could be considered as more or less attached permanently to the district" (1942:309).[5] Of these, only ten were planters and traders. Four belonged to an oil prospecting firm, two were recruiters, nine were government officials, and one was the district radio-telegraphist. Forty—or nearly two-thirds of the district's settled whites—were, if Sturgeon's figures are correct, Catholic missionaries of the Society of the Divine Word. In a country where commercial interests dominated, the liability of the Sepik is evident from the occupational composition of its colonial population alone. Nationality should also be mentioned. Most of the twenty-six "secular" residents were of Australian or British origin, while most of the forty missionaries were from German-speaking coutries of Europe, a fact of increasing significance as World War I receded and World War II approached.

Australians, of course, feared excessive German influence on the natives at both ends of the interwar period, but the missionaries were also a reminder of the differences between the two colonial regimes. The industrious, if somewhat visionary, character of the later period under imperial German rule was not lost to the region when the Australian military occupied Aitape in 1914, nor when German planters were sent home at the end of the war. The "German" term of the contrast was embodied throughout the interwar period by these Catholic missionaries, whose neat establishments along the coast stood in anomalous juxtaposition to the rough-and-ready Australian establishments, and whose efficiency and industry were frequently noted with ambivalent approbation by secular observers of the Sepik scene.

CHAPTER 3

The Catholic Mission
and its Material Base

*According to historical experience, without a money economy the
bureaucratic structure can hardly avoid undergoing substantial internal changes. . . .*

—MAX WEBER

*No matter what kind of job comes up, the story is always the same:
if we don't take care of it ourselves, no one else moves a finger.*

—EBERHARD LIMBROCK

The experience of colonists in the Sepik prior to World War II was
dominated by their awareness of the region as a frontier, distant not only
in miles and comforts from the centers of colonial society, but separated
in structure and spirit from the strictures of metropolitan ideals. Romola
McSwain has said that Europeans in the neighboring district of Madang
"saw the economic, political and religious systems as discrete entities,"
that "individuals involved themselves in only one aspect of the economy,"
and that the "missions restricted their activities almost entirely to religious and educational change" (1977:29). This is certainly an adequate
rendering of social ideology among colonial Europeans, but it is not an
adequate rendering of how the "bureaucratic structure" developed on the
Sepik frontier. As the quotation from Eberhard Limbrock, the Catholic
mission's first leader, suggests, it was no simple matter to construct reli-

The epigraphs at the head of this chapter are from
H. H. Gerth and C. Wright Mill's *From Max Weber:
Essays in Sociology* (New York: Oxford University
Press, 1958), 205.
Ralph M. Wiltgen's "Catholic Mission Plantations in
Mainland New Guinea: Their Origin and Purpose,"
in *History of Melanesia* (Canberra: Australian
National University Press, 1969), 340.

gion as a separate institutional domain in a region lacking active administrative and commercial support. Under Limbrock's direction, the mission became the most active economic agent in the region, providing not only sermons and schools for the natives, but sawn timber for government stations and private establishments, transportation services on its steamer, agricultural experimentation, and, of course, coconut plantations for its own financial support.

Understandably, such a display of self-sufficiency violated the model of organic solidarity implicit in the secular European social ideal. As we have already seen, the mission's pursuit of land for plantations brought it into competition with the Neu Guinea Compagnie early on, while the later success of the mission's plantations and industries formed a distinctive part of the mission's identity in the eyes of other colonists as well. Yet, the same combination of enterprise and evangelism that was subject to ironic, and sometimes politically dangerous, comment from the outside, also involved internal contradictions for the mission itself. This chapter, then, examines the development of the mission's material base not merely in itself, but as a vehicle for discussing the ambiguous and paradoxical relations that constituted important aspects of the colonial experience for missionaries on the Sepik frontier.

FRONTIER SOCIETY AND THE OCCUPATIONAL CODE

Frederick Jackson Turner's attribution of central features of American society to Americans' experience on the American frontier might have found willing ears among European residents of the Sepik during the years before World War II. The reports, letters, and memoirs produced by Europeans in the area during that time all dwell on the region's singular character, the difficulties faced by the writers, and the lengths to which they had to go to adapt. No one was exempt, it seems, from the prevailing rusticity of life "in this wilderness at the farthest ends of the earth" (Wiltgen 1969a:339). In the words of a young American priest who had joined the Catholic mission in 1935, New Guinea was "a land of the unexpected" (Angelus 1936), a theme as frequently illustrated by the peculiarities of its European denizens as by the exotica of native life. Traveling in the Sepik during the 1920s and 1930s one might meet, according to travelers and memoirists, a Catholic bishop in shirtsleeves checking in the cargo from a coastal steamer (Marshall 1938:221), a government officer on a tax raid outside his jurisdiction (Townsend 1968:159), a planter who had left his coastal estate to roam the interior recruiting labor (Mead 1977:103), or an illiterate drifter running the district's major store (McCarthy 1963:137).

Perhaps nothing was used so frequently by memoirists to characterize the singularity of life in the Sepik as such "standard" deviations from the proprieties of the division of labor that underlie European ideas of the status quo. The Pacific historian, H. E. Maude, has suggested that "to divide [colonial] agents . . . into occupational categories—beachcombers, missionaries, whalers, traders, planters, government officials, and so on" is no more than a "convenient abstraction" because the categories "merge in their constituent personnel and overlap in time" (1968:134). Whatever shortcomings such practice entails for historical analysis, however, it is clear that these occupational categories deserve attention by the anthropologist because they constituted a code used by the colonists themselves. If the historiographical utility of this code is limited by a lack of fit between convention and reality, it is precisely this lack of fit that made occupational categories so useful to colonists as a rhetorical device for depicting the unusual and unconventional aspects of life on the frontier.

Separations in the Code

Categories such as "missionary," "government officer," "planter," "miner," and "recruiter" are used so pervasively in the memoirs and letters of Europeans in New Guinea that they can be said to represent the principal lines of classification in colonial society and to reveal much about the kind of order colonists were attempting to create or recreate in New Guinea. The use of occupational categories in that literature suggests, in particular, that separation between the sectors represented by such occupational types was expected as "ideologically correct." J. K. McCarthy, for example, virtually *begins* his memoirs with his first lesson in the colony's occupational code. When he boarded the ancient steamer in Sydney that was to take him to Rabaul in 1927, a "pale, wizened steward" took one look at him and guessed on sight that McCarthy was headed to the territory's capital at Rabaul as "Government:"

> "... How did you know I was Government?"
> "When you've been on the run as long as I have . . . you get to know the types. You haven't got the missionary look . . . you're not a planter or trader, else you would be in the bar by now with the rest of 'em, getting full. And you're not a member of bloody Parliament, so you must be Government" [1963:5].

It is not really important to ascertain whether this exchange actually took place, because the anecdote's significance derives less from its role in McCarthy's life than from its role in McCarthy's text. Like most writers in the genre of the travel memoir, McCarthy begins his story with a brief account of leaving home. The episode here fulfills the rhetorical function of the traveler's first incorporation into the new society for which he is bound. Just as the boat, "an elderly coalburner . . . permanently permeated with the smell of copra" was the author's physical means of transport to New Guinea, so the rough and ready code produced by the steward was the key to McCarthy's place in the colony. McCarthy's occupation was the vehicle for the experience to follow in his memoirs, and it would be a different experience (that is, separate) from that of a missionary, a planter or trader, or a visiting VIP.

Boats and ships figure frequently in memoirs and letters of the period, not only as the principal means of passage to and from New Guinea but also as the principal means of moving from one part of the territory to another. Many writers thus used boats and ships as a vehicle for commenting on changes in the social order that accompanied a movement from a local center to a local frontier as well. Margaret Mead, for example, contrasted life in the capital of the territory with life on the frontier in a succinct description of the passengers aboard a steamer in 1938 heading from Rabaul to mainland New Guinea, at Madang:

> . . . we had five days on the Montoro and our first touch of out-station life again. Rabaul is very civilized and full of cocktails these days. On the Montoro there were two sisters come to inspect their order, two Methodist missionaries who didn't drink anything, a huge Australian priest who looked like his German brethren and whose Queensland accent was like a blow in the face, so unexpected it was, a mob of miners who told one the names of imaginary public schools they had once attended and how their fathers refused to let them go out of Africa with Cecil Rhodes because it was 'like going into trade' and who solemnly discussed the charms, probably never seen, of Budapest, and an earnest-faced boy coming up to do two years at a lonely trading station in Papua [Mead 1977:219].

If the transition from the center of colonial society to its frontiers could be characterized by the sudden appearance of types with whom one would not normally have mixed, a spell of frontier life could be so isolating that a sea or river journey within its bounds could offer the illusion of a jarring return. Some months after his arrival in New Guinea, for example, a young priest who had been staying at the mission station on Tumleo Island, marveled at the mixture of passengers aboard a schooner making a coastal run: "Captain . . . anthropologist, district officer, recruiter, and a Yankee priest" (Angelus 1936). The collage effect was also evident to Mead herself who, after spending some months among the Mundugumor with the anthropologist Reo Fortune, found herself bemused by the social flotsam dumped by traffic on the Sepik River for an overnight stay at the government station at Ambunti:

> . . . we [Mead, Fortune, and the anthropologist Bateson] stayed with the wholly adorable District Officer, Robbie, who is loved by and loves everyone. He had as a guest, chance-sent on a recruiter's pin-

*nace, a most ambiguous female with a rattrap mouth, mascara eyes
and a wholly suspicious and deadly restraint of manner, who was, I
think, pretending to pretend that she wasn't a reporter or spy from
the League of Nations. . . .*

*Then there were recruiters and pinnace owners and a ship's
captain who could talk our Arapesh language, having blown up all
the drums in one of their villages years ago as a government officer.
There was a mad, proud recruiter and a slightly truculent little one,
and government officers—some good boy scouts and some not. Altogether it made quite an odd party [Mead 1977:140].*

As Mead's passage obliquely suggests, however, frontier life as symbolized by the collection of passengers on the Montoro and at the odd party
assembled in Ambunti does not match the expectations that one might
have of normal society as symbolized by the cocktail parties at Rabaul or
as one might expect from the occupational code. "Mystery," in Kenneth
Burke's terms, is the "obverse expression of the disrelationship among
classes" (Burke 1965:278), but Mead's suggestion that people on the frontier were not always what they pretended to be or what one might expect
them to be, is a critique of colonial society achieved by translating mystery into sham. The priest on the Montoro, who looked like his (dignified) German confreres, had an (undignified) Australian accent; the
"mob of miners" only pretended to respectability; the "ambiguous female" at Ambunti was a poor excuse for a spy; government officers were
just "boy scouts," and some of them bad ones at that. Mead recognizes
that separation between occupational types constituted the colonial order, but she questions the authenticity of that order on the frontier by
moving the differences between the types from the realm of drama to that
of charade.

Distortions of the Code

Mead, of course, was not the only chronicler of life in the Sepik to sense
that the nice distinctions of European society might be distorted on its
frontiers. G. W. L. Townsend recalled with some scorn how in his early
years as a government officer stationed at Aitape in the 1920s, "Government" had had to use prison labor to run the plantations that had been
expropriated from German owners by the Australian Expropriation
Board. He recalled the story of the plantation at Sissano, west of Aitape,
as a particularly rich example of colonial social logic carried to its most
absurd extreme. This plantation, too small to merit an expensive European manager, was finally assigned by the District Officer to a Chinese
prisoner in his charge:

*In order that the [District Officer] might faithfully report the pres-
ence and wellbeing of the prisoner in his charge to the authorities in*

> Rabaul, a native runner came down from Sissano each week—
> sometimes two of them came bearing baskets of oysters and prawns
> from the Sissano lagoon; and fowls, duck eggs and vegetables from
> the prisoner's garden. The oysters and prawns were the gift of God,
> and therefore free; but the remainder were the property of the pris-
> oner, and for these we paid a moderate price.
>
> The runners, having reported that the prisoner was still present
> and in his usual good health, took back with them the prison rations,
> rice, tinned meat, sugar, tea, salt, etc.; also whatever trade goods
> had been ordered from Ning Hee's store on the beach. The Chinese
> prisoner-manager, with his sale of produce to us and his sale of trade
> goods to the Sissano natives, had worked up a nice little business as a
> sideline, and his Aitape bank-balance grew steadily. It was sug-
> gested, at one time, that he should take out a trading-license, as
> required of all traders; but his objection that he did not require one,
> 'as he was Government,' was impossible to overrule [Townsend
> 1968:63; emphasis mine].

Like the purist in Townsend's story, who suggested that he who traded be treated as a trader regardless of his official status, most colonists who wrote and published memoirs and letters, expressed concern at keeping the domains of government, commerce, and religion separate and in proper relationship to each other. Yet, like the prisoner, who insisted that he be treated according to his official affiliation of "government" rather than according to his actual activities, most colonists realized that slippage in the alignment between official sectors and functional domains was inevitable in the conditions in which they lived and worked. As seen in the last chapter, vigorous business activity was the sine qua non of even barely adequate shipping service to the Sepik as well as of increased monies and personnel for the government. Without a visible business community, and in the virtual absence of a local market economy, colonists in the Sepik had to fend for themselves.

One effect of this situation was a convergence in the kinds of enterprise undertaken by people in the three major sectors of the society. Plantations might be run and labor recruited by government agents and missionaries as well as by private planters and recruiters. Each sector ran boats for its own transportation needs and storage sheds for its own materials and supplies. To be sure, although the convergence was not complete it was widely noted by colonists with an eye for the incongruous, and was considered unseemly by many and dangerous by some. One might admire the efficiency with which missionaries ran their stations and plantations, for example, but still question the propriety of a religious institution with "Ltd." following its name (Marshall 1938:225). Conversely, some German missionaries appear to have been concerned that Australian patrol officers were conducting their duties in a manner more befitting a lowly trader than a representative of the state. Townsend recalls that in his patrols up and down the coast, he often received the loan of a horse from Catholic fathers and brothers who felt that "Government" ought to have more dignity than to trudge along on foot (Townsend 1968:114).[1]

Given that the ideology of separate domains was most often evidenced by its breach, competition between Europeans in the Sepik during the period before World War II frequently involved accusations of sector impurity. Margaret Mead once expressed relief that she would be able to avoid a trip to the coast where all the whites "feel that the native should be reserved for their special varieties of exploitation" (1977:124); partly to this end, Europeans of different sector affiliations generally expressed their preference that the others restrict their activities to narrowly limited concerns. The British naturalist, A. J. Marshall, for example, felt that there was really no need for the Catholic missionaries to conduct so wide a range of activities in the late 1930s, when the government, in his opinion, was firmly in control (1938:225). Despite frequent acts of cooperation between individuals in the different sectors, there was great concern that natives not "misunderstand" the division of labor that Europeans were so imperfectly trying to establish in their midst. Missionaries might loan horses to the government officer, or carry him part way on the mission steamer, but they preferred to avoid the appearance of involvement in a government patrol (Townsend 1968:95). As we shall see later, the concern that natives might not learn to make the appropriate distinctions between different types of European could have serious political repercussions, as it did for the missionaries after World War II.

Yet, the problems that underspecialization might cause among different groups of Europeans, or the problems that Europeans feared that underspecialization might cause between themselves and the native people, could fade in comparison to the problems that might be caused within a single sector or institution. This may have been especially true for missionaries and government personnel, who were enmeshed in large organizations that exercised control over their agents by upholding specialized models as goals for their activity and as measures of their success. To purists in headquarters at home or in the capital, the many and varied occupations and alliances required for their field agents to establish and maintain their enterprise on the frontier could appear as diversions, threatening the identity of the enterprise itself. The problem of justifying the inevitable detours that conditions forced on their projects would, of course, have been even more critical for agents who had internalized the goals of their sending agencies than for those who may simply have wished to keep their jobs. The ironic expressions through which so many colonists represented their experience in the Sepik could thus have political import in regard to internal as well as external political affairs.

Although Barnett and Silverman (1979:13) have argued that "separations" in modern ideology in categories such as the family, business, religion, and government distort the relations of modern society by suggesting divisions among institutions that are actually internally linked, the point here is not whether the categories of the occupational code are or are not adequate to a discussion of colonial society in some basic analytical sense. Rather, my point is to show that actors understood their work and the work of their fellows in terms of such categories, and that their confusion created an important problem in frontier life. It is partly for this reason that Father Ralph Wiltgen, a missionary historian of the Society of the Divine Word, could so fruitfully focus his discussion of the early history of the Catholic mission in the Sepik on the development of its plantations and industries. To anticipate the following discussion, however, I must note an important category shift. If, for secular colonials, it was the mission's combination of "business" with "religion" that rankled or rang untrue, the internal problem for the mission had less to do with such secular categories than with their theological cousins, "spiritual" and "material" work.

EBERHARD LIMBROCK AND THE MATERIAL BASE

It is significant that Father Ralph Wiltgen wrote his article on "Catholic Mission Plantations in Mainland New Guinea: Their Origin and Purpose" in 1969—after the deliberations of the Second Vatican Council and the papal encyclical "On the Development of Peoples" (Paul VI, 1967). The latter, especially, enabled Wiltgen to depict the mission's first prefect apostolic, Father Eberhard Limbrock, as a man ahead of his times. As architect of the mission's system of plantations and industries along the north coast, Limbrock had been a controversial figure among his contemporaries. As the mission's prefect (acting as a bishop), Limbrock had been responsible for both the effectiveness and the authenticity of the Catholic mission project, yet had for a long time been found wanting on both counts. It was, in fact, only after Limbrock's "farming system" enabled the mission to survive the isolation of World War I that his foresight was recognized within the community. And it was only after Vatican II that one who views the kind of work directed by Limbrock as "development" could present Limbrock's policies as theologically prescient as well.

A glance at the history of Catholic views on the role of economic development in mission work may illuminate the internal context in which Limbrock's policies received their initial interpretation. Arbuckle (1978:284) provides a useful summary of theological emphases on this issue over the past century or so:

Period	Emphasis
Post-Vatican II	"Development is an essential part of mission work"
Vatican II	"Development is useful to show people that the church is relevant"
Pre-Vatican II	"Development work helps the missionary to make pastoral contact with people" or "it has no direct connection with missionary work, but it can be useful"
Extremely Pre-Vatican II	"Development work is dangerous, it distracts the missionary from his real work"

It is necessary to move to the bottom of this list to characterize the dominant emphasis in Catholic missiology in the 1890s when the mission to New Guinea was officially begun. Of course, Catholic mission theology has never been univocal. However, even such "liberal" theologians as Joseph Schmidlin of the Münster School, who became associated with the Society of the Divine Word in 1911 (Bornemann 1975:482), placed "economic and charitable missionary activity" last in his catalog of "indirect missionary means" (Schmidlin 1931:435–440).

To understand the controversy surrounding Limbrock's plantations and industries, it is necessary to see that they were initially conceived in conformity with contemporary emphases in missiology, not as "development work" with "charitable aims" but as sources of finance and supply that would enable the missionaries to get on with the "spiritual" work of salvation—that is, bringing people into communion with the Roman Catholic Church (Ferguson 1984:117). It was expected, in other words, that "material work," while necessary, could be contained within the conventional hierarchy of missionary means, remaining subordinate to such direct means as prayer, example and sacrifice, preaching, and the catechumenate and baptism (Schmidlin 1931:340–391).[2]

It is important to note at the start that this hierarchical model of missionary means created a missionary situation different from that of missionaries fielded by some evangelical groups at the same time. Beidelman's historical ethnography of the Church Missionary Society in Tanzania, for example, places great emphasis on the contradictions that the technical requirements of frontier work caused for missionaries whose spiritual identity rested upon a rejection of the achievements of secular culture and science (1982a:99–126; Nemer 1981:22). Unlike these ascetically inclined missionaries, the Catholic missionaries of the Society of the Divine Word were not embarrassed by the necessity of using modern technology and science, nor of engaging in commercial activity to maintain themselves in the mission field. The problems caused by Father Limbrock's plantations and industries in New Guinea resulted not from any contradiction between the work required and the Society's spiritual orientation, but from the fact that the work grew too large to be contained within the Society's division of spiritual and material labor between priests and brothers—a division that embedded the theologically approved hierarchy of missionary means within the class structure of the countries from which its missionaries were drawn.

The SVD: Internal and External Affairs

The New Guinea mission was only the fourth foreign mission fielded by the Society of the Divine Word, one of several Catholic mission-sending societies founded in Europe during the revival of Catholic foreign mission work in the second half of the nineteenth century (Schmidlin 1933). Established in 1875 as a seminary for training German priests and seminarians (students for the priesthood) for mission work, the institute's statutes were revised in 1885 to establish the group as a full-fledged religious congregation dedicated to serve and staff Catholic missions in foreign lands (Bornemann 1975:166–175). The Society's first missionaries began work in South Shantung, China in 1882; in 1888, they began to send missionaries to South America; in 1892, missionaries were sent to the German colony of Togo in Africa; and in 1896, the first SVD missionaries arrived in the German colony of Kaiser Wilhelmsland in New Guinea. Two aspects of this brief chronology demand our attention here: first, that the Society was still devising its methods and procedures for administering foreign missions when the New Guinea mission was established, and second, that the Society had little prior experience in the extreme conditions like those that prevailed on the Sepik frontier.

Perhaps the most important implication of the SVD's relative youth in 1896 was the Society's extreme self-consciousness concerning matters of spiritual identity and organizational form—matters which, in the world of Catholic religious congregations, have always been inextricably linked with the special purposes for which the Society has been founded. The sociologist E. K. Francis has, for example, contrasted the "Gemeinschaft" type of monastic community constituted by rules that emphasize stable local communities, whose members are separated from the outside world, and the "Gesellschaft" type of religious order with rules that facilitate geographical mobility and engagement with the outside world (1950:438–439). Although Francis rightly points to the long-term historical trend away from communities shaped by the former type of rule to those which are shaped by the latter type, one can see from the early history of the SVD that a particular society may move between these poles, and may even come to be composed of separate groups characterized by different types of spiritual orientation and rule.

The first important shift in these matters of spiritual identity and organizational form came for the SVD in the mid-1880s. At that time, the group changed its constitution from one appropriate to a small group living in a single seminary to one appropriate to a complex religious society composed of priests, brothers, and sisters living in a number of "houses" in different European countries as well as abroad. Rudolf Pöhl has referred to this as a shift from a "spirit of apostolic spirituality" to a "spirit of institution." The former is characterized by strict observances in regard to fasting, silence, and devotions, while in the latter the rules of the community are altered to facilitate a more active life style and to conform to Vatican standards for the constitution of a modern mission-sending religious congregation (1977:57–79; Fischer 1925:267–279; Bornemann 1975:166–175). Although the more communal, contemplative model of religious life was formally resurrected by the creation of a group of cloistered sisters to pray for the success of Catholic missions, the inherent tension between internally oriented "community" values, and externally oriented "institutional" values would reappear in other polarities over the years—such as, brothers versus priests, missionaries serving at home versus those serving abroad, and missionaries sent out by the Society versus their leaders representing the Church abroad.

A brief glance at the organization of the Society will help to situate the predicament later faced by Limbrock in his frontier mission. Its outlines will appear more clearly if certain features are contrasted with a Protestant model, following the method of Lawrence Nemer (1981), who has compared the Mill Hill Society (a British Catholic missionary society that served as a model for the SVD) and the Church Missionary Society (the evangelical group whose ascetic spirituality was mentioned above). Nemer's first line of comparison is the conception of membership. As opposed to the CMS, which was primarily a society composed of laymen who, in effect, hired missionaries to run their training institutes and go abroad, both Mill Hill and the SVD were religious orders of the Roman Catholic Church whose members *were* the home workers and missionaries—priests and seminarians, brothers, and sisters in the case of the SVD—all under vows of obedience to the superiors of their society. These differing notions of membership conform with differing notions of governance, for although the CMS was administered by lay committees that supervised the work of the missionaries, both Mill Hill and the SVD were governed by individuals—a Superior General and his administrative appointees (Nemer 1981:32–64). This indeed was a key feature of the spirit of the SVD, which from the beginning utilized the Roman Catholic view of monastic obedience that elevated submission to ecclesiastical authority from a human to a theological plane:

it is to be a spirit of dedication, and especially of faith and trust, of humility and self-denial. For only if our company is a completely submissive instrument in the hands of God can it accomplish anything good. Therefore it holds firmly to the principle that God makes his will known most certainly through the will of superiors and through external circumstances. Although superiors should not presume that every command they give is the will of God, it is nevertheless God's will that subjects obey [Bornemann 1975:97].

Of considerable historical importance is the fact that during most of Limbrock's tenure as leader of the New Guinea mission, the governance of the SVD was in the hands of the Society's founder, Arnold Janssen, who had first been rector of the mission seminary and then, when the Society was formally organized in 1885, had been elected Superior General for life.

To be sure, Janssen's freedom of action was profoundly attuned to, if not precisely curtailed by, the necessity of securing approbation for the Society's establishments at home and abroad by local political and ecclesiastical authorities. In particular approval was needed from the curial body in the Vatican, then known as Propaganda Fide, which was responsible for assigning and administering Catholic mission territories. If Societies like Mill Hill and the SVD could move quickly and dramatically owing to the powers of decision vested in their individual Superiors, endowed as they were with an "almost military chain of command," both had to deal with this rather slow-moving curial bureaucracy for assignment to mission territories, for some matters of staffing and finance, and for problems that could not be internally contained (Nemer 1981:52–56 on Mill Hill's relations with Propaganda). As Nemer notes, the advantage to Catholic missionary societies of Propaganda was that it gave mission interests an influential voice in the Vatican, an advantage lacked by many Protestant societies in relation to their own governing church bodies. The disadvantages were that Propaganda limited the control that Societies had over their missions abroad. Propaganda, itself, was subject to pressures from European governments concerned with missionary activity in their protectorates and colonies, and was also an arena for competition among the several Catholic mission-sending orders. Perhaps more important was that through Propaganda's control of ecclesiastical offices, it formed an alternative source of power to the Societies and their superiors in mission lands.

These features of the organization of Catholic religious orders and foreign missions in the nineteenth century meant that as the number of SVD establishments in Europe and abroad expanded—that is as the Society emerged from the obscurity of a newly founded mission seminary to a successful missionary organization—it had to operate in an increasingly public world, subject to an increasing number of challenges to its capacity for internal control. It is significant that Janssen initiated his missions to China, Togo, and New Guinea under a plan that was designed to minimize such problems. As opposed to the long-established Jesuit practice, Janssen opted to combine the offices of ecclesiastical superior (the Vatican appointment, responsible for public decisions), and religious superior (the Society appointment, responsible for the private, or "inner," life of Society members), in a single man. This enabled Janssen to communicate with the ecclesiastical superior, whose policies were clearly vital to the welfare of the Society's members and to the success of the mission, through his capacity as religious superior of the SVD community—the office "most directly subject to him" (Bornemann 1975:416). Although this combination of offices later succumbed to its inherent contradictions, the lesson had not yet been learned when Eberhard Limbrock led the mission to New Guinea. As was true of the even more controversial leader of the Society's mission to China under whom he had already served for thirteen years, Limbrock would find that his perceptions of what would be necessary to establish the Church in the New Guinea mission field would sometimes contradict the view of his SVD staff of what was necessary for an "orderly" life as a religious community.

The Division of Labor in the SVD

Although the SVD was separated in matters of spirit and organization from the larger ecclesiastical and secular communities of which it formed a specialized part, its conception of an "orderly" life drew on the social and cultural resources of these larger communities, especially those related to the division of labor by class and by gender. From the start, priests had a valorized role in the SVD, just as they had in the Church at large, and just as educated, cultured men enjoyed in the Germanic societies of Europe during the late nineteenth century. The seminary with which the Society began originally was dedicated exclusively to educating seminarians and priests for the foreign missions. Later, when the Society was constituted in 1885 to include brothers as well as priests, all administrative and supervisory offices were reserved for priests. The brothers, who originally served just the mission seminary, were raised to missionary status by these new rules, but their role was still conceived as that of servant, providing material labor to enhance the spiritual services, such as teaching, preaching, and administration provided by the priests. As befit the position of women in the Church and in the larger society, Arnold Janssen created a completely separate organization of sisters, with one branch cloistered for prayer and contemplation, and another branch, the Sister Servants of the Holy Spirit (SSHS), for active sisters who would pursue "women's work" in the Society's establishments at

TABLE I
Membership in the Men's Divisions, SVD, 1875–1909

Year	Priests	Brothers	Students
1875	2	0	4
1880	4	12	79
1885	21	64	195
1890	33	159	235
1895	30	248	310
1900	43	290	286
1905	43	329	277
1909	48	301	293

Source: Fischer 1925:232

home and abroad. A complete community consisted of each of these types (excepting, of course, the cloistered nuns) performing their respective tasks, as well as students in the minor and major seminaries, and candidates in various stages of readiness for full membership in one or another of the component groups.

Underlying and supporting this fairly conventional division of labor, however, were some fairly innovative practices for the provisioning of the Society and for the performance of its work. Janssen, apparently, was one of the first in Catholic mission circles to understand the power of the home press. There was, we are told by an early biographer, "no monastic institution that could have served him as a model "in this regard (Fischer 1925:233). Indeed, it appears to have been largely through the revenues and publicity generated by the sale and circulation of magazines and pamphlets published and printed by his own press that Janssen was able to fund and attract members and students for the rapid growth of his Society. The expenses were great because during his lifetime Janssen was responsible for founding six European establishments (the mother house at Steyl, Holland; a college or residence for members studying in Rome; two houses in Austria; two houses in Germany), and for sending missionaries to seven foreign fields (China, South America, Togo, New Guinea, North America, Japan, and the Philippines). The statistics in Table 1 concerning membership in the men's divisions also indicate the Society's rapid growth in scale.

There is no doubt that this expansion, in full swing when the first mission left for New Guinea, both limited the resources available for its support and at the same time formed a model for rapid expansion in the mission field. Yet, before turning to the experience of the pioneer missionaries in New Guinea, a few more points should be raised about the value placed on technology and science in the home establishments. First, as I have already noted, the Society promoted printing and the other trades in which the brothers were primarily engaged, not as an exercise in pious humility, but as serious business. The very best equipment available was used and, for the magazines, the brothers developed highly efficient (and controversial) sales and distribution techniques (Bornemann 1975:159). Although the ideal type for a mission brother remained that of a "simple, natural, prayerful" man engaged in "manual labor and farming," Bornemann notes that the growing reputation of the press "contributed to the healthy increase" in the number of brothers and that "their influence, while scarcely noticed, grew apace" (Bornemann 1975:161–162).

> Carpenters, locksmiths, tailors and shoemakers, caught the spirit and wanted to employ the latest technical improvements in their shops. In the course of the years they made it their aim to become master craftsmen in their respective trades and skills, while following the vocation of Brother in a missionary society [Bornemann 1975:162].

If the nineteenth and early twentieth century equivalent of "high technology" was approved for SVD brothers who nevertheless were expected to remain "simple" men, scientific studies were highly regarded for the Society's priests who, in like fashion, were expected to retain their spiritual orientation. Janssen, it may be noted, was by profession a teacher of mathematics and though he disapproved of rationalism in theological studies (to the extent that it controverted the authority of the sacred texts and of the Church as their interpreter and exegete), he encouraged his most talented priests to study at the best German universities and promoted the various sciences that could contribute to missionary work. The anthropological journal *Anthropos,* for example, was founded under SVD auspices during Janssen's lifetime and, as we shall see, priests especially trained in geology, surveying, and tropical agriculture, as well as in linguistics and ethnology, all found their way to the New Guinea mission during its early years.

Plans for the New Guinea Mission

It should be clear from the preceding discussion that Janssen was not a man likely to discount "material" considerations in sending members of his Society on a mission abroad. Unlike the Marists, who appear to have relied on the spirit of sacrifice in fielding their first, unsuccessful mission to Melanesia in the 1840s (Laracy 1976:69; Arbuckle 1978:279), the SVD made extremely careful material preparations to facilitate the capacity of its missionaries to establish themselves permanently in the field. There had already been two abortive attempts by undersupplied Catholic missionaries to establish a foothold on Umboi Island, south of New Britain, as a base for evangelizing the mainland (Wiltgen 1969a:329). Janssen himself studied the annual reports from the Neu Guinea Compagnie, then virtually the only source of printed information available about conditions in Kaiser Wilhelmsland, and personally sought the advice of men who recently had been there. After delicate negotiations with officials of the Neu Guinea Compagnie, Janssen then obtained permission for his missionaries to establish a base near Friedrich Wilhelmshafen, the capital, so that they would have access to shipping services and supplies (Bornemann 1975:310–311). As mentioned in the last chapter, he proposed that land for a coconut plantation be obtained so that the mission would have a local base of financial support. Janssen also applied to the "collection agency" known as the Pious Work for the Propagation of the Faith in Lyons, France, for funds to "help defray the costs involved" (Wiltgen 1969a:330).

Other material preparations for the new mission resulted in a "veritable mountain of boxes and crates," including a prefabricated two-story house, with a "complete kitchen, beds, lockers, etc." as well as the "necessary equipment for a carpentry, blacksmith shop and foundry" (Bornemann 1975:309). To man the mission, Janssen selected three brothers—a mechanic, a carpenter/cabinetmaker, and a cook/tailor, as well as three priests, one of whom would serve as prefect apostolic and religious superior of the new community. As Wiltgen has noted, "the priests were to concern themselves primarily with the spiritual upbuilding of the mission and the Brothers primarily with building it up materially" (1969a:330). Sisters were not to arrive for another year or two: they had to wait until the men had prepared a convent for them, and until the work had progressed far enough for their female services—school teaching, ministry to women and young children, and housekeeping—to be of use (Bornemann 1975:314).

If the work expected for the new mission was to be divided in conventional ways among the different classes of the Society's personnel, the mission superior was to be capable of supervising and planning the work in all of its different aspects. The choice of the man to head the mission was clearly critical for the structural reasons already discussed. Eberhard Limbrock already had served for thirteen years in China, where he had supported Janssen in a divisive controversy over the independent behavior of the superior of the community in South Shantung. In addition, Bornemann tells us that Limbrock had a "friendly disposition, was prudent in his conduct and speech, and was an able administrator. Genuinely religious, he was at home in the scriptures and was every inch a priest" (1975:308). While Limbrock's "priestly" deportment was no doubt an important consideration, Janssen's own recollection of the reasons for his choice allude more directly to Limbrock's farming background and to his brother-like studies in locksmithing that preceded his entrance to the seminary at Steyl:

> When the question came up of assigning someone to head the mission in New Guinea, the thought kept coming back to me: Father Limbrock would be good for the job. For he is both devout and practical minded, and both of these qualities are very necessary. And also he will interest himself with those things which will be necessary for the support of the mission there [Wiltgen 1969a:360–361].

Janssen did not limit himself to material preparations for the mission. In regard to the spiritual well-being of the community which, like the home community, was expected to be based on a spirit of obedience, Janssen advised Limbrock that he should "not rely too much" on the advice of his consultors, the other two priests accompanying the pioneer party (Bornemann 1975:312). He was also charged with the task of looking after the health of his personnel, so as not to "endanger the welfare of the entire mission" (Bornemann 1975:312). Janssen's conception of the kinds of work required for the spiritual upbuilding of the mission may be gleaned from some of the other advice that he sent to Limbrock before the latter left China for the New Guinea field. A school system was anticipated, for Janssen sent some sample schoolbooks for Limbrock to inspect. Janssen also considered the linguistic problems that would affect spiritual work in a situation where "for every seven hundred or one thousand people, there is a different language." The Our Father, Hail Mary, and Apostles' Creed, Janssen thought, should be taught in the different local languages, but "the catechism, Bible History and prayerbooks should be printed in only one language," whether German, English, or a native language being left for Limbrock to decide (Bornemann 1975:312–313).

Geopolitics and Mission Policy: The Early Years

If there was little in Janssen's conception of how the Catholic mission system should be established in New Guinea that might enable one to foresee the internal problems that would soon arise, this is partly because no one anticipated the political problems that forced the mission to *begin* work not near the capital town as planned, but in the wilderness approximately 275 nautical miles away. It should be noted that there had been an intense period of strife, known as *Kulturkampf,* between the Catholic Church and the German government during the 1870s (Sperber 1984:207–252). In fact, Janssen had founded the Society of the Divine Word in Holland rather than in Germany because of the repressive situation at home. By the 1890s, however, a slow reconciliation between church and state in Germany was underway, and the SVD's problems in New Guinea stemmed more directly from the peculiar position of the

Neu Guinea Compagnie, which still administered the territory for the German Reich and which still held monopoly rights to the acquisition of land. The Company's earlier difficulties with the French Catholic missionaries in the Bismarck Archipelago not only had been partly responsible for Germany's request to the Vatican that German missionaries be sent to the mainland, but also partly responsible for the Reichstag's decision to transfer sovereign control in New Guinea to the Imperial Government. The politics of sector purity even played a role in Berlin. For example, it is reported that the Reichstag itself concluded that "it seemed *improper* that a private company, organized primarily for commercial purposes, should exercise sovereignty over the Church as well" (Bornemann 1975:310).

At any rate, this was precisely the situation that obtained in Kaiser Wilhelmsland when Limbrock and his party arrived. And if some took offense at the fact that the Company itself confused the categories of government and commerce, local Company officials were apparently not prepared to brook an institution that confused the categories of religion and commerce, especially when the mission's plan to establish a coconut plantation would entail competition for the Company's own budding copra industry along the north coast. Limbrock was not permitted to begin mission work near the capital (ostensibly because of Lutheran mission interests), nor was he permitted to purchase a large block of land. Thus it was that Limbrock set up his first mission station on the distant island of Tumleo, near the harbor of Berlinhafen [Aitape]. Janssen's reaction to Limbrock's first important decision was suffused with ironic disapprobation: "So they succeeded in moving you to the north near Berlinhafen, where you are now ensconced on an island. May it all turn out for the best. At least there are some people there, which is not the case to the south" (Bornemann 1975:313).

Although there were indeed approximately 300 people on the island of Tumleo, about 400 on the neighboring island of Ali, and small groups of villagers living along the mainland coast nearby, Limbrock himself had no desire to be thus confined. Yet in 1897, when the Neu Guinea Compagnie took over the property and interests of the trader, Ludwig Kärnbach, it soon became clear that such confinement was likely to result from the Company's plans. P. Luecker, the Company's agent in Aitape, not only informed Limbrock that the Company itself would take over land that the mission had just arranged to purchase at Aitape, but also went on a buying spree that gave the Company titular rights to virtually all the coastal land between Aitape and Friedrich Wilhelmshafen. Although Limbrock lobbied successfully in Berlin to regain his title to the land at Aitape, it took nearly a decade of intense political activity to attain the foothold that both Limbrock and Janssen had desired to the east—in particular, land for a plantation in the environs of the colonial capital (Wiltgen 1969a:330–347).

One consequence of this situation was the skewed distribution of the stations established by the mission during its first ten years. These included four stations in the vicinity of Berlinhafen and three in the vicinity of Friedrich Wilhelmshafen. Limbrock was effectively prevented by the Neu Guinea Compagnie's claims to land along the coast from establishing a single station in the central part of the region. Limbrock did attempt to purchase land on the two offshore islands of Koil and Mushu, but even these transactions were disallowed by the new Imperial Government. As Limbrock explained to his Superior General, "We thought that a change in government would also bring with it a change for the better in these matters, [but] Governor von Bennigsen immediately upon his arrival said very outspokenly: 'We are not in favor of the mission acquiring much land' " (Wiltgen 1969a:337). It was not until many of the Neu Guinea Compagnie's purchases were themselves disallowed by an Imperial Court, and not until the second Imperial Governor, Albert Hahl, had finally been convinced that mission enterprise was consistent with his own program for extending government influence that the mission's requests for station and plantation land in this region were approved.

In the meantime, however, Limbrock had been forced to develop arguments for his requests that would persuade influential persons in Berlin to intervene on the mission's behalf. Perhaps the most imaginative example is the letter that Limbrock wrote on 5 February 1900 to Franz Ludwig Prinz von Arenberg, "an influential Catholic member of the Reichstag," explaining why the mission needed to obtain more land (Wiltgen 1969a:336). The points raised by Limbrock in this letter include: a) that if missions were self-supporting, less money would leave Germany, and the missions would be protected against war and depression at home; b) mission plantations would serve as a model for the natives, so that the land would be improved, the people would learn to live orderly lives, and businessmen would have a larger market for their goods; c) the mission would be the most effective agency for bringing about these benefits because of its proximity to the people and the longevity of the mission's stay; d) that the mission's investment remained in the colony for reinvestment, thus increasing the proceeds and allowing the mission to spread a variety of other benefits among the natives; and e) that other governments had a policy of aiding missionaries in their colonies, by facilitating their acquisition of land and reducing their import duties and taxes (Wiltgen 1969a:336–338). It is clear that for public presentation, at least, Limbrock was well on the way to viewing his work as a "civilizing mission." Although Limbrock acknowledged in his letter to Arenberg, that "this problem of getting the mission established on a material basis is a question of life and death" (Wiltgen 1969a:338), he wrote more openly about the internal benefits of plantations in his letters to his Superior General, Father Arnold Janssen, during this period of uncertainty and despair.

Evangelism and the Economic Frontier

If a frontier can be defined as a zone where normal boundaries between the conventional sectors of society are easily confused, it can also be described as a zone which in itself is hostile to serious attempts to constitute these sectors as separate domains. Renato Rosaldo has suggested that "civilized society is most likely to infer the social character of indigenous peoples from those acts that impede commerce and that are completely at variance with civilized social norms . . ." (1978:240). I shall take up the question of the mission's appraisal of native character in the next chapter; here we shall examine Limbrock's picture of the "frontier" in its broadest sense, for this rather than native character is the subject of his most intense complaints. It is the "frontier" or, in his phrasing, "New Guinea," that is conceived in terms of features that impaired the functioning of his own project and thus threatened the structural integrity of the mission itself.

Undoubtedly, even had he been able to begin work near the capital, Limbrock, like the Lutherans of the Rheinische Mission Society who were working there at the time, would have found New Guinea an extremely trying mission field. Yet, by starting in the Aitape area where, save for a few traders, colonial influence had not yet been extended, the difficulties and expenses were greatly increased. With no local source for the supplies that the missionaries believed essential to their well-being, everything, including building timbers, had to be imported. Although Aitape became a port of call for the bimonthly ship on the Singapore route and of less regular visits by Neu Guinea Compagnie coastal steamers, the missionaries were on their own as far as regular transportation from the islands to the mainland was concerned. They were responsible for their own medical work, for their own fresh food, and for their own land transport as well.

The costs were high, and Limbrock needed money, as he frequently reminded Janssen:

> *Poor, poor New Guinea! Here every foot of ground still has to be cleared, every road has to be made, every bridge built, every really worthwhile plant imported, every hen, every duck, and every other domesticated animal including the horse, has to be brought in from the outside. . . . Every thread on our backs has to be gotten from Europe or elsewhere [Wiltgen 1969a:339].*

Although Janssen warned Limbrock that the Society's own funds were severely stretched owing to the expenses incurred in expanding the society's houses in Europe, Limbrock was persistent and aggressive in his demands. For example, although Janssen offered to donate the first pair of cows to the mission in 1903, one of the new priests arriving via Djakarta brought with him *ten* head of cattle, for which Limbrock promptly sent Janssen the bill (Wiltgen 1969a:354; Fischer 1925:395).

To be sure, the fact that a civilized infrastructure did not exist was not the only problem posed by the frontier. The low cultural level of the natives, the climate that sapped the missionaries' strength, the linguistic diversity and political fragmentation among the native villages that made it necessary to establish a large number of stations—all these were on the list of "obstacles" faced by the new mission (Schmidlin 1913:160–161). Limbrock himself complained that not only did the mission have to establish the first schools ever in each area, but that "we have to use exceptionally great patience and effort to make the people even somewhat understand the very notion of schools and their usefulness" (in Wiltgen 1969a:339). As to obtaining native labor and supplies, the plaint is the same:

> *Everywhere else you can buy everything or almost everything with money; here they don't even know what money is. . . . And if we want someone to work for us and help us, we have to do it ourselves first, and then press the shovel or hoe into his hands, indicating that he should do it exactly the same way. At first the novelty of it interests him and he goes along beautifully. But if we turn our backs and return half an hour later, the bird has flown the coop and is gone . . . [Wiltgen 1969a:339–340].*

Limbrock's letters to Janssen (as excerpted by Wiltgen), speak constantly of the overwhelming burden that such circumstances placed upon mission finance and personnel. It is clear that even Limbrock himself was afraid of losing control over the critical relation between material and spiritual work that defined his mission as a religious enterprise and gave it a specific denominational and spiritual form. Certainly, he found few supports for the specialized evangelical work that his priests were supposed to pursue:

> *The most diversified demands are made on us. . . . We have to be farmers and planters; we have to import, care for, and breed cattle. For sea journeys we must understand sailing and steering. There are many wounds to bind, sicknesses to study, and sick colleagues to care for. . . . Then we have to study accounts and find places where we can buy things at a low price. . . . As soon as we leave the mail steamer, we need our own ships, our own surfboats, our own oarsmen, our own landing places, boathouses, and piers with cranes and winches. . . . What cost and trouble and work is caused by these boats alone and all that goes with them. . . . We ourselves have to unload the steamers, bring our cargo ashore, and put it where it belongs. . . . In addition to this there is the usual work of caring for souls . . . [Wiltgen 1969a:340; emphasis mine].*

Frontier conditions had already begun to deconstruct, or invert, the conventional hierarchy of mission means. Spiritual tasks were being relegated to the background of "usual work," and material tasks were placed in the forefront of the mission superior's concerns. If Limbrock came to believe his public statements about the civilizing effect that mission plantations might have upon the natives and about the various benefits that would thus accrue to the colony at large, it is also clear that he had come to believe that the mission could not fulfill its spiritual aims without the aid of "civilization." Limbrock seems to have decided that a civilized infrastructure was required for missionary work, and that, given the impotence of government and commerce, he and his missionaries would simply have to provide it themselves.

Construction and Deconstruction

Many mission histories look back upon their pioneer years as a "heroic" period, punctuated by trials and sacrifice, when the founder and his associates triumphed over myriad obstacles to establish a spiritual ascendancy in the mission field. Historians of the SVD mission in New Guinea do not, however, locate its heroic period in the first ten years of mission work, but in the second decade, after the political situation had improved and Limbrock was able to obtain the land that he required for mission plantations and for mission stations. For this mission, the heroic period is not represented as a time of spiritual prowess unencumbered by material concerns, but as a time of unprecedented material upbuilding instead.

The immediate crisis that impelled Limbrock to take action appears to have been the announcement in the fall of 1904 that Norddeutscher Lloyd would discontinue Aitape as a port of call. At that time, all of the mission's outstations were dependent on the mission headquarters for their supplies but, as Limbrock noted, the news that henceforward Friedrich Wilhelmshafen would be the only stop on the mainland placed the mission in a "horrible dilemma" (Wiltgen 1969a:346). Not only would the mission have to weather considerable delays as they waited for a ship that could move their goods and provisions from the capital to Tumleo Island, but the delays would involve much spoilage of their provisions and, because such a great portion of their supplies were imported, there would be heavy storage costs in Friedrich Wilhelmshafen as well. En route to see the governor about this situation, however, Limbrock heard that land near Friedrich Wilhelmshafen would soon become available, and that neither Neu Guinea Compagnie nor the faltering Lutheran mission was interested in taking it up. By November 1904, Limbrock had obtained the governor's permission to acquire approximately ten hectares of land for new headquarters near the capital, and the governor had sent Limbrock's request for an additional 500 to 1,000 hectares to the colonial office in Berlin (Wiltgen 1969a:347–348).

Mission writers become rather breathless in describing the pace of mission achievement in the years after the mission's political fortunes had changed. Limbrock was then able to move closer to Madang, and his new headquarters at Alexishafen soon became a showcase for missionary enterprise as well. The land was acquired and surveyed in June 1905, and by the end of the month the missionaries had cleared one acre of forest and built a rough two-story residence with chapel, carpentry, and a storeroom on the ground floor. By December 1905, they had received, housed, and dedicated a sawmill, imported from Europe, including a steam locomotive and sawing machinery. In only four days of operation, they were able to send a load of planks to Tumleo, and in eighteen days had sawn enough timber to begin construction of a two-storied residence for workers. No longer dependent on costly imported building timbers from Australia, the saw mill hummed "from six o'clock in the morning until six o'clock in the evening," utilizing the best of the wood that was being cleared from the expanding station's site (Hagspiel 1926:119).

By the end of 1906, Alexishafen was graced with not only its original "bushwood" residence and its sawmill, but also a workers' residence, a new kitchen, two timber sheds, a carpenter's shop, a locksmith's (machinist) shop, a new chapel, and a vertical frame saw. In 1907, more machines were added, including planing and boring tools, circular and ribbon saws, and rail tracks to facilitate the transport of timber from the receding woods. Gardens were planted around the station—coconuts at thirty-foot intervals were interplanted with yams, taro, and sweet potatoes, so that locally grown produce could be added to the laborers' fare. A central warehouse also was constructed in 1907, as were buildings for the nuns' convent and the central school. By 1909, the central school opened with students who previously had been housed on Tumleo, and in 1911, the first graduates either became apprentices in the various crafts, or began studies in the new catechetical training school. The first small hospital, built in 1907, was replaced by a hospital with twenty beds in 1910, but by 1912 a larger hospital was erected, including a dentistry and an X-ray studio (Hagspiel 1926:116–124). Brother Clarence was the *only* dentist in all of mainland New Guinea, and it is reported that partly through his services to planters and their workers the name of Alexishafen gradually spread (Hagspiel 1926:124). The success of the new mission headquarters as a center for industry, however, is shown by the fact that in 1910, after the North German Lloyd had resumed its old schedule of stops on the mainland, Alexishafen was added as a new port of call (Hagspiel 1926:132).

This was not all, however. In 1904, Limbrock had sponsored both geological studies by specially trained priests in the Aitape area, and mapping expeditions along the coast. By 1909, he was experimenting with rice production in the hope of substituting locally grown rice for the 150 to 200 tons that were annually imported to support approximately 600 laborers on mission farms and plantations as well as for the students at the mission schools. One priest studied rice cultivation in Java but, although their first crop grown with the aid of Indian laborers was successful, the experiment later failed owing to illness among the workers and crop disease. Two priests were then sent to the United States to study rice cultivation in Louisiana, and the first machines for an experiment in capital-intensive rice culture arrived just before the beginning of World War I (Hagspiel 1926:132–136). The number of stations also was increased: by one list they included two additional stations in 1908, five in 1909, two in 1911, and another two in 1912 (Schmidlin 1913:162–163). One of these, incidentally, would become the seat of the new regional superior, for by this time the wisdom of dividing Limbrock's double office had been recognized—as early as 1908 by Limbrock himself (Bornemann 1975:504).

There are three points that can be cited to justify rehearsing the long list of projects that were undertaken at Limbrock's behest between 1905 and 1914. First, the list is extremely impressive when compared to how little capital development was being sponsored by other agents and agencies in the region during that time. Indeed, anticipating his own program, Limbrock had twice in 1905 provided memoranda to Governor Hahl advancing his ideas on "what the Governor might do for the cultural and economical development of the New Guinea mainland" (Wiltgen 1969a:350). These plans undoubtedly were influential in convincing the governor "to authorize land purchases for [the mission] anywhere" (Wiltgen 1969a:349), while Limbrock's subsequent success in developing these lands and his various mission industries understandably gave the mission its reputation for "efficiency" in the region at large (Hagspiel 1926:12, 16–17).

The second point is that if this mission's success in nonreligious pursuits could impress secular observers, it could also be interpreted as failure by purists within the mission itself. Hagspiel noted that the "very principle underlying [Limbrock's] scheme was attacked by a number of his own missionaries who disliked the idea of devoting their precious time to farming, planting palms, and raising cattle, instead of giving themselves to mission work proper—to the saving of immortal souls" (1926:128). As Wiltgen explains, there were at least two priests managing mission plantations by 1906 and, as there were not enough brothers to take charge of all the building and development work that Limbrock's program entailed, "other priests, too, had to do much manual work, and all did not like the idea. Complaints found their way to Steyl, and Father Janssen questioned Father Limbrock about his policy" (Wiltgen 1969a:352).

Limbrock himself was modest in his claims about the accomplishments of the "spiritual" side of the mission's work. Evangelism was recognized to be slow and difficult. Although supporters might note that more and more contract laborers were being exposed to Catholic teaching and might spread the word when they returned to their villages, the benefits of Limbrock's program had not yet outweighed the costs. Limbrock acknowledged that the spiritual and material aims of pioneer work were proving contradictory rather than complementary in the conditions that obtained. "Someone might well object," Limbrock wrote in reply to Janssen:

> and state that we missionaries ought to withdraw ourselves more from material occupations . . . . Of course, we try to let the Brothers do as much of this work as possible, so as to keep ourselves free for divine services and evangelizing. But unfortunately up till now the good Brothers are just not numerous enough. . . . If a house is to be built, then a foundation is also necessary. For better, then, or for worse, we have had to accommodate ourselves to what was unavoidable and to take over the work ourselves. It pained us deeply, however, that in the meanwhile the mission work had to suffer greatly [Wiltgen 1969a:352].

While Limbrock's plan received the approbation of Janssen who, it may be recalled, was himself renowned for impressive feats of institution building in Europe and abroad, the controversy apparently encouraged Limbrock to propose at the Society's next General Chapter meeting (held every seven years) to separate the offices of prefect apostolic and regional superior. It also motivated Limbrock to offer to resign several times. Janssen, it appears, was able to encourage Limbrock to stay on, despite the latter's desire (expressed in a letter of 12 February 1907) to "leave the world's stage and disappear . . . and find for myself a quieter and more agreeable place than was allotted to me here" (in Wiltgen 1969a:357).

This brings us to the third point, for while the machines, agricultural projects, and mission stations were designed to eventually make the mission self-sufficient, its initial result was to place the mission deeply in debt. When Janssen died in January 1909, he was succeeded as Superior General by the Nicholas Blum who, as the Society's Procurator General, had long been responsible for the distribution of funds to the missions (Bornemann 1975:385–387). Janssen was willing to put up with Limbrock's determination to pursue his somewhat visionary scheme no matter what the cost, but it appears that Janssen's successor was not so sympathetic (Wiltgen 1969a:356).

When Limbrock's resignation was accepted in 1913, then, it was merely the last of several reversals that the mission had experienced in its pioneer years. An institution defined through the religious character of its mission actually came to excel in the work normally expected of commercial or even government agencies. A program designed to assure the mission's capacity for self-support had placed the mission in debt, priests had performed the labor of brothers, and the ecclesiastical superior—Limbrock, himself—had resigned to live out the rest of his life "working in New Guinea as any other priest . . ." (Wiltgen 1969a:356).

CONCLUSION

I have argued in this chapter that European society, as it became constituted in the conditions obtaining in the northwest region of New Guinea, was characterized by a blurring of boundaries between sectors that were normally expected to concern themselves with clearly defined and ultimately complementary functions or tasks. In examining the case of the early development of the Catholic mission, I have further suggested that these conditions induced, as Weber put it, "substantial internal change" within the institutions involved.

This blurring of boundaries had tremendous political impact. We have seen, for example, how Limbrock's requests for land were first denied and then encouraged by successive administrations with different priorities for the region in mind (that is, profit for itself, characterizing the Neu Guinea Compagnie; the establishment of influence and control over the native population by Hahl's Imperial Government). The ambiguity with which the mission was subsequently regarded stems partly from its very success in becoming an important presence in the Sepik. The Australians, who were taking over from the German administration in Rabaul at just about the same time that Limbrock was resigning as the leader of the mission, wished to establish themselves in control in the Sepik, and to make it clear to the natives that the Germans were gone. For the first aim it is arguable that like Hahl before them, they needed the missionaries with their many stations, boats, horses, knowledge, and influence, but that for the latter aim, they would have preferred to have seen them gone.

As it was, the mission had to fight for its life against an Australian ruling that would force all German missionaries to leave the country in 1923. To be sure, the main battles involved those in power abroad. But the missionaries in New Guinea had contributions of their own to make, in particular regarding attacks on their engagement in "business" from the new Australian regime. Father Puff, who was appointed temporary administrator of the mission after Limbrock resigned, found it necessary to marshal the same arguments in favor of mission enterprise that Limbrock had earlier used to obtain the land required to start the mission system in the first decade of mission work.

In a letter to the first administrator of the Australian civil government (which succeeded the military occupation force in 1921), Father Puff even quoted a "modest proposal" that Father Limbrock had first written in a letter to Governor Hahl:

> *If the envy of other business firms asserts that such educational establishments are of material advantage for the mission, it would be recommended that a public request be made, that all such business enterprises everywhere should found such and similar educational establishments. The more the better! And if they so desire, we shall be ready to put at their disposal any number of Sisters, Fathers and Brothers for the supervision and direction of those schools and for teaching in them. . . . Whatever gain and profit there may be, we shall gladly leave to the business firm that undertakes the happy enterprise [Wiltgen 1969a:359].*

Clearly, the oppositional climate that had characterized "old" New Guinea still prevailed, and clearly, too, the missionaries were as capable as any of their secular opponents of treating the occupational code ironically, to defend their interests in the political field.

Perhaps most important to note here, however, are some of the ways in which the mission managed the internal contradictions that frontier work had posed. To return to Arbuckle's classification of Catholic theological positions on development work (1978), we must recall that it was still an "extremely pre-Vatican II" period when Limbrock retired. Another writer on Catholic missionization reminds us that as late as 1919 "the charge of the Catholic missionary, as it was formulated in the encyclical of Pope Benedict XV . . . was to 'open the way of heaven to those hurrying to destruction' " (Hezel 1978:256). Yet, the very same projects that could be represented to colonial authorities as promoting economic development (as commonly understood at that time), could also be represented as means for self-support. Indeed, when Limbrock informed the Cardinal Prefect of Propaganda Fide in 1889 that he had just obtained permission to purchase land for his first plantation, the Cardinal commended him for his good judgment that "has provided for your mission funds and lands which shall henceforth secure for those following after you a stable patrimony" (Hagspiel 1926:128; Wiltgen 1969a:342).

Limbrock's projects soon went beyond the modest level of a single plantation, but so too, somewhat later, did the demand for self-support. As World War I approached, Limbrock's policies began to look prescient to others as well. In 1913, a convocation of Catholic missionary bishops from German Oceania resolved that they should all "start plantations," 'so as to make the mission as financially independent as possible from Europe' " (Wiltgen 1969a:356). As the war progressed, it soon became evident that Limbrock's plantations and industries were responsible for the mission's capacity to continue work. Within his own mission, Limbrock ceased to be a figure of controversy and became a hero, instead. By 1922, an official mission observer was able to report that Limbrock was now called "the man of Providence," even by priests on the staff who had opposed him a few years before (Hagspiel 1926:127).

Finally, one may note a similar process occurring in regard to principle as well. At one point in the mission's internal struggle, the Superior General and founder of the Society had himself advised the community that "physical work is an honor for the first missionaries and a great example for those that follow" (Wiltgen 1969a:352). By using "an old trick of all hagiography" (Barthes 1972:31), in other words, Janssen was able to represent the missionaries' situation in light of the long and distinguished tradition in Christian religious culture of representing "high" virtues in the garb of the "low." As Barthes has said, "The singularity of a 'vocation' is never better displayed that when it is contradicted—but not denied, far from it—by a prosaic incarnation" (1972:30–31).

CHAPTER 4

Hierarchy and the Mission Station System between the Wars

And finally, this very lack of any universal binding characteristic among the people . . . sets up real barriers of difficulty among the Fathers and Brothers themselves. . . . What is meant here is that each mission [station], being so entirely segregated from the others, has its own distinct problems to such an extent as to be almost a distinct mission by itself.

—BRUNO HAGSPIEL

In the preceding chapter I argued that the economic situation along the north coast of New Guinea required colonial pioneers to eschew some of the distinctions in conduct that conventionally marked different sectors of European society and, in the case of the Catholic mission, different classes of personnel. One result of this situation was that distinctions that were expected to be "transparent," or evident to the eye from external signs, became "opaque" and subject to special justification if they were to be maintained at all. In this chapter I will argue that the indigenous social and cultural situation caused similar dislocations in the colonists' political organization. For the Catholic mission this meant that the hierarchical constitution of their community was as vulnerable as their division of spiritual and material labor to conditions on the Sepik frontier.

It has often been suggested that the small scale of Sepik societies, together with their great diversity of social and cultural forms, make it difficult to generalize about the effects of colonial penetration (Roscoe and Scaglion 1984). Yet, one implication of the Catholic mission's experience in the Sepik is that this situation affected the very systems that supported colonial penetration. The above quotation certainly suggests that the Catholic mission's capacity to make and implement central policy was impaired and that the role of individual agents was simultane-

---

The epigraph at the head of this chapter is from
Bruno Hagspiel's *Along the Mission Trail*. Vol. 3, *In New Guinea*. (Techny: Mission Press, S.V.D.), 69.

ously enhanced. This chapter examines some of the ways in which this diversity was interpreted within the mission, how the mission attempted to contain diversity, and how its expectations about the expression of hierarchy were altered in the course of its experience during the interwar years.

Father Ralph Wiltgen's article on the interest of land to the pioneer mission along the north coast of New Guinea is nicely balanced by the emphasis that Father Bruno Hagspiel, writing in 1926, places on the sea. Hagspiel had toured the New Guinea mission in May and June of 1922, as chronicler for the grand tour taken by William Gier, the Society's third Superior General, through the SVD's mission territories in the Pacific. Although Hagspiel devotes much attention to the plantations and industries developed by Limbrock as a "feature which distinguishes [New Guinea] from most of the other mission fields of the world," (1926:125), these enterprises had by then proven their value and the greatest challenge to the mission now came from the geographical size and the cultural diversity of the Society's New Guinea field. These were evident to Hagspiel as he and the Superior General made their way down the coast from Sissano, the mission's westernmost station, to its headquarters at Alexishafen in the southeast, visiting the stations and talking to the missionaries along the route.

Like the travelers I mentioned earlier, Hagspiel devotes much attention to the ship that proved "one of the principal performers in the bringing to pass, as far as transportation goes, of the greater part of our missionary experiences in New Guinea" (1926:28–29). In this case it was the *Gabriel,* a ninety-three-foot steamer obtained by the mission in 1909. Her dimensions are reported in full detail, as are the arrangement of space on board, stowage capacity, fueling needs, engine machinery, navigational equipment, captain (a mission brother), and native crew. Yet, in contrast to Limbrock whose frontier had been economic and to whom the mission fleet represented a great deal of trouble and expense, Hagspiel's frontier is political, and his ship undergoes a subtle transformation as his passage proceeds. Initially a very physical copra- and cargo-carrying workhorse, the *Gabriel* is transformed into a vehicle of communication and ministry, and finally emerges as a metaphor for the mission itself. In other words, the *Gabriel*'s monthly round of the mission's twenty-two stations comes to represent that "binding characteristic" which held the mission together, but which Hagspiel found lacking among a native population divided not only by geography, but also language, custom, and sentiment (1926:37–38;69).

It is significant that Hagspiel, a representative of central authority in the Society, should choose to emphasize the integrative capacity of the *Gabriel* and, indeed, to praise all aspects of mission practice that might serve to contain diversity within the mission field. Just as the division of labor among the different classes of mission personnel embodied its hierarchy of spiritual and material goals, the local orientation of its missionaries to a common center embodied the structure of authority in the larger Church. In New Guinea, however, the latter had proved as difficult to maintain as the former. As an earlier writer on this mission has already pointed out, the spatial arrangement of its stations isolated the missionaries from one another, while social, cultural, and linguistic diversity among the native people made centralization a virtually unattainable ideal (Schmidlin 1913:161).

The pioneer missionaries had been the first to face the strategic problems posed by both the small scale of Sepik societies and the linguistic and cultural diversity that they recognized along the north coast. Like other missionary groups—the Lutherans near Friedrich Wilhelmshafen, for example—they might have concentrated their efforts in a smaller area. Under Limbrock's direction, however, the pioneers had opted for broad coverage in their field, accepting the economic costs of establishing numerous sites rather than just a few. It was largely through their enterprise that the mission had been able to establish itself over the long stretch of coast visited by Hagspiel and the Superior General in May and June of 1922. Yet, if the pioneers had resolved some of the problems of finance and supply necessary for establishing and maintaining a system in so large an area, it was for their successors to deal with the political problems of constituting the territory in authentic ecclesiastical form. If Limbrock's plantations were the touchstone of the pioneers' efforts to create an effective material base for the mission's spiritual work, Hagspiel's *Gabriel* can be seen as the "defining technology" for the mission's work on this new, political frontier.

The Station System in 1922

It should be noted at the outset that there was nothing in the station system per se to trouble an official observer of the New Guinea mission. This system, understood as a precursor to a mature territorial diocese, consisted quite simply of a central station to serve as the bishop's seat, and outstations, manned by priests, which served in turn as centers for proto-parishes. By the time of Hagspiel's visit, this basic structure had been embellished by the addition of several stations that served primarily as plantations or farms, by the use of one of these stations as a separate center for the Society's regional superior, (whose function, it will be recalled, was primarily to look after the spiritual welfare of Society personnel); and by the fact that most of the outstations also had their own

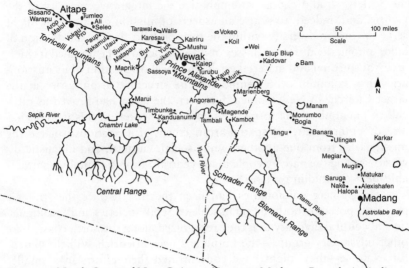

Figure 4. North Coast of New Guinea, Aitape to Madang. Boundaries indicate Catholic Mission Vicariates prior to World War II.

set of "bush" stations to facilitate Catholic observances in distant village areas to which the priest periodically traveled to deliver the sacraments and to teach. A main station would typically include a chapel or church and a missionary's residence; depending on its age, location, and the enterprise of its personnel, it also might contain a school, dispensary, sisters' residence, gardens, and so forth.

It is possible to be fairly precise, thanks to Schmidlin (1913) and to Hagspiel (1926), about the number of main stations that the mission supported first in 1912 and then again in 1922 (Figure 4). We can see from Table 2 that the mission was not only able to maintain itself during the stringent years of World War I, but also managed to establish several new stations.[1] Occasionally a main station was demoted in status. Hagspiel, for example, was able to add a footnote to his book before it went to press to explain:

> *In February, 1925, the Father and Sisters gave up Monumbo as a central station, and instead have settled on the volcanic island of Manam, which faces Monumbo. Monumbo has, in consequence, now become an out-station of Bogia (1926:110).*

On the whole, however, the process was more likely to go the other way, both from the mission's understandable reluctance to abandon a substantial investment in labor, materials, and cash, and from a strong sense of spiritual responsibility. As Father Janssen had told Limbrock back in the

TABLE 2
Mission Stations: 1912 and 1922

	1912	1922
(1911)	Sissano	Sissano
(1912)	Warapu	
(1911)	Arop	Arop
(1919)	Malol	Malol (?)
(?)	Aitape	Aitape
(1896)	Tumleo	Tumleo
(1901)	Ali	Ali
(1897)	Walman (Pro)	
(1909)	Yakamul	Yakamul
		Ulau
		Suain
(1908)	Boiken	Boiken
(1908)	Yuo	Yuo
(1912)	Wewak	Wewak
		Murik
		Marienberg
(1899)	Monumbo	Monumbo
(1901)	Bogia	Bogia
(1909)	Megiar	
(1909)	Mugil	Mugil
(1909)	Matukar	
		Halopa
		Nake
		Saruga
(1905)	Alexishafen	Alexishafen

Sources: Column 1, Schmidlin 1913:161, 163
Column 2, Hagspiel 1926
(Locations are shown on Figure 4)

earliest years of mission expansion, it was better to be conservative now than to face the possibility of having to give up a station later:

> Of a people to whom the Gospel has never been preached, the Lord does not demand more than the observance of the natural law. After it has received the Gospel, it will be less excusable if it falls back into paganism. Therefore it is your duty, if you once begin anywhere, to continue the work, except where your preaching is refused [Fischer 1925:398].

The mission's capacity to maintain old stations and to open new ones, ultimately depended on the number, health, and welfare of its personnel. Numbers, health, and welfare, however, were of great concern in the early 1920s when the Superior General and Hagspiel paid their visit because no new missionaries had been able to join or relieve the original ones during the years of World War I. Of the ninety-three missionaries who had been in New Guinea in 1913, only seventy-four were still alive. The four new American sisters, who had come in 1921, increased the total to seventy-eight missionaries, but many who had been there for the duration were either elderly, tired, or sick. Even worse, the Australian government had decreed that all missionaries of German nationality would have to leave the country in 1923. Although this ruling was first softened to forbid only the arrival of new missionaries from Germany, and was later rescinded altogether, it is clear that the question of personnel was critical in 1922.

It is difficult to say exactly how many missionaries would have been considered optimal at that time. In Hagspiel's opinion, the current force was insufficient. Nearly half of the missionaries then in New Guinea were sisters, seventeen of whom were working at the central station of Alexishafen, and three each at seven of the main stations—Bogia, Monumbo, Wewak, Boiken, Yakamul, Ali, and Tumleo (Hagspiel 1926:207). Hagspiel gives great credit to these sisters, without whom "all the priests' missionary activities in New Guinea would be . . . incomplete and, in the long run, doomed to failure" (1926:206). Yet as valuable as their work among the native women and children may have been, the basic tasks of maintaining the mission's material base, of keeping the stations open, and of delivering the sacraments fell to the forty brothers and priests. Their tasks included filling administrative offices, managing plantations and workshops, and running central institutions such as the high school and catechetical training center at Alexishafen in addition to the other stations. Given that one must allow for some to be sick or on leave at any one time, this number was not enough. Indeed, Hagspiel noted that some of the main stations were temporarily without a resident priest and that many of the brothers had responsibilities which previously two, or even three, men would have split among themselves (1926:144).

Yet if the question of optimal staff size were a simple arithmetic problem, Hagspiel would have taken more comfort than he did from the fact that new missionaries from America were expected soon. Indeed, thirteen more, including brothers and priests, arrived in the following year. Additional numbers of missionaries, however, could not resolve what Hagspiel saw as a more fundamental problem than the personnel crisis created by the recent world war and its political aftermath. The station system, like the Church which it was expected to prefigure and bring about, was authentically formed only to the extent that it remained a centered community. Contradicting this requirement in New Guinea, however, was the fact that the native people themselves occupied a uniquely decentered social and cultural world. As Hagspiel so eloquently observed in the quotation with which I have opened this chapter, the principal effect of this fact was to make each mission station "almost a distinct mission by itself" (1926:69).

Fragmenting Forces in the Mission Field

Hagspiel identifies language, culture, and what may best be called social scale as three lines of division among the native people of the coastal region that exposed the mission to internal fragmentation. Perhaps the most basic of these was social scale, for the preexisting social divisions of indigenous society, unlike those in the larger and more lustrous fields of China, India, or Japan could not be resolved into overriding categories like class or caste, nor—as in Africa—into large political units like tribes. Although Hagspiel himself uses the term "tribe" in lieu of a ready alternative, it is clear that the missionaries with whom he spoke on his tour had impressed upon him that tribes in New Guinea rarely comprised more than a few hundred people living in a small number of villages in close geographical propinquity. The villagers living on one small island like Tumleo (population of 300 in 1922) or Ali (population of 400 in 1922) are examples; others would include the 800 people of the coastal village of Arop, who were noted for their proclivity to suicide when shamed (Erdweg 1919/1920), or the neighboring people of Malol village, renowned throughout the region as "murderers and thieves" (Limbrock 1909/1910).

The use of such geographical and cultural criteria for unit definition is testimony to the fact that political relations among groups in the area were seldom constituted hierarchically. The consequent absence of a ruling elite, or even of what Hagspiel calls "any universal binding characteristic" (1926:69) meant that missionaries had to negotiate their position anew among each new group, however small. They also were more exposed to political conditions in any particular locality than they might have been among people organized as a chiefdom, for example, with a wider range for the exercise of indigenous leadership and authority. Of course, missionaries made use of the networks that connected individuals and communities through marriage, trade, and ritual alliance; yet, these could not assure the missionary of a friendly reception any more than influential converts in one village could assure that other villagers would follow suit. It is, perhaps, only in such a context that Hagspiel could express great praise for such "random access" methods as might be provided by mission laborers returning home to unmissionized areas at the end of their contracts: "When the missionary has, later on, made his appearance in their villages, he has found most of the pagans friendly; thus the greatest obstacle to intercourse is found to be removed, and the ground prepared, for future spiritual work" (1926:129).

The next obstacle that such a missionary might face was likely to be language, for the fragmenting force of small social scale was greatly exacerbated by the fact that language and dialect groups were almost as numerous as political units and, at least on the coast, almost as sparsely peopled. To illustrate the dimensions of the problem, we can examine the location of the sixteen mission stations in 1922 that lay in the region covered by Laycock's linguistic survey of the Sepik, published in 1973. The possible distortions that could be caused by linguistic change, or by population movements, or both in the intervening years can be discounted here, for most of Laycock's sources on the languages in the immediate vicinity of these stations were written by the early missionaries themselves. What differences appear between the findings of these missionaries and Laycock's own investigations approximately fifty to seventy years later appear to be solely of technical interest (for example, possible changes in Murik noun classification, Laycock 1973:33–34) and do not in any case suggest that the number of languages proposed for the region by Laycock in 1973 was any different from the number that obtained in 1922.

The results, presented in Table 3, yield a minimum figure of ten distinct languages for the villages and village areas from which these sixteen main stations took their names. It is important, however, to understand that this number can be modified in different ways. For example, the languages that Laycock numbers 2 through 6 and 10—fully sixty percent of the total—are closely related Austronesian languages, while numbers 88, 116, 57, and 51 are non-Austronesian languages of at least four different families. If these considerations suggest somewhat less diversity than the number of languages per se, Laycock's notes on dialect suggest that the situation be considered more diverse, instead. Within the Sissano group of Austronesian languages, for example, Laycock notes Father Kirschbaum's observation of 1910 that Malol "shows more non-Melanesian elements than the surrounding languages, and says that the language of this group is to be distinguished from that of Arop, Sissano, and Sera," while Laycock himself notes that "there is considerable dialect divergence between the [mainland] villages, and between [these] villages and the islands" which comprised the Ali language group (1973:5). Certainly Hagspiel's own estimate of "twenty-five to thirty more or less widely divergent languages and dialects" is unexceptionable on Laycock's grounds, especially given that Hagspiel was taking into consideration the languages spoken along the entire 320 miles of coast that formed the mission's territory in 1922, and not just the languages spoken in the immediate vicinity of the sixteen stations selected for discussion here (Hagspiel 1926:121).

TABLE 3
Languages in the Immediate Vicinity of Mission Stations
in the Sepik Region, c. 1922

	Stations	Languages	
1.	Sissano	Sissano	(# 2)
2.	Arop	Sissano	
3.	Malol	Sissano	
4.	Tumleo	Tumleo	(# 3)
5.	Aitape	Ali	(# 4)
6.	Ali	Ali	
7.	Yakamul	Ali	
8.	Ulau	Ulau-Suain	(# 5)
9.	Suain	Ulau-Suain	
10.	Boiken	Boiken	(# 88)
11.	Yuo	Kairiru	(# 6)
12.	Wewak	Boiken	
13.	Murik	Murik	(# 116)
14.	Marienberg	Buna (?)	(# 51)
15.	Manam	Manam	(# 10)
16.	Monumbo	Monumbo	(# 57)
17.	Bogia	*	
18.	Mugil	*	
19.	Halopa	*	
20.	Nake	*	
21.	Saruga	*	
22.	Alexishafen	*	

*Madang area languages
Sources: Column 1, Hagspiel 1926
Column 2, Laycock 1973

Although it is clear that professional linguistic criteria for defining what are and are not distinct languages would allow a number of different conclusions about the extent of linguistic diversity in the area, the fact that no sharp disparity between Hagspiel and Laycock can be found on this point suggests that the missionaries' assessment was not skewed by any special bias. Of course, the missionaries' *attention* to linguistic differences was closely tied to their conception of the role of language in the missionary task. For the Catholic mission in the Sepik, a dual role is suggested by its policy of teaching German in its schools, while teaching catechism and elementary religion in the local languages of the villages themselves. If the former reflects the mission's metropolitan orientation and the centering role that language can play, the latter reflects the necessity for effective communication and the fact that in this area no single native language enjoyed sufficient currency to serve as a lingua franca, even given the mission's help. The rapid spread of New Guinea Pidgin soon reduced the missionaries' dependence on local languages for conducting daily affairs. Prior to 1931, however, when Pidgin was adopted as the language for the schools and for religious instruction, missionaries were required to attain competence in local languages to conduct their spiritual work.

Compounding the problems of access created by the narrow geographical range of political influence and authority among native societies, and the problems of communication created by linguistic diversity, were a final set of problems created by variation in the customs that affected the missionaries' assessment of the quality of native moral and religious life. In this regard, customs and beliefs concerning childbirth and childrearing, maturation and courtship, marriage and divorce, friendship and enmity, and illness and death were no less important, and no less variable than those concerning religion (that is, the supernatural) itself. Clearly, if missionaries were to achieve a position of moral authority, they had to address the conditions that obtained among the people in each local scene. What this meant for the station system, however, was that each situation invited a different focus for evangelical effort, and that the selection could be made only by the missionary with local contacts, local linguistic competence, and local "ethnographic" expertise.

To return to the question of personnel, we can see that additional numbers of priests might enable the mission to staff new stations or, if deployed as secondaries to old stations, might at least ease the problems of replacement when a missionary became ill or went on leave. What additional numbers could not do, in Hagspiel's opinion, was alter the forces that made each *station's* situation unique. Hagspiel, for example, visited one area in which the missionary had made special efforts to induce villagers to abandon their "methods of birth control" (presumably infanticide); Father Kirschbaum on the Sepik River was preoccupied with headhunting; the missionaries on Tumleo Island had apparently taken a particularly virulent form of sorcery as a major focus of their concern (1926:189, 38–45, 177–182; Puff 1912/1913). These differences, in Hagspiel's opinion, limited the capacity of the missionaries to benefit from the companionship and advice of missionaries working at different stations in the area. They are also the differences at the heart of what Hagspiel meant when he proposed that each station had become "almost a mission by itself" (1926:69).

The Representation of Diversity

Although I have, in effect, absolved Hagspiel and the missionary authors and informants from whom he obtained his information of any "special interest" in their representation of the language situation in the Sepik, we must tread more carefully if we are to assess Hagspiel's representation of the cultural scene. Clearly, these early missionaries lacked the comparative material from other parts of the Sepik that later allowed ethnologists such as Frank Tiesler (1969) to represent the north coast as one of the region's more coherent culture areas. It is also true, as we shall see, that Hagspiel's concern for the coherence of the mission system was sharpened by the likelihood that it would soon begin to expand from the coast into the "vast interior" that "still remains, for the most part, an unknown region" (1926:70). Yet, Hagspiel's representation of the extent of cultural diversity in the mission field does appear excessive—even given the state of ethnographic knowledge at the time. Consider, for example, the following statement that he provides as a summary to his presentation of the general features of native cultural life:

> *The traits of the people of various tribes, often separated by but a few miles of one another, will frequently vary to such an extent as to appear to be diametrically opposed; and even within a single tribe sometimes beliefs and motives are to be observed [sic], as being held simultaneously, which are inconsistent within themselves and often contradictory, the one to the other [1926:64].*

One must note that by 1922 the Society's missionaries in New Guinea had already published a great many essays and articles containing more or less systematic observations on the material culture, language, social organization, religious life, health, habits, folklore, and history of the people in the villages among whom they worked and in the areas through which they traveled for purposes of exploration and expansion. Many contributors naturally restricted their outlets to Society magazines that circulated among "mission friends" and that maintained only minimal standards of evidence and, in fact, discouraged scientific writing styles (Höltker 1940/41:2–3). Yet quite a few also published ethnographic articles in professional ethnological journals, including *Anthropos* which was, as I have already noted, published under the auspices of the SVD, itself. Mention should also be made of the missionaries' contributions to collections of objects housed in Society museums for public display and scientific study and, especially, of their collaboration with professional ethnologists to whose inquiries they replied and for whose evidence and conclusions the missionaries' observations provided support (Brandewie 1985).

Although formal ethnographic study was understood to be an adjunct to, or a by-product of, a field missionary's professional—spiritual or material—work, its scientific justification should not be underestimated; at any rate, it is relevant for understanding the theoretical context in which the material they collected was placed. It must be recalled that the founder of the journal *Anthropos,* Father Wilhelm Schmidt, was himself an SVD priest. He was also the leading figure of *Kulturkreislehre* in Vienna, an ethnological school that followed the lead of Fritz Graebner of the Ethnographic Museum at Cologne in using culture-historical methods to trace the geographical origins of the languages, art styles, religions, and customs found in the various cultural regions of the world. As envisioned by Schmidt, the ultimate aim of this exercise was "to reconstruct a limited number of original cultural circles" from "the known distribution of contemporary culture traits" (Harris 1968:384). Understandably, the mission's work in New Guinea, an area previously unknown to ethnology, provided an intriguing scientific task for professional ethnologists of the *Kulturkreislehre,* and the Society's missionaries clearly were in a position to provide the detailed data necessary for scientific scrutiny at home (Brandewie 1985). Schmidt organized much of the linguistic data provided by missionaries in the New Guinea field and corresponded with them himself on various points concerning native religion and character (Hagspiel 1926:63,65).

Although the task of documenting local variation among the region's contemporary cultures was thus accorded positive *scientific* value, it is also true that Schmidt's version of *Kulturkreislehre* accorded a negative *moral* value to cultural diversity in and of itself. A cultural evolutionary theory, for example, might see evidence in cultural variation of finely tuned adaptations to specific local environments. Schmidt's culture-historical theory, however, considered variation the degenerate product of an original and, as far as religion was concerned, essential (that is, revealed) set of cultural forms.[2] In contrast to Graebner who viewed culture circles as themselves products of history, "Schmidt's culture circle was a possible starting point for history: it was the original culture of an area, which was to be disrupted by the subsequent intrusion of other cultures" (Andriolo 1979:135).

Although Hagspiel's book on New Guinea was a contribution to public relations and not to professional ethnology, he used the latter (citing Schmidt and the findings of other ethnologists) to set his scene. Allowing for the kind of simplification that inevitably accompanies popularization, Hagspiel's representation of diversity follows the orthodox ethnological line. That is, rather than seek a pattern in the present-day distribution of objects, traits, and beliefs in the New Guinea field, Hagspiel represents its contemporary culture as a disordered and virtually meaningless array. Following in the spirit of his Society's most distinguished ethnologist, Hagspiel explains:

after original unity, subsequent separation, and later infiltrations of
mixed cultures through the migration of the peoples . . . and after
their gradual intermingling, it is not especially strange to find here
one people whose characteristics are often so complex, perverse, and
even self-contradictory, that it is extremely difficult to give them any
definite place in the great social family [i.e. the people of the South
Seas] in which they are centralized [1926:62].

The question of how much Schmidt's ethnological theories owe to his Catholicism remains a subject of contention among historians of anthropological thought (Kluckhohn 1936:173–174; Harris 1968:390–392; Braukaemper 1979:560). Certainly the notion of degeneration, especially as elaborated by Schmidt in regard to religion, subjects contemporary diversity both as form (different beliefs among different people) and as content (belief in many supernatural beings) to a moral interpretation which was by no means at odds with the missionary aims of Schmidt's Society. Nor was the idea that order requires placement in a larger social unit at odds with the universalizing orientation of the Roman Catholic Church. By denying to native culture its own set of ordering principles, the road was opened for a publicist like Hagspiel to shift from a scientific to an ecclesiastical frame. By a simple substitution of Catholic hierarchical principles for "original unity," Hagspiel transforms Schmidt's ethnological version of paradise lost into a missionary vision of the paradise to be gained.

Strategies of Containment

Whatever the effects may have been of cultural diversity on the mission system, I think that we must conclude that Hagspiel's *representation* of cultural diversity in the mission field serves primarily to rationalize the new order that the missionaries were attempting to impose. Yet, the nature of his bias is precisely the point. Hagspiel's vision of the spiritual benefits that Catholicism could bring to the natives of New Guinea was one that viewed salvation as a state to be mediated through inclusion in a hierarchically ordered whole.[3] Thus, we can see why his concern that this "whole" was weakened among the missionaries themselves takes on a larger eschatological significance than it might otherwise appear to have. To be sure, Hagspiel finds a "sweet consolation" in the sad fact that missionaries could frequently baptize dying infants so that their souls could go directly to heaven. Yet, the mission's real ministry was to the living whose own chances for heaven were mediated by the social and cultural conditions in which they lived. Consequently, Hagspiel's real praise was reserved for those mission activities that ordered those conditions in a recognizable, that is, "centering," way. The German taught at mission schools, for example, had "established a first bond of intercourse and the sharing of common interest among the tribes," and even the plantations and industries had "contributed their quota of influence to bring the people more and more into a common relationship" (1926:70).

The "ordering" role of the mission stations themselves was critical to the process in Hagspiel's eye, and was best exemplified by some of the larger stations along the coast. The station at Boiken, for example,

> seemed to me a perfect model of all that a station among uncivilized people should be. Cocoanut [sic] groves abounded, and there were sheep, geese, ducks, chickens, etc. Everything that would conserve life and assure a future supply of food was set out here in orderly and well-planned fashion [1926:95].

Wewak, further down the coast, was another "ideal missionary settlement . . . even more efficient than Boikin [sic]" (1926:95); while at Bogia, where he spent a week traveling through the surrounding area with the station priest, Hagspiel saw the reflection of mission order in the villages themselves. Oneputa, for example, was "exceptionally beautiful. All the houses are in one group, not scattered over a number of plantations [i.e. gardens] as is generally the case" (1926:183). The Dagoi people impressed him with the "orderly arrangement of the houses. They had been erected in one place . . . " (1926:192). He visited a Tsepa village in which one hundred and fifty Catholics "gave every evidence of living wholesome Catholic lives. Holy pictures and crucifixes were in every hut into which I peered, and everywhere I found the women busy, contented, and happy" (1926:190). Hagspiel was especially gratified to inform his readers that five hundred villagers assembled *together* at Bogia for Sunday service, some coming by canoe on Saturday and the others, in reply to the mission's own slit-drum signal, walking for hours along bush tracks to be there on time. "What an example for many Catholics at home!" (Hagspiel 1926:198–199).

In stark contrast to such long-established coastal stations, however, were some of the newer stations, like Marienberg on the Sepik River, which Hagspiel visited only briefly, but the conditions of which are described in a long letter from its famous missionary, Father Kirschbaum. In fact, the letter was written from a village on the Karowai (Karowari) River, which Kirschbaum visited periodically to purchase materials for his Marienberg station. So gruesome did Hagspiel consider Father Kirschbaum's account of the headhunting peoples in that area, that he warned his readers that although "the narrative . . . is not precisely suited to fireside reading and reveries . . . its very roughness goes to show as perhaps nothing else can just what real missionary life is when one *gets down to business*" (1926:38). As he notes elsewhere, "the ordinary routine of life in New Guinea has always been as one continuous panorama of death and slaughter, save where mission influence has penetrated" (1926:37).

Given the moral power that the missionaries attributed to their own religion, it is not surprising that many of the tragic features of this "ordinary routine" were attributed to pagan religious practices and beliefs. To be sure, the presence of cultic life in itself was taken as evidence that "there is really a kernel at least of religious feeling within the whole" (Hagspiel 1926:89), and Hagspiel could appreciate the spiritual sensibility embodied within a native cult house as well as its craftsmanship:

> the top of these spirit houses is usually decorated with a bird with large beak and wings turned upward, seemingly lifting itself up to higher regions, as if the souls of these stone-age artists had a longing for a higher motive than to be found on this earth . . . At any rate . . . the very size and position [of the carving of the spirit to which the house is dedicated] prove the fact that these uncivilized natives have some conception of, and belief in, a higher being [1926:194].

Despite such traces of what Schmidt's ethnological school would interpret as original revealed truth, contemporary native religion amounted in Hagspiel's opinion to little more than a "means of preventing the vengeance of an angry god from falling upon his mortal subjects" (1926:86). "These powerful manifestations of the god . . . serve to fill the minds of the people with fear, rather than love" (1926:86).

The moral consequences of this complex could be seen throughout the area, Hagspiel believed, in the natives' understanding of misfortune and in the logic which led from misfortune to treachery, revenge, warfare, and death. Along the eastern part of the coast, for example, adepts with magical control over the sun and the rain might wield great influence, but native logic dictated that if a man's magic should fail, it was because of a spirit's displeasure. Thus, the magician would have to be killed to prevent even greater disaster to the village as a whole (Hagspiel 1926:175). On Tumleo Island, sorcerers venerated a wooden figure that could be used to cause illness and which, in turn, fueled the desire of a victim's relatives to take revenge (Hagspiel 1926:180–182; Puff 1912/ 1913). Hagspiel's most spectacular exhibit in this regard came from Father Kirschbaum's account of headhunting. "It is," Father Kirschbaum explained,

> part of their religion; they simply have to do it according to their belief, in order to escape the evil spirit's revenge, which would [otherwise] be exercized in the ruin of their own village. Poor people! Their lord, Satan, keeps a tight hold on them—a very tight hold indeed! [Hagspiel 1926:40]

Breaking this "tight hold" was one of the principal goals of all mission work at that time. The schools, workshops, gardens, and plantations at the stations or at the headquarters in Alexishafen could help. The missionaries, we are told, were extremely pleased when girls from their area who had been given the opportunity of studying with the mission sisters, married Catholic boys who had been working for the Fathers before they returned home: otherwise the girls would be forced by their families to marry a pagan and they and their children would be lost to the church (Hagspiel 1926:158). Yet, completely removing children from their villages to control the influences upon them was possible only in the case of the orphans whom the sisters had under their care in Alexishafen. For the majority of the population, such an extreme technique was neither practical nor moral. As Father Kirschbaum wrote, reflecting on a Karowari River lad who was already in possession of one human skull:

> . . . there is no use in reveling in the conjectures as to how many years of advance for Christian civilization would be assured if all the elders could be at once transported or otherwise disposed of, for good and for all. We must give them, as well as the youngsters, the best chances possible to secure heaven; but nevertheless, the cold, hard, facts of the situation have to be faced, and they have to be reckoned with, also [Hagspiel 1926:42].

Isolation and Community

Exactly how such conditions were to be reckoned with was, by the station system's own logic, left to the individual missionary priest. This should not obscure the fact that missionaries conformed to similar patterns in many areas of practice, but—contra Hagspiel—it should suggest that the differences in spiritual focus that arose among stations may have been as much a result of differences in temperament and outlook among the priests as they were of differences in "objective" cultural facts. Bryant Allen provides a fine example that illustrates both of these points, albeit from a few years later, when two new priests—Father Edmund Kunisch at Ulau and Father Richard Kunze at Yakamul—were both making "strenuous efforts" to spread mission influence south of their coastal stations, behind the Torricelli range. Already known to men from the interior who had earlier come through their stations "en route to and from contract labor assignments, or who visited the coast for salt and trade goods," the two priests, Kunisch to the east, and Kunze to the west, "began establishing camps, houses, chapels, and school buildings, all made of local materials at selected sites throughout the northern half of the area." They often left behind them a catechist or teacher from the coast (Allen 1976:82).

Although both priests were in pursuit of similar ends, and although both employed formally similar strategies at about the same time, their assessments of the situation diverged radically, and led to radically different evangelical styles:

> *Informants in Kunze's area describe how he immediately attacked the* tambaran *cult, pulling secret paintings and ritual objects out of the spirit houses and forcing women to view them. At times he broke up initiations, swinging a stout stick and sprinkling holy water over the participants and the enclosures in which the ceremonies were taking place. Participants were told that it was 'wok bilong Satan,' the devil's work, and that they would be consumed by fire if they persisted. Older men had to be physically restrained from killing him by younger men, who, having experienced something of the European world beyond . . . , realized both the futility of killing one European, and the likelihood that terrible retribution would follow.*
>
> *Kunisch, on the other hand, although he spoke against the* tambaran, *appears to have been more concerned about sorcery, a theme which found some sympathy with many villagers. Informants speak of him with respect, as a quiet person, who never attempted to force change [Allen 1976:82].*

Although this account is a reconstruction of events that occurred a decade after Hagspiel's trip to New Guinea, it underlines his concern—as great for the missionaries, as for the natives—about the effects of isolation and autonomy from a center of hierarchical control.

Hagspiel could have treated the isolation of SVD missionaries in their respective outstations as an occasion for them to develop in terms of religious models of separation from the world. Yet, this was clearly not within the scope of the "spirit" of this Society. Hagspiel's own spirits were lightened not by separation but by ordered inclusion as, for example, by the stateliness of the mission's headquarters at Alexishafen where the fruits of disciplined labor could be seen, and where one could witness, as he did, a Corpus Christi procession in which "the order maintained throughout was splendid" (1926:213). He could only rue the forces that normally kept missionaries away from such "edifying and dignified" spectacles, and which left them alone, on their own, in the bush. Hagspiel did not enjoy muddy roads, dirty hands, nor mosquitoes (1926:165,188,100), and he did not view isolation as a spiritual opportunity, but as an invitation to spiritual disaster, instead:

> *Proportionately remote from one another lie the mission stations: so it is seldom that the missionaries are able to come together for a friendly conference. And this consciousness of remoteness, of solitude, of standing quite by oneself in the midst of the low cultural state of the heathen, of being severed from every good influence which serves to uplift and to elevate—this consciousness, I say, tends*

in the long run to weaken the missionary, both in spirituality and humaneness. 'In the midst of the wilds and surrounded by the wild,' declared a missionary priest, 'one runs into danger of becoming more or less wild and lawless' [1926:130].

It should, of course, be clear that if the mission community in 1922 appeared to be in danger of exceeding the bounds of its organizational competence, this was not only because of external conditions ("obstacles"), but also because of the Society's own organizational values and ideals. I have already suggested that Father Hagspiel's position as a representative of the Society's center directed his eye to its political, and hence spiritual, coherence. Although his image of clerical community may have been appropriate to seminary life, however, it was neither a real possibility for effective missionary work in New Guinea, nor was it necessarily appropriate for a mission in the process of constituting itself as a Church. When, approximately ten years later, the Sepik became a jurisdiction of its own, separate from Alexishafen, notions about authentic community were brought more into line with conditions that actually prevailed in the mission field.

ECCLESIASTICAL SPACE, STATUS, AND TIME

The Catholic mission in New Guinea was in a period of transition when Hagspiel and the Superior General paid their visit in the spring of 1922. I have already mentioned the critical external change in civil administration and Australia's threatening pronouncements in regard to personnel. Yet, at the same time that Hagspiel was visiting New Guinea, significant changes in the mission's territorial jurisdiction and ecclesiastical status were also underway. Hagspiel's perception of the community as regrettably decentered had some justification on this basis alone, for the community was still operating with a temporary administrator and was still awaiting the appointment of a new ecclesiastical head. This time, however, the leader was to be a vicar apostolic instead of a prefect apostolic as Limbrock had been, in recognition of the mission's success in creating both a material base for its spiritual work and for creating through this spiritual work a native laity of some size. The new bishop was not to be conceived simply as the leader of a small clerical community; rather, he was to provide the "unifying principle" for the entire Catholic community in the region as it moved towards its goal of attaining the diocesan structure of a mature Catholic church.

Changes in Ecclesiastical Space

The 1920s were marked by rather striking changes in the ecclesiastical organization of the New Guinea field, the character of which may best be explicated by noting their family resemblance to the kinds of changes that have marked the history of other colonial agencies, whose systems were developed in the same general area over about the same period of time. In this regard, it may be helpful to refer to Levine and Levine's description of the historical development of the Australian administrative system in British New Guinea (Papua) in response to problems already familiar from our discussion above, that is, "a general lack of finance and staff, the rough terrain, small isolated nature of indigenous groups, lack of chiefs who could influence large numbers of followers, [and the] great diversity of local languages. . . ."

> As a mechanism for the gradual integration of British New Guinea, a policy of dividing the country into districts was put into effect. . . . Each administrative district was assigned a headquarters and resident magistrate whose duty it was to dispatch patrols throughout the area to investigate disturbances, hold trials, take census, and ensure that government edicts affecting the villages were obeyed. As areas were penetrated and patrolled, new districts and district headquarters were gazetted and these were further divided into subdistricts [Levine and Levine 1979:13].

Allowing for the obvious differences between a magistrate's concern with "law and order," and the "spiritual" work of a priest, the external similarities between the two systems are obvious, with mission stations, their priests, and their station areas appearing as structural equivalents for the headquarters, magistrates, and districts of the administrative system devised by Sir William MacGregor for Papua, and later used for the Australian administration of New Guinea, as well.

At first glance, one might think that the similarity extends to higher levels of Church organization as well for, like the government, the Church begins the process of integration with a predefined "whole" and, again like the government, proceeds to elaborate this "whole" into a hierarchically ordered system of divisions and subdivisions. For example, we have already seen how the ecclesiastical territory of Kaiser Wilhelmsland was itself created by the Vatican through detachment from an earlier territory, including both the mainland and archipelago regions of German New Guinea. As Figure 5 shows, the history of this new territory was likewise punctuated by numerous similar divisions, the first of which occurred in 1913. We have also seen that by that time the SVD itself had been able to effectively occupy only the area between Aitape and Friedrich Wilhelmshafen (Madang). Thus, when another missionary society declared itself ready to take on a mission in the region, the Vatican detached the western portion of the ecclesiastical territory, created for Kaiser Wilhelmsland, and assigned it to this new group. From 1913 until the end of World War II, then, there were two ecclesiastical districts for the Territory of New Guinea rather than just one.

We shall return to the fate of this western district shortly, but first it

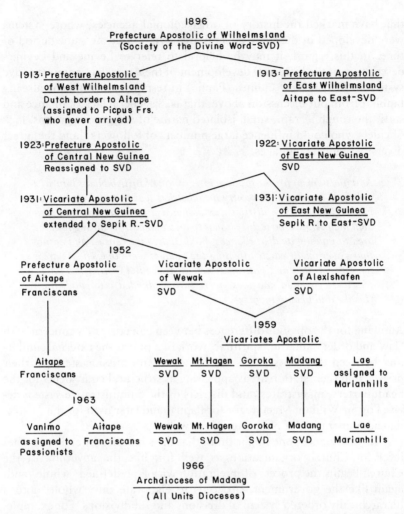

1896
Prefecture Apostolic of Wilhelmsland
(Society of the Divine Word-SVD)

1913: Prefecture Apostolic
of West Wilhelmsland
Dutch border to Altape
(assigned to Picpus Frs.
who never arrived)

1923: Prefecture Apostolic
of Central New Guinea
Reassigned to SVD

1931: Vicariate Apostolic
of Central New Guinea
extended to Sepik R.-SVD

1913: Prefecture Apostolic
of East Wilhelmsland
Aitape to East-SVD

1922: Vicariate Apostolic
of East New Guinea
SVD

1931: Vicariate Apostolic
of East New Guinea
Sepik R. to East-SVD

1952

Prefecture Apostolic
of Aitape
Franciscans

Vicariate Apostolic
of Wewak
SVD

Vicariate Apostolic
of Alexishafen
SVD

1959
Vicariates Apostolic

| Aitape | Wewak | Mt. Hagen | Goroka | Madang | Lae |
| Franciscans | SVD | SVD | SVD | SVD | assigned to Marianhills |

1963

| Vanimo | Aitape | Wewak | Mt. Hagen | Goroka | Madang | Lae |
| assigned to Passionists | Franciscans | SVD | SVD | SVD | SVD | Marianhills |

1966
Archdiocese of Madang
(All Units Dioceses)

Figure 5. Prefecture Apostolic of Wilhelmsland, Changes in Territory and Status, 1896–1966. (Based on information from Divine Word Missionaries 1969: 49–57.)

is necessary to point out the critical difference between the apparently similar systems developed by the government and the church for the integration of their respective fields. While each new administrative district was part of a *single* administrative system, each new ecclesiastical district formed a separate system of its own. The "unifying principles" (to borrow a term from Father Hagspiel) of the two systems thus operated at quite different levels, and had quite different practical results. When it was formed in 1921, the Territory of New Guinea was a single unit, centered at Rabaul, and all of the districts within this territory were under the control of that center and all of its staff were formally governed by the rules and regulations of a single Territory Service. By contrast, in the ecclesiastical system integration took place below the level of this political entity. As conceived in the period before Vatican II, at any rate, each ecclesiastical entity was formally independent of others in the same geographical region, with each bishop separately and directly responsible to Rome.

The ecclesiastical system was complicated by the Vatican practice of assigning the ecclesiastical units it created to missionary societies. Because each Society had its own center, its own resources, its own training institutions, its own national regions of recruitment, and its own "spirit" or style, ecclesiastical units that were assigned to *different* Societies were naturally more separate in practice than those assigned to the same Society. Indeed, because the mission-sending Societies staffed these units, they tended to be the principal recorders and guardians of their mission history. Thus, primary historical sources are more likely to contain information on a single Society's missions in different parts of the world than material on neighboring missions maintained by different Societies in one part, politically or geographically defined. The fact that these units were all units of the Roman Catholic Church is extremely important ecclesiastically. However, mission historiography reflects the fact that the sociologically effective units were the separate ecclesiastical districts and the Societies to which they were entrusted, whose reputations were—at least in the early stages—augmented or diminished by the performance of the missions that they sent to work within these ecclesiastical bounds.

To return to the particulars of the two ecclesiastical districts of interwar New Guinea, it was extremely important to their history that the Picpus Fathers (to whom the western district was first assigned) had been prevented by World War I from taking up their assignment, and that the new ecclesiastical district was in 1923 reassigned to the Society of the Divine Word. Considering the situation that Hagspiel had described in the previous year, it is understandable that work in this "new" territory was not immediately begun. It was not until 1928 that one of the SVD priests was selected as its prefect and not until the eastern boundaries of the district were extended from Aitape to the mouth of the Sepik River in 1931 that it could claim sufficient resources to be effectively constituted as a separate district on its own. Because of their joint history and their joint affiliation with the SVD, however, the Sepik and Alexishafen jurisdictions maintained a closer relationship in practice than would have been the case had another Society taken over in the west as originally planned.

Changes in Ecclesiastical Status

At about the same time that the western district from Aitape to Vanimo was being returned to the SVD, the Society's original territory was being raised in ecclesiastical status, marking official recognition by the Vatican of its progress over the past twenty-six years. As can be seen from Figure 5, the western region was likewise dignified after its extension to the mouth of the Sepik River brought part of the previously established mission system within its bounds. Instead of one prefecture under the leadership of one perfect, then, the SVD's mission field in New Guinea eventually included two vicariates under the leadership of two vicars. In contrast to the earlier prefect, Eberhard Limbrock, who (merely) *acted* as a bishop, these vicars were *consecrated* bishops, in accord with the dignity conferred upon the ecclesiastical districts that they led (Winslow 1967a:727). A variety of diplomatic considerations in regard to the Vatican's relations with the SVD and Australia may have entered into the decision to elevate these districts in New Guinea to the rank of vicariate at this particular time. However, the result was that they were now endowed with *real* bishops whose task it was to represent and to ensure the future of these missions as authentic parts of the diocesan structure of the Roman Catholic Church.

It should be mentioned that the process of differentiation whereby the Church was to emerge from its Society cocoon had already begun with the somewhat belated designation of an officer separate from the prefect to serve as Regional Superior of the New Guinea community of the SVD, and by the designation of certain local resources as the property of the Society as distinct from property belonging to the prefecture, itself. The elevation of the prefecture to vicariate status was an important step in this process, quite apart from the gratification that the missionaries obtained from the Vatican's recognition of their work. We have already seen how the first prefect had depended for the actual exercise of his power to direct the mission on the mediation of the Superior General of the SVD. The new vicars, too, were selected from the Society's members and, like their predecessor, depended on the Society for personnel, financial aid, and spiritual support. Their higher status, however, clarified their position as independent officers of the Church, and enhanced their authority within the communities they led.

Although a bishop's powers in a vicariate were exercized "in the name of the Pope" (and not directly, as in a diocese, "in the name of Christ"), the extent of the vicar's authority over the spiritual and temporal affairs of the Church in his district was considerable, and was founded on the same theological and historical bases as that of a residential bishop in a diocese (Winslow 1967b:638–639). Canon law specified certain obligations, such as the administration of the sacrament of Confirmation, the periodic visitation of the "parishes" in his jurisdiction, a five-year report to the Vatican, and a visit to Rome every ten years. The general terms of the office were, however, widely conceived. The bishop was responsible for "the worship of God, preaching the word of God, the administration of the Sacraments . . . safeguarding the faith and morals of the faithful, and the religious instruction of the faithful. . . . " and it was up to the bishop to decide how the priests on his staff would share in this work (Faulkner 1967:587; Winslow 1967b).

Naturally, custom and established practice constrained the way new bishops could order these affairs. Yet, the extremes to which he would be entitled by his symbolic role alone may be suggested by the following passage from the New Catholic Encyclopedia, about the history of the role of the bishop in the church:

> *from the time of Ignatius [Bishop of Antioch, 1st century A.D.], the bishop has been the living and visible symbol, the center and effective principle of unity. . . . There is indeed a spiritual union of souls to Christ, but this necessarily expresses itself in a visible union with the one who for a given community is the image of what Christ is for the Church and whose role it is to make concrete the mystical union with Christ. Ignatius time and again insists that to maintain such union no liturgical celebrations are to be held, no communal actions taken, no doctrine received except in union with and submission to the bishop, who as surrogate of Christ is the pole of unity around which Christian life centers [Faulkner 1967:589].*

To be sure, New Guinea in the 1920s and 1930s was far distant from Antioch in the first century A.D., and no one would expect a new bishop to insist on such extremes. The point to be made here, however, is that because of the virtually unlimited fund of symbolic capital created by the presence of a bishop, the mission communities between the wars could be centered on the bishops themselves. This is not to say that there was less concern about the practical matters of communication and isolation, but simply that these no longer bore the ecclesiastical significance they had for Hagspiel in 1922. After the territory was raised to vicariate status, and following the arrival of its first bishop in 1923, the mission and the Church were more clearly differentiated. The unifying principle was no longer embedded in the authority structure of the religious community. It was divided between an ecclesiastical superior (the bishop) and a religious superior, whose jurisdiction was limited to the personal well-being of the missionaries as members of the SVD, but who was not, like the bishop, in charge of the mission as a vicariate of the Roman Catholic Church under the bishop, Propaganda Fide, and the Pope.

Like changes in ecclesiastical territory, such changes in ecclesiastical status are reflected in the ways in which missionaries themselves recall and record the events of mission history. One cannot help but note the official bias that pervades missionary historiography and provides the means for depicting the progress of time and the direction and spirit of mission work. Even in articles written for a general academic audience, the mission's historians and memoirists provide bishops with a privileged role. Father William Ross's paper (1969) on the mission's pioneer work in the New Guinea highlands in the 1930s, for example, refers to a bishop in more than one-third of its thirty-eight paragraphs, to wit: 1) the idea of exploring the highlands is *suggested* to Bishop Wolf at Alexishafen in 1930; 2) Bishop Wolf *applied* for government permission to proceed; 3) Bishop Wolf *appoints* the first missionaries to open stations there; 4) a letter from the miner/explorer Dan Leahy describing Mt. Hagen is *shown* to Bishop Wolf; 5) the Leahy brothers *visit* Bishop Wolf and encourage his enthusiasm for further exploration; 6) the missionaries *return* and *report* their experience to Bishop Wolf; 7) Bishop Wolf *wished* certain missionaries to accompany others on the trip to Mt. Hagen; 8) Bishop Wolf *ordered* a station to be built at Mingende; 9) Bishop Wolf gave official approval *authorizing* a new mission in the Mt. Hagen area; 10) the violent death of a missionary in the highlands is *reported* to Bishop Wolf; 11) Bishop Wolf *releases* Father Ross from other obligations so that he could return to the highlands; 12) In 1959 the western highlands becomes a separate Vicariate with a new bishop named as the first Vicar Apostolic; and 13) last but by no means least, "With a resident bishop at Mt. Hagen the work of the Catholic Mission has made continual progress" (1969: passim; quotation from p. 327).[4]

This is not "heroic history" of the kind to which Sahlins refers in his discussion of hierarchical polities focused on a king (1983). Yet, just as Sahlins argues that accounts of "kings and battles" should not be dismissed as mere mystifications (1983:520–521), so I would argue that the official bias of Catholic mission historians not be regarded as a merely pious convention. In both cases, historical representation derives from a particular kind of society and illuminates the very features that made possible the kinds of events it recalls. As all of the "suggesting," "applying," "appointing," "showing," "visiting," "reporting," "wishing," "ordering" and "authorizing" in Father Ross's account suggest, the bishop's role, like that of the king, derives from a "cultural order that, multiplying [his] action . . . by the system of society, gives him a disproportionate historical effect" (Sahlins 1983:520). Father Ross's assertion that "continual mission progress" was made in the Western Highlands once the region became a separate vicariate with a resident bishop is a statement about this "disproportionate historical effect."

HIERARCHY AND THE SEPIK MISSION COMMUNITY

Given these considerations, 1931 must be seen as a most significant year for the Catholic missionaries in mainland New Guinea. It was in 1931 that Eberhard Limbrock, the pioneer prefect, died (in Sydney, en route to Europe for medical care) and it was in 1931 that the Sepik region proper was effectively created as a *local* jurisdiction with its own *locally* resident bishop. If, following Ross, we take expansion as an index of local mission progress, or at least vitality, we can see from the roster of stations that for the mission community in the Sepik the ecclesiastical changes were a success. The last main station in its territory had been opened at But in 1924. Now, however, we find the creation on the coast of an island station (actually, a circuit) named Vokeo in 1932 and of Turubu, on the mainland between Wewak and Murik, in 1933. The mission's first main station behind the coastal range was opened at Sassoya in 1933, Timbunke (up the Sepik River from Marienberg) opened in 1932, and Kambot (on the Yuat River, one of the Sepik's major tributaries) was founded in 1933 (Figure 4). The *Steyler Missionsbote* also reflects the pace and direction of this activity, for descriptions of trips through the hinterland, and reports on the land and people in the vicinity of the new inland stations, predominate the magazine's coverage of this region in the 1930s. Given the dangers of diversity that Hagspiel had anticipated in the event of such expansion, however, we may well ask what effects it had on the coherence of the mission community, itself.

It is not clear exactly how Bishop Wolf dealt with these problems in the Vicariate of East New Guinea, which was expanding into the highlands at the same period of time. We may note, however, that the frequency with which he is mentioned in Father Ross's article suggests that Bishop Wolf chose to take an active role of control, and we may also note that this role would have been facilitated in 1935 when a German organization gave him a "two-seater monoplane called *Paulus,* and one year later a larger plane called *Petrus.* They reduce[d] 14-day treks between Alexishafen and the Bismarck Mountains to 80-minute rides" (Divine Word Missionaries 1969:52).

Of course, Bishop Wolf's territory also remained in possession of the most profitable plantations and of the elaborate headquarters built by Limbrock at Alexishafen. Something of Wolf's style may, in fact, be suggested by Nancy Lutkehaus' comment that in his ecclesiastical territory "the traditional Catholic hierarchy was replicated in miniature," with Alexishafen serving as "its 'Vatican City' where the [bishop] resided," (1983:29), and by a traveler's observation that Alexishafen's new cathedral was "a replica of St. Peter's in Rome" (Marshall 1938:222).

The new jurisdiction created for the Sepik was less prosperous than the territory to the east, and was capable of meeting only one-third of its material needs from local resources (Angelus 1936). Although Alexishafen was built close to the major port town of Madang, the region within which the Sepik mission worked still had no towns worthy of the name and still had only a rudimentary commerical community. Although this mission's field of expansion was not so distant in miles from the coast as the Bismarck mountains of the New Guinea Highlands, it had no plane with which to replace lengthy journeys either on horse or foot, or by river or sea. The new jurisdiction did include some of the stations that Hagspiel had found most impressive on his tour in 1922, but neither Tumleo, nor Boiken, nor Wewak were comparable to Alexishafen in scale.

In short, it appears that although the eastern district could support a large center set apart by pomp and circumstance from the general state of the surrounding frontier, the western district could not. In the Sepik, neither the old center at Tumleo nor the new headquarters constructed on Kairiru Island in 1936 appears to have assumed anything resembling a "miniature Vatican" role. The integrating images in the Sepik were more like the old ship *Gabriel,* partaking of the frontier's rustic character; and in contrast to Alexishafen, the bishop's seat in the Sepik was not as important an image of the community's center as was a former captain of the *Gabriel,* the new bishop himself.

"The Fighting Bishop"

Joseph Loerks, the new bishop in the Sepik, was an old New Guinea hand. Unlike Francis Wolf, who came to lead the New Guinea mission from Africa (where he had previously served in the SVD's Togo field), Loerks had spent his entire career as a priest in New Guinea, having arrived there in 1900 at the age of twenty-four as one of the mission's early pioneers. According to Limbrock's report on the mission in 1906, Loerks was then managing the Alexishafen plantation, and he was later one of the group sent to study methods of rice cultivation in the southern United States (Wiltgen 1969a:352,355). When Hagspiel came through in 1922, Father Loerks was resident at the "model station" of Boiken, which had the fine gardens that Hagspiel admired as a good example of industry and planning for times ahead (1926:94–95). Later that year, Loerks succeeded Brother Casnius as captain of the *Gabriel,* and also served for twenty years as mission procurator, the officer in charge of central supply (Hagspiel 1926:217; Angelus 1936).

Loerks's practical experience feeds well into the hagiographical formula already established for Eberhard Limbrock. In a chronology of mission history published in 1969, for example, we are not simply told that he was appointed to lead the new mission district in 1928, but that when he received news of his high appointment, he was washing dishes in Epping, Australia, at the SVD's convalescent home for New Guinea missionaries (Divine Word Missionaries 1969:51). Loerks's experience gave him an unrivaled knowledge of the state of mission operations, of conditions in far-flung stations, of commercial supply houses and shipping schedules, not to mention the Australian administration—all factors with which the man selected to establish the Sepik as a new and separate jurisdictional territory would have to deal. If Limbrock's belated reputation as "the man of providence" had reflected his success in establishing the mission on a sound material basis, Loerks's reputation as "the fighting bishop" reflects the verve with which he attacked the political problems that became his to solve.

It is important to recall from Chapter 2, that after an exceedingly slow start, the Australian administration had accelerated the pace of its activity in the Sepik at approximately the same time that Loerks was directing the mission to expand. Although relations between the mission and the new administration had improved since the early 1920s when Australia had threatened to bar German nationals from the territory, events continued to occur that the missionaries viewed as unwarranted incursions into church matters. As we shall see in the next chapter, the cargo cults (millenarian movements) that were first reported in the region in the 1930s were widely interpreted by the colonial public as "waves of mistaken enthusiasm" connected with "religious teachings," calling for more effective regulation of mission activities in the country (Thomas 1935:25–26). As Bishop Loerks's epithet implies, he was not averse to staging an active defense. In a letter to his seminary community back home, one of Loerks's younger priests provides the following portrait of the bishop's style when the community's interests were threatened:

> Our Masonic Government recently turned ultra-Bolshevistic by issuing an ordinance that clergymen may assist at marriages but before the law the only marriages recognized as valid are those contracted before a government official and marriages in the native fashion. But we have real Catholic Action here under the leadership of the Bishops. Our Vicar Apostolic [Loerks] is known as the 'fighting Bishop' and he relishes such occasions. I hope I am present when he meets the administrator [Angelus 1936].

Loerks's style was not always confrontational. We are fortunate to be able to go outside the mission for comments on this point. G.W.L. Townsend knew Loerks both before and after his consecration as bishop. When he had been captain of the *Gabriel* in the 1920s, Loerks had met and traveled with patrol officer Townsend several times. And later, when Loerks had become Bishop and Townsend the chief District Officer, the latter reports that they had worked together to solve the "inevitable" conflicts "with young [government] field-staff who hoped to bring the District under 'complete control' by Christmas; and earnest young, and not so young Fathers who hoped to convert the whole of the population by Easter at the latest" (1968:226). Townsend writes that it was "Thanks to [Loerks's] tolerance and wisdom [that] no conflict between persons ever had to go beyond our conferences" (1968:225), and reports an incident in which compromise was achieved when a young and zealous priest had condemned the only practical means of handling the dead— cremation—in a flood-prone region of the Sepik River (1968:226). While Loerks's capacity to contain such crises may not have endeared him to the more fervent missionaries on his staff, the wisdom of his cooperation with Townsend was shown later when Townsend agreed to soften the burdens on the mission of the government's restrictions on the freedom of German aliens after war in Europe was declared (Townsend 1968:243).

To outsiders like Townsend and the British naturalist and memoirist, J.A. Marshall, Bishop Loerks's special qualities were exemplified through the many practical skills that brought him into contact with their own secular world and distinguished him from a stigmatized, "other-worldly" missionary stereotype. Marshall, for example, reports:

> On steamer day, so the story runs, you'll see him there on the beach checking the mission cargo, lending a hand, shifting the cases, coat-less, in shirtsleeves. Perhaps the South Seas is the only place where you can see a bishop's shirt-sleeves. But it makes little difference what Bishop Lorks [sic] wore, for he has a noble bearing, a fluent scholarly tongue, and the look of the man of the world in his frank direct eyes [1938:221].

Townsend also appreciated the bishop's appearance and gave high marks to Loerks's skill as a boat captain and raconteur. The bishop, Townsend concluded, was "a fine figure of a man who bore little resemblance to the conventional idea of a missionary bent on converting Pacific Islands heathen" (1968:224–225). In fact, Loerks's deviation from this conventional missionary type was so great that the Australians wanted to imprison him when they occupied New Guinea during World War I. "From his excellent [horse] riding," so the story goes, "they thought he was a German officer. He had to prove to them that he was only a missionary priest" (Laumann 1939–40:121).[5]

Within the mission, of course, Loerks's manner contrasted less with the outsiders' stereotype of a fervently impractical missionary than with an insider's stereotype of a prelate, set apart from his community by ceremony, servants, and wealth. The audience of Catholic faithful in Europe who read the *Steyler Missionsbote* would have been expected to appreciate the irony in an article describing a confirmation trip taken by Loerks to Sassoya, one of the new inland stations. They are treated here to a bishop saddled with a skittish horse, sliding down muddy hillsides, delayed by tardy carriers, and poured upon relentlessly by rain. "His Excellency" is distinguished from his companions only by his honorific titles and the natural grace with which he encounters the frustrations of a typical journey through the bush (Laumann 1939–40). Clearly, conditions were not favorable to the conventional expressions of dignity which bishops in less rustic areas might be able to afford. Clearly, too, Loerks's eschewal of the conventional code for episcopal conduct had consequences for the idea of community that his missionaries entertained.

The Servant of the Servants of God

I was fortunate to obtain a copy of a long letter in which a young American priest tells his former seminary colleagues about his first five months in the Sepik mission in 1936.[6] The value of this letter is that it reflects collective representations within the mission, for Father Angelus was a newcomer whom more experienced missionaries had just been "breaking in." If we recall that the pioneers had used the confusion between "spiritual" and "material" work to represent the frontier, it is notable that, although Father Angelus spends much time talking about material matters, he seems not to find them remarkable. When he wishes to characterize his experience in New Guinea as strange, Father Angelus turns to confusions in the hierarchical structure of the mission, instead. "Plans seldom materialize in New Guinea," Father Angelus writes, so instead of becoming a junior member of headquarters staff (still located on Tumleo Island), he was suddenly left alone:

> *When the schooner pulled out . . . I remained behind with a three-fold title, namely pastor of a flock that speaks pidgin, German, and the Tumleo languages; newly appointed procurator of the Vicariate, and the Rector of the Central station. That's New Guinea all over. It surely seemed strange to hear Father Blas on his return asking me for permission for certain articles and to arrange the order for confession, etc; he is ten years my senior and ordained six years before me [1936: emphasis mine].*

Father Hagspiel, who took such delight in the ceremonial display of community order at Alexishafen in 1922, would have found little comfort in the Holy Week ceremonies over which Father Angelus presided in 1936:

> *. . . I hadn't the least idea a couple of weeks ago that I'd have the entire Holy Week services among other things to do this year. It starts something like this: the Celebrant with a couple dusky lads leaves the church on Palm Sunday and strikes up the Gloria . . . and the responses come from the sister and kiddies within [1936].*

Father Angelus's letter is clearly shaped by a different conception of mission community than that which informs Father Hagspiel's book. The young priest, for example, has been instructed about the dangers of isolation in New Guinea but, significantly, displaces the danger from the missionaries to secular Europeans who "having little social life and many servants" become idle and either take ill or to drink. Like Hagspiel, Angelus believes that community support is the best defense against such a fate. The support sought by Father Angelus, however, is not the warm companionship of a "friendly conference," or the "blessed aid and consolation of frequently being able to meet together," so dear to Father Hagspiel (1926:130;69). For Father Angelus, the blessings of community are instead ensured by internal discipline "to the orderly life that is prescribed by the rule of the Society [SVD]."

Nowhere does Father Angelus better express his views on the nature of the Sepik mission community in the mid-1930s than in his remarks on its "principle of unity," Bishop Loerks himself. Angelus had been told that as bishop, Loerks was the "father of the mission," while as procurator, he, Angelus, was its "mother." Father Angelus tells his readers that he sees the logic in the latter designation "since all the needs and requests must pass through the procure." Yet the model of community solidarity expressed through such familial imagery apparently struck neither Angelus nor Loerks as appropriate to their situation or to the bishop's style. The bishop preferred to be known as "the servant of the servants of God:"

> The bishop calls himself the *Servus servorum Dei* . . . One soon sees that the title becomes him well. Ever alert from 4:00 AM till 9:45 PM pondering over the many problems that present themselves daily. . . . Besides the spiritual cares of his flock he is especially vigilant about the clothing, food, and housing conditions being aware that good tropical missionary work cannot be accomplished without them. While at the table with newcomers he sees that each has the kind and the amount necessary, denying himself, he will pass on the last of some dish with the remark, 'the rest for the best' or something similar. The shirts and helmet wanting to my gear were supplied from his private wardrobe [Angelus 1936].

In light of his own role vis-à-vis the bishop, Angelus says that he, too, would prefer an alternative designation—"a servant of this servant of the servants of God."

Clearly these alternatives do not in any way deny hierarchy as the principle of order in the mission community. Indeed, they are more strikingly vertical than the "father and mother" imagery, which both the bishop and his procurator reject. What the bishop does with his alternative is precisely what we have seen happen before with the hierarchically related pair of "spiritual" and "material" work: the hierarchy is affirmed by inverting the models that express it in socially conventional form. Just as "physical work" becomes an honor for the first missionaries, so it is an honor for the bishop to represent himself not as the "father" of the missionaries in his district, but as their "servant" instead. As Father Angelus's comments on isolation imply, the community is not adequately represented by concrete familial imagery but is etherealized as a "rule of order" to which individuals can separately adhere. Its center has become less a place for companionship and ceremony than it is a state of mind.

The subject in this chapter has been the organization of the Catholic mission in the Sepik region of New Guinea, and its representation by missionaries and other observers in the period between the wars. Beginning in 1922 with Father Bruno Hagspiel's observations on the problems of the Catholic station system, we moved to ecclesiastical developments that separated the Sepik mission from the mission centered on Alexishafen, and closed with observations on the personality and style of the bishop who led the mission in the Sepik through the 1930s and up to World War II. I have accepted Hagspiel's argument, with some qualifications, that conditions in New Guinea made it difficult for the missionaries to constitute themselves as a "centered" community, but I have also argued that the conception of how the community should be centered changed over the course of time.

Hagspiel's conception of a centered community was constructed in opposition to those conditions of native community that constrained the flow of mission personnel and isolated the missionaries from each other for relatively long periods of time. Missionary priests, especially, were placed in positions of great responsibility among people who were fragmented politically and linguistically and whose customs, though diverse, were also depicted as lacking civilized sentiment and orderly form. Because they spent many years at a single post, missionaries devoted their often considerable energies to "doing something for 'their people' " and became "deeply attached . . . to the work and surroundings by which their activities are defined" (Hagspiel 1926:172, 171). Although the missionaries could periodically enjoy civilized comforts and Christian companionship at Alexishafen, the prevailing opinion was that it was not at headquarters but at the outstations that "*real* missionary work" was done (Hagspiel 1926:171). To Hagspiel, then, the requirements for effective mission work in New Guinea tended to contradict the requirements of authentically centered *community* life, and Hagspiel used the forces that loosened the bonds of fraternal fellowship as the main motif for his depiction of New Guinea as a difficult mission field.

There is little reason to suppose that these forces were lessened in the Sepik jurisdiction during the period that followed the reorganization of the New Guinea field. Whatever fellowship may have gained by the division of the territory was more than likely lost in the Sepik as the missionaries expanded into the hinterland, searching, as one missionary—using a timely analogy—phrased it, like prospectors "for the gold of the soul" (Laumann 1939/40:121). We have heard from Townsend that some of the missionaries afoot during this expansive period were "earnest young, and not so young fathers who hoped to convert the whole of the population by Easter at the latest" (1968:226). Although the "fighting bishop" was willing to curb those of his staff whose excesses brought them into conflict with Townsend's officers, it is clear from the case of Father Kunisch and Father Kunze that this was a time and a community in which great differences in evangelical strategy were allowed to prevail (Allen 1976:82).

Although conditions in the Sepik during the 1930s still appear to have encouraged a situation in which each mission station functioned as "almost a distinct mission by itself" (Hagspiel 1926:69), the image of mission community that we find in later writing lacks the tension of Hagspiel's earlier work. This is true in part because ecclesiastical changes have shifted the burden of "unity" from the group as a whole to its bishop, and in part because of the character of their bishop, Joseph Loerks, himself. Perhaps further research will show that voices like Angelus were already present in the mission in earlier years. The point, however, is that after bishops were appointed to the territories in New Guinea, alternative views of mission community could be authenticated by a particular bishop's style. Because Joseph Loerks eschewed conventional expressions of hierarchy that would set him apart, missionaries in the Sepik could see in their bishop a reflection, rather than a negation, of the conditions that shaped their ministries and their lives.

CHAPTER 5

Missionaries in Between

The Colonial "Triangle," Cargo Cults, and The War

Not necessarily involving a conflict of personalities, but certainly implying a conflict of roles, a missionary, who is subject to the pulls of both environments, must first evoke the values of the local environment if he is to bring his charges to an appreciation of the values of the environment of which he himself is a child; and in cases of conflict he must choose according to his conscience and to his role— which are not always compatible. Having made his choice he must accept the consequences which must inevitably flow from the values of both environments. He is so placed that he must be maligned whether he is helping one side or the other, both, or neither. He is a favourite target, not least because he cannot riposte without damaging himself.

—KENELM O.L. BURRIDGE

One of the most notable features of colonial society along the north coast of New Guinea during the period preceding World War II was the predominant position commanded by Christian missions—especially the Roman Catholic mission—in the region from Alexishafen west through the Sepik to Vanimo. This was partially a result of the poverty of the Australian administration during the interwar years, and also partially a result of the organization of the Catholic mission, itself. Through the mission's relatively dense network of stations, outstations, and schools, and through the considerable autonomy accorded its station personnel, missionaries in the coastal region of the Sepik (and in other areas to which the system was extended), enjoyed a measure of local knowledge and influence that many other colonists envied, or feared, or both. Although the mission system placed its personnel in an advantageous position in regard to establishing influence in native communities, however, it is important not to confuse missionary influence with missionary control.

The epigraph at the head of this chapter is from
K.O.L. Burridge's *Mambu: A Melanesian
Millennium.* (London: Methuen & Co. Ltd., 1960),
145–146.

The place missionaries gained in local communities was a source of both vulnerability and strength. The missionaries' aim was to bring native people into their own moral community. Yet, as K.O.L. Burridge argues in the quotation above, missionaries had to "evoke the values of the local environment" to make their case. Missionaries had to bargain in local currencies to win trust and cooperation from potential parishioners, but were in turn subjected to the logic of local values they did not always fully understand. Because missionaries attempted to enter the native world, other Europeans saw them as inconstant allies. Because missionaries never completely left their own world, native people sometimes concluded that missionaries had dealt with them in bad faith.

If missionaries' vulnerability to a rupture in relations with other Europeans had been demonstrated most decisively in the political threats that followed World War I, their vulnerability to a rupture in relations with native people became most disturbingly evident during the 1930s, when "cargo cults" were first reported along the north coast. In *Mambu: A Melanesian Millennium* (1960), K.O.L. Burridge discussed how the "triangle" of relations between missionaries, government officials, and native villagers was implicated in one of the early cults that appeared in the Catholic mission territory centered on Alexishafen. This chapter examines how this structure developed in the Sepik, how it placed the missionaries in relation to the "cargo" incidents of the 1930s, and how the triangle was disassembled by the catastrophic events of World War II. Wherever possible these issues are discussed from the vantage point of Wewak, a small colonial outpost, which became the center for district administration in the mid-1930s and for the Catholic mission in the Sepik after the war.

THE DEVELOPMENT OF THE TRIANGLE IN WEWAK

K.O.L. Burridge introduced the term "triangle" as a shorthand designation for the local configurations of political power that developed among villagers, missionaries, and government officers in colonial New Guinea. These three parties are singled out not because recruiters, traders, and planters were insignificant, but because government officers and missionaries desired more from villagers than the simple quid pro quo that normally characterized business and labor relations (1960:140–146). The notion of the "triangle" should not, of course, obscure divisions within the mission, government, and village worlds, but is merely meant to highlight the fact that relations between any two of these three parties were subject to qualification by the relations each had with the third. The specifics, of course, could vary over time and place.

"To Break the Spears"

In the area around Wewak, colonial penetration appears to have followed the general pattern outlined in Chapter 2 for the region as a whole. Trading interests preceded the mission and the government here as they had around Aitape, but the time scale must be pushed forward by several years. This is somewhat paradoxical, because Wewak had the best harbor between Vanimo, near the Dutch border, and the colonial center at Madang. However, because the Neu Guinea Compagnie had acquired much land in the Wewak coastal area during the 1880s, when Dr. Otto Finsch had traveled through, the area was not available for the first settlers later on.

As we have already seen, Eberhard Limbrock was barred from the area around Madang, and chose to build his first mission station on one of the islands offshore from Aitape, near the establishment of the trader, Ludwig Kärnbach. The Neu Guinea Compagnie took over Kärnbach's station on Seleo Island when the trader died the following year. Thus, when the Imperial Government finally established its own station in the region in 1906, Aitape was selected as the site for the government's main post despite the poor anchorage afforded by Aitape Bay. During most of this period, the Wewak area remained "bush," isolated from intensive European influence by legal inaccessibility, and by its reputation as an area where native warfare of "brutal ruthlessness" raged (Gerstner 1953:429).

The Neu Guinea Compagnie's network of stations, centered on Seleo Island near Aitape, was sufficiently scattered to reach the periphery of Wewak (Figure 4). Indeed, by 1899 when the Company finally ceded its land monopoly and governing charter to the Imperial Government, the Company had acquired an additional 2000 hectares in the Wewak area (Sack 1973:153), and had established at least four of its six trading posts just to the west. These included a small plantation of 700 palms and a store under the management of a Malay trader on Tarawai Island, a trading station on Walis Island, a Chinese trader on Mushu Island, and a station on the mainland at Dallmanhafen, near the village of Wom, where there was another small plantation of 500 palms (Sack and Clark 1979:166,180, cited by Roscoe 1981–82:11).[1] The Company's Seleo station reported exports for 1899 of copra, trepang, and green snail shell—probably won mostly through trade, but to these must be added men recruited for labor, most of whom were probably sent to the Company's large plantations to the east.

Although it is important not to underestimate the possible effects of early labor recruitment,[2] it is unlikely that the presence of Company traders in itself impinged heavily on village life in the Wewak area at this time. As for the missionaries, we have already seen that colonial politics forced them to concentrate their efforts elsewhere during their first decade. And, although government intervention via shelling from warships is recorded to the east and the west of Wewak around the turn of the century (Tieseler 1969–70:117–118; 129), it was not until after Hahl established a post at Aitape in 1906 that conditions were prepared for a sustained government presence along the Wewak coast.

The mission's early relations with the colony's governing authorities had been complicated by competitive economic interests, but the situation changed when Hahl's administration took over. Limbrock was delighted with Hahl's willingness to permit the mission to obtain land for stations and plantations, and pleased when Hahl promised him in 1904 that a police station would be erected at Aitape (Wiltgen 1969a:349,345). Pacification had not been systematically pursued in the area around Aitape at that time, and native communities along the coast and even on the island where the missionaries had built their first station still retained the capacity to pursue their own ends by means of force:

> "For ten years, the missionaries there had no police protection, although tribal murders of revenge were repeatedly being committed in the immediate vicinity and even on the island where they were living" (Wiltgen 1969a:345).

As Wiltgen points out, Hahl's plan to build a post at Aitape may also have been motivated by native uprisings in the Bismarck Archipelago and near Friedrich Wilhelmshafen in 1904. In the first case, ten Catholic missionaries had been killed, and in the second, a native plot to kill the whites in Friedrich Wilhelmshafen had been narrowly averted (Wiltgen 1969a:345).

Rapprochement between Hahl's government and the mission flowed not only from simple calculations of self-interest, but also from similarities in outlook. According to Firth:

> Governor Hahl thought Limbrock was the ideal missionary, a man of action committed to the economic development of the colony and to the spread of German language and culture . . . Hahl's criterion of a mission's usefulness was patriotic, not religious . . . Keeping the Germans in a position of cultural supremacy in New Guinea would depend on training New Guineans to accept German as a lingua franca and on ensuring that the civilization of Europe reached the villager 'in our language and with our thoughts' [1982:154].

Hahl's idea of "control" was not distant in spirit from the mission's idea of civilization as inclusion in a hierarchically ordered whole. For both, submission to authority and civilization went hand in hand, even if Hahl's image of the latter tended less towards church congregations and religious processions than to German culture, and labor crews for building stations, bridges, and roads.

The government's project, however, was no more immune than the mission's to the difficult conditions along the north coast. Taming the elements that repeatedly frustrated their efforts to bridge the Aitape River was a task relieved for the officers only by efforts to tame the natives who, as Roscoe puts it, went through "cycles of subjection and revolt" (1981–82:13). Firth has noted that "on the Aitape coast villages were simply too big and their warriors too numerous for fifty police to manage" (1982:93). Indeed, the administration's report for 1907–08 complained that the natives

> are completely uncivilized, have had only very little contact with Europeans and are extremely warlike . . . In these circumstances, it was very difficult for the station to gain any influence or to achieve any recognition of its authority. It was openly challenged to fight and the troop was exposed to ridicule [Sack and Clark 1979:266; cited by Roscoe 1981–82:14; Firth 1982:93].

Native recalcitrance in the face of authority soon led to a series of punitive raids by the government, which, "like a blind giant . . . thrashed out in the general direction of the enemy without really knowing who he was" (Firth 1982:94).

If people in the vicinity of Aitape were the first victims, it was not long before the government attempted to extend its rod further afield. In 1908, there was an incident involving the mission, which had recently purchased land for a copra plantation on the mainland opposite its Yuo Island station. Some mountain villagers, claiming that they, rather than the Yuo Islanders, were the rightful owners of this land, burned down the mission's sheds at Boiken and the mission was threatened with "drastic reprisals" if it did not leave the area immediately. Although it was never clear who exactly was responsible for the threat, "German officials and the police landed . . . a few weeks later, climbed to a hill village, which they found deserted, and set fire to it"(Firth 1982:94). Nor were native attacks on each other taken less seriously. In another case in the Wewak area at about the same time, the government burned down two hamlets of a village on Kairiru Island where, it was believed, some men from Karesau Island had sought refuge after staging a raid with allies from Mushu Island on yet another Kairiru Island village (Anonymous 1980:117–118, cited in Roscoe 1981–82:13–14).

As the government thus achieved recognition, it moved to consolidate its position by appointing headmen and headmen's assistants (luluais and tultuls), who would henceforward be responsible to the government for village compliance with government demands. It was reported in 1910 that all coastal villages within reach of Aitape had luluais (Sack and Clark 1979:308, cited in Roscoe 1981–82:14). Whether or not this included the Wewak area is difficult to say, but it cannot have taken long.

As the government's road and its rod went together, it is likely that *luluais* were in place in the vicinity of Wewak by 1912, when the bridle path had reached Boiken and had been linked with another path that had recently been constructed through Wewak to Moem (Roscoe 1981–82:13).[3]

The government's efforts to extend its influence eastward from Aitape surely facilitated the mission's efforts to build stations in the area as well. The dates, at any rate, are suggestive. The Yuo Island station was established in 1906, under the direction of Father van den Hemel, who later in the year conducted his own expedition to map the coast and islands from Tumleo through the Wewak area and east to Turubu. In 1909, the mission opened its station at Boiken, and in 1911, the mission purchased approximately 500 hectares of land along the bay between Wewak Point and Boram. The mission opened a new station and plantation at this site in 1912—the same year in which the government track through Wewak was linked with the road from Aitape to Boiken.

With the exception of a few villages located on the coast and on some of the offshore islands where Austronesian languages were spoken, the people in the general vicinity of this new government road and mission station were speakers of non-Austronesian languages, principally Boiken. When the missionaries first arrived, it appears that the Austronesian speakers of the mainland villages of Wom, Wiwiak, and possibly Moem, were all living in hamlets located on the coral headlands that punctuate the coast in this area and which still bear their names. Behind the bays between Wom and Wewak Point to the west, between Wewak Point and Boram in the center, and between Boram and Moem to the east, was swampland and a relatively narrow plain that rose abruptly into the northern foothills of the Prince Alexander range. In these hills, not far from the sea, were the northernmost villages of the Boiken-speaking people, whose relationships extended north to the off-shore islands and south behind the coastal range.[4]

The major ethnographic reports on the "Wewak-Boiken" people were published in the early to mid 1950s by Andreas Gerstner, a Catholic priest who had been stationed for nearly twenty years at Wewak and at But, in the neighboring Arapesh-language area. The principal features of Wewak-Boiken society according to Gerstner's accounts (1951, 1952a, 1952b, 1953, 1954–1955, 1958, 1963), were a dual organization into patri-moieties regulating marriage; an elaboration of exchange relationships between constituent groups, and between trade friends and affinal/matrilateral relatives, especially mother's brothers and sister's children; art and ritual life focused on initiation into the spirit cult; and the frequent escalation of disputes into warfare. The settlement pattern appears to have involved villages comprising hamlets that were sometimes, but not always, identified with one or the other moiety (1953:418). Yet, what is most important to note here is that the many case histories Gerstner marshals to illustrate his ethnographic points document a situation in which intervillage relations were extensive, aided by communication via slit-gongs (drums), frequent visits between friends and kin, and a lively ceremonial life fed by competition between "big men" for wealth and prestige (Gerstner 1953).

Gerstner's reports document a gradient of sophistication for the Wewak-Boiken villages that was higher at the coast than in the hinterland. Yet, while Gerstner's examples involve changes in colonial time that had understandably worked from the center of European influence on the coast and only spread gradually inland (that is, cessation of warfare, diminution of the spirit cult, labor migration, mission influence, and so forth) the gradient may also have been of traditional standing, as Mead suggests of the Arapesh people, whose territory borders that of Boiken speakers to the west (1970:178–179). The northernmost villages of the Wewak-Boiken group, like the Arapesh, appear to have participated in the regional network of coastal trade. They served an important middleman role in funneling products from the inland to sea-going traders from the offshore islands and eastern coast, and sending products obtained from islanders and distant coastal villagers to their own partners living farther back in the coastal range.

It was, of course, through such relationships that events on the coast could attain a significance far wider than local boundaries might imply. Roscoe, writing of the Boiken-speaking people inland of the Boiken mission station (approximately ten miles to the west of Wirui and Wewak), suggests that:

> [i]t seems very probable that Yangoru villagers, especially those in the north, were aware of a German presence on the Boiken coast from its very beginnings. Among the northern villages, immigrants from the coast still maintain relations with clan brothers there and, in the ancestral past, visited these relatives for trading purposes. . . . Following any one of several routes through the mountains, bands of villagers moved between Yangoru and the coast, carrying out pots, netbags, and pigs, and importing uncut shell wealth and salt, in the form of brine carried in short bamboo containers or waterlogged driftwood. By all accounts, there was also a brisk trade in songs, dances, fashion and gossip and it is therefore likely that, shortly after the appearance of Europeans, trading parties were returning to Yangoru bearing tales of the mysterious new creatures [Roscoe 1981–82:15].

Allusions to the earliest effects of the mission's arrival among the coastal Wewak-Boiken were offered by native witnesses in a legal case concerning a property dispute between the mission and the government in 1958 (East Sepik Provincial Office, Land Files 1958). This hearing reveals that the missionaries made two payments of 627 and 265 marks for land in

Wewak in September 1911, probably to representatives from two different villages claiming ownership rights in the 500-hectare tract obtained by the mission at that time. It is apparent that this land had served coastal villagers as a sago swamp and as a hunting ground before the missionaries' arrival, and that during the following years the mission continued to permit natives to cut sago on unimproved portions of the property and occasionally permitted villagers to plant a garden on more distant sections of its land.

Perhaps the most interesting testimony in the case, however, is from two men of Kremending village, who said that they were born at a place near the coast called Suambanyan, and had been children when the missionaries first arrived. One of these witnesses claimed that his people had acquired the territory around Suambanyan as a consequence of tribal warfare, but when the missionaries had come and taken the land, his people were afraid and ran away to the hills to a place their ancestors had occupied long before. The other witness was more concise about the reasons for the move: "In those days," he told the court, "very few disagreed or argued with the Germans so our people left."

Considering what we have seen about the German government's attitudes in regard to native self-assertion, the Kremending villagers' move was no doubt a prudent response to their position in the "triangle" of colonial relations as it began to form. Gerstner informs us that the name of the mission's land, Wirui, means, in the Wewak-Boiken tongue, "'to break the spears.'" He goes on to explain: "When through the influence of the mission and the government in our area, the continuing wars and feuds came to an end, the men broke their spears in this place. Therefore the name!" (Gerstner 1954:472, n. 24). Certainly, it was an appropriate name, not only because of the ceremony, but because "to break the spears" was a succinct summation of the positions of the three parties at that moment in the triangle's development.

Shifting Alliances

As we have seen, relations between the government and the mission were subject to new complications after World War I brought in the Australians, an event that occurred between two and three years after the opening of the Wirui mission station. Although the years of war were difficult for the mission, the Wirui station and its new plantation grew quickly to become one of the mission's larger and more prosperous establishments. First built on the narrow plain between Wewak and Boram Point, the station was in full swing in 1922 when William Gier, Superior General of the Society of the Divine Word, and his companion, Bruno Hagspiel, steamed in on the mission vessel *Gabriel*. We may recall that Hagspiel found Wirui an "ideal missionary settlement indeed":

Fathers Hesse and Averberg, with Brothers Bartholomew and Elre-
dus, awaited us at the landing-place in Wewak; and after a walk of
about fifteen minutes through the cocoanut [sic] plantations, we
were again at home in one of our mission stations. The place is
wonderful, set in the midst of another plantation which yields some
eighty tons of copra a year, with a prospect of eighty more tons, two
or three years hence . . . In addition to domestic stock of all kinds,
there are many European vegetables. Father Hesse gave me a won-
derful butterfly collection—over fifteen hundred specimens—for our
museum. He had collected every one of these himself, thus becoming
a veritable "butterfly missionary" [Hagspiel 1926:95].

The mission's aim in regard to the Wewak-Boiken people was to bring
them within the moral compass of the Church. Although we have already
seen that different missionaries initiated this process in quite different
ways, there were identifiable areas of social and cultural life with which,
whatever their personal styles, the missionaries were bound to be concerned. The missionary-ethnographer, Andreas Gerstner, noted in one of
his articles on Wewak-Boiken society, for example, that the moiety system regulating marriage had persistently presented a problem for the
mission, because while the church disapproved of marriage between
"blood" relatives, the natives did not recognize "blood" relationship as an
obstacle to marriage between people of different moieties (1953:418).
Subtle problems such as this may have arisen later on, but other customs
mentioned by Gerstner, such as arranging marriages when children were
young or sending betrothed girls to live in the homes of their future
parents-in-law, required a less intimate knowledge of local practice to be
perceived as a danger both to morality and to the mission's aspiration to
provide young girls with a Christian education and to see them married
in the church.

   At any rate, aside from copra and butterflies, the only other information that Hagspiel provides about the Wirui mission concerns the
nexus of relations occasioned by the mission sisters' attempts to retain
young girls from the general area at the Wirui Mission's school. The first
of the two stories that Sister Aloysiana told Hagspiel was about Sangai, a
girl who had so impressed the sisters with her intelligence and attitude
that they had secured permission from her father to keep her at the
school for an extra year. Three days later, however, the father demanded
the girl's return: "She has to cook sago for me. Besides, I did not understand that she was to live here." The reference to sago may have alluded
to the wedding custom whereby the bride's relatives bring sago to the
hamlet of the groom (Gerstner 1953:442), for Sangai was married forth-
with. When she ran away soon thereafter and sought refuge with the
sisters, they could do nothing, "for her husband could invoke the aid of
the government" (Hagspiel 1926:96–97). The second story was even more

dramatic than the first. When this girl failed to return home on time from the mission school:

> all the people of her village swarmed into the station—father, mother, brothers, the chief, old women, and young men and boys. They rushed into the kitchen, seized [her], and were bearing her away down the hill, when, fortunately, Father Averberg met them. He compelled them to release the girl, reminding them that they had agreed to allow her to remain, and that now her wishes must be consulted. The gist of the matter was that some wild fellow of the bush had decided to marry her, and her people had consented to the union. . . . She refused to go home, and refused to marry. Later, the matter was brought before the government official, and in his presence [the girl] declared that she would not marry anybody, but desired to remain with the Sisters. The parents, seeing the uselessness of their efforts, then permitted her to stay for two more years [Hagspiel 1926:97–98].

Although there are not enough details provided in these stories to permit analysis of the cost of such incidents to mission-village relations, they do illustrate that at least by 1922, the roles of the administration and of the mission had differentiated to the point where shifting alliances among the three parties were possible. In these two cases, the mission was placed in the middle between village girls and their fathers or husbands, with administrative intervention (or its possibility) favoring the village men in the first case, and the girl and the sisters in the other. In principle, then, when faced with the kinds of sanction available to the government, neither missionaries nor village leaders were in a position of control.

"Control," however, was not the sole aim of Australian administrative officers in the Sepik; to the extent that they competed with missionaries for the confidence and loyalty of native New Guineans, they were placed at a disadvantage by the relative poverty of their resources, by frequent transfers from one post to another, and by the practical requirements of their duties in pacified areas (Burridge 1960:141–142). Certainly the government station at Wewak in the 1920s was not an attractive post for officers endowed with either an adventuresome or missionary spirit, or both, judging from the memoirs of G.W.L. Townsend and from the Australian government's reports on the state of its Mandate to the League of Nations.

Although the site for the government station on Wewak Point, approximately two miles west of Wirui, had been marked by the Germans just before World War I, it appears to have been the Australians who built the first permanent police post or substation at Wewak—on land belonging to Wiwiak villagers whose hamlets were located on the point's high plateau. By 1924, the Wiwiak villagers had been induced to move off the hill, leaving the officer's ramshackle bungalow standing amidst the villagers' "coconut and betel-nut palms, the breadfruit and other food trees, most of which [remained] on top in the Administration area" (Townsend 1968:109).

Townsend himself arrived as Acting Deputy District Officer in Wewak in 1924, but his memoirs record little about local people and events at this time. While at his post, Townsend seems to have been engrossed with domestic concerns—rebuilding his house and "hearing the small complaints of the Station; listening to District gossip; casting an eye over the sweet-potato gardens; and vainly attempting to reconcile the authorized scales of issues of native rations and stick tobacco with what the totally illiterate policemen could remember having done with them . . ." (1968:114–115). The station was "virtually run" by one of his native police sergeants, and, as supplies for the government post at Wewak were delivered on the mission vessel *Gabriel* and stored in the mission's warehouse at Wirui, Townsend was free to spend much of his time on patrol (1968:110, 109).

The Australian administration's report to the League of Nations for 1923 to 1924 says of "Weewak" only that "[c]onsiderable progress was made in this portion of the district, and it is now practically all under Government influence,"—an inaccurate claim if it was meant to refer to the southern as well as the northern foothills of the coastal range (Commonwealth of Australia 1925:41). Yet the only "penetration patrol" from Wewak noted between 1923 to 1924 and 1927 to 1928 was conducted by Townsend in July 1924 as part of an urgent investigation into the depredations of two labor recruiters in the region south of the mountains of the coastal range (Commonwealth of Australia 1926:37; Townsend 1968:110–113). Townsend writes of this area:

> . . . at that time there had been little or no contact between the people of this foothill country and the Administration on the coast. Not only were there no regular patrols into the area but government had not reached them second-hand either, through the appointment of any of their men of influence to be Luluais (chiefs) or Tul-Tuls (assistants to chiefs). Therefore, the very existence of these people was not 'recognized' by the Government, which suited the majority of the villagers who preferred not to 'belong' to anyone but themselves [1968:111].

Unfortunately for officers posted to Wewak, the challenge of "first contact" was not to be had in the course of the normal patrols they were likely to pursue. Townsend's routine at Wewak, for example, took him

> "Eastward along the coast to the Murik Lakes, returning to Wewak by zig-zagging among the villages in the coastal hills; westward along the coast to Matapau, and returning in a similar zig-zag among the hills; and thirdly a visit to the offshore islands. . . ." [1968:109].

Aside from visiting the plantations where the government officer was responsible for inspecting the condition of native labor, these routine patrols brought an officer into the villages for tax collection and census; for ensuring the general cleanliness of the villages, inspecting latrines, and instructing the villagers in "sanitary" ways of burying their dead; for hearing disputes concerning land or sorcery; for insuring the upkeep of portions of track or road, and so forth (Commonwealth of Australia 1923:63; Burridge 1960:141–142).

We should recall, of course, that the same villages, subject to such oversight and interference by officials in coastal areas under government control, were also likely to be in the range of the mission station system. Although government officers had the threat of police action behind them, their capacity to establish personal relationships with the villagers was limited by their generally short stay in the area, by the large territory for which they were responsible, and by the fact that their main conduits were village officials (*luluais*) with whom they dealt in Pidgin or through an interpreter. The missionaries did not have force at their disposal to make villagers conform to mission routines. However, they stayed for long periods in a single station area, learned local languages, and achieved influence not only through their role as teachers but also through personal relationships that might be sustained for many years at a time (Burridge 1960:140–145).

CARGO CULTS

Precisely how villagers in the region experienced the new order is uncertain, although one thing is clear: villagers began early on to seek access for themselves to the powers Europeans appeared to control. The term "cargo cult" is generally used to refer to this quest when it has taken the form of a full-fledged movement, usually in response to prophesies of an imminent upheaval, in which native people will finally gain access to the secrets of "abundance" (Knight 1982:405), which Europeans know but have not been willing to share. In these movements, abundance has typically been symbolized by images of "cargo" (*kago*): excessive quantities of goods of European import, manufacture, or design. These movements have also included programs of action, typically involving participation in a variety of innovative ritual forms.

Patrick Gesch, a Catholic priest and student of cargo cults among Boiken-speaking people in the Sepik, has indicated the parallel between cargo cult and initiation in indigenous traditions: "In both cargo cult and initiation there is a kind of secret which will yield a more exciting life" (1985:143). The search for the secret to a fuller life in the new order has not, however, only been manifest in cults of the classic type. As Gesch notes, Sepik people have also looked, at various times and places, to such apparently straightforward activities as civil disobedience, grass-roots nationalism, national political participation, alternative local administration, army patterns, chain letters, commercial enterprise, cooperative societies, women's clubs, schools, bible usages, and church practice for "the secret key to the good times" (Gesch 1985:128). Although this list is drawn for the most part from the period following World War II, we shall see that a similar list, drawn from a somewhat different cultural repertoire, could be compiled for the 1930s as well.

Quite reasonably, "cargo cult" scholarship has focused on understanding these movements from the natives' point of view. Yet, Europeans in New Guinea were also deeply implicated in cargo situations, which they often did not recognize as such, and which deeply challenged their own capacity to comprehend and control. Roy Wagner has argued that cargo thinking represents a kind of "reverse anthropology," a native interpretation of western ways, which sees in our products, techniques, and routines a "profound human significance" that we ourselves are wont to ignore (1981:31–34). To Europeans, the ambiance created by cargo thinking has been both profoundly disturbing and profoundly obscure. Their most common artifacts and routine activities may be invested with a significance that seems excessive, they may be accused of withholding secret knowledge, and their explanations may fall on deaf ears. In some instances, they might enjoy a surprising turn of enthusiasm for a program they have long been supporting; in others, they might find themselves suddenly abandoned and years of work gone awry.

As Burridge has argued, "Europeans and the roles they play [are] parts of a total complex from which Cargo movements may emerge" (1960:140). To be sure, such movements have fed on indigenous modes of religiosity and on the proclivities of the region's peoples to import and try out new ritual forms. There are some cases on record in other regions in which millenarian activities have arisen outside the context of the triangle, galvanized by other manifestations of alien power, such as the "aircraft situation" in the highlands (Burridge 1969:143). Along the north coast, however, in territory within the reach of the Catholic mission, leaders of cargo cults and related enthusiastic movements have had to "carry out their tasks" within the complex of political power which the triangle "implies" (Burridge 1960:141). In the process, these leaders and those under their influence have attempted to address the problems posed by alien power through manipulating the possibilities presented by the triangle and, thus, sometimes subjecting its "normal" tensions to severe strain.

Cargo Cults and the Mission

The principal contemporary accounts of early cargo activity in the Sepik and in the SVD territory centered on Alexishafen to the east were written, with few exceptions, by SVD missionaries themselves. Credit here belongs especially to the SVD ethnologist, Father Georg Höltker, whose lengthy and detailed discussion of the Mambu movement (1941) in the territory of the Alexishafen mission provides our only contemporary case study, and whose summaries of other missionaries' contributions to the *Steyler Missionsbote* (1940–41) have made the gist of most other contemporary reports more widely available. Fuller summaries of some of the relevant *Steyler Missionsbote* reports are provided by Eckert (1940), Lommel (1953), Worsley (1957), and Steinbauer (1971). However, the early missionary reports, together with a short account of The Four Black Kings movement in Australia's Annual Report to the League of Nations for 1930–31 (Commonwealth of Australia 1932:96), and brief allusions to the same movement in two issues of the *Pacific Islands Monthly* (1932; Thomas 1935) and in Mead (1970: 247) constitute the only contemporary references that I have found. Mention also should be made of a few later works such as Burridge's study of cargo movements in the same area in which Mambu had once been active (1960); Allen's discussion of cult diffusion in the Dreikikir area of the Sepik (1976); Lawrence's history of cargo cults in the southern Madang district (1964); and Gesch's ethnography of a modern movement in the Negrie area of the Sepik (1985).

Although these later writings are indispensable for the interpretation of the contemporary materials, the fact that most of the authors of the early reports were missionaries deserves further consideration. Undoubtedly, interesting administrative reports have been lost owing to the vagaries of history, and perhaps Margaret Mead made further inquiries into the cult activities of the Arapesh of Alitoa village which I have not found in her published work. Yet, the fact remains that it was the missionaries who were "on the spot," in more ways than one, and who had a ready outlet and audience for relatively casual reports of their own doings, the customs of the people among whom they worked, and the personalities and events with which they had to deal. To be sure, an ethnologist/ missionary like Höltker, who fortunately was in the region on a three-year research tour when the Mambu movement was ending, could recognize its scientific value and its connections with similar phenomena elsewhere in Melanesia. However, most of the missionaries, who wrote for the *Steyler Missionsbote,* noted them less as ethnographic facts than as either peculiar incidents or problems in which they themselves were involved.

That these recorded incidents were peculiar, and that they frequently involved the mission, there can be no doubt. Seven such incidents, reported in the *Steyler Missionsbote* up to, but not including, the events surrounding Mambu (which was reported by Höltker in the journal *Annali Lateranensis*), have been marshaled by one analyst or another as cases relevant to the general theme of "cargo cult." These include (see Figure 4 for the place names mentioned):

1930: at Suain, in connection with an epidemic (perhaps of flu),[5] a native received revelations from "God Father." The destruction of the spirit houses had caused the illness, and "heathen offerings" were made under a tree (Kunisch 1930–31; Höltker 1940–41:24,25; Höltker 1941:212; Lommel 1953:30; Worsley 1957:99; Allen 1976:175).

1931: In the Kaiep hinterland prophets known as "the four black kings" gained a large following, and taught that the goods (cargo) now in the hands of Europeans had been made by New Guineans' own ancestors and had been unjustly deflected by the whites from New Guineans (the intended recipients). The prophets claimed miraculous powers for themselves, and preached against the head-tax, the administration, and the mission, prophesying that the administration station would soon sink into the sea. At Walman, on the coast near Aitape, villagers buried their pots because, according to the prophecies of the "four black kings," new pots and tinned foods would grow out of the ground (Bartholomaus 1932–33; Höltker 1940–41:23, 36–37; Pacific Islands Monthly 1932; Commonwealth of Australia 1932:96; Thomas 1935; Höltker 1941:212; Lommel 1953:30; Worsley 1957:100–101; Steinbauer 1971:40–41; Allen 1976:175).

1931/32: A man from Garankom, in the Mugil hinterland, was taken ill with the flu while on a plantation. His co-workers reported that he had died but then returned to life. Although not a baptized Christian, the resurrected man claimed that the Archangel Raphael was now by his side, and that the natives should follow the missionaries in all things. After delivering this message, the man died again (Baar 1931–32; Höltker 1940–41:58; Höltker 1941:213; Eckert 1940:35–36).

1932: In the course of a "Christian awakening" in villages on the lower and middle Sepik River, the villagers decided to destroy the cult objects from their spirit houses. Father Kirschbaum intervened to prevent this destruction and steamed upriver in the mission vessel, *Stella Maris,* to collect the objects (which were later sent to the Lateran Museum). At Moagende village, a long line of men and women removed the masks and carvings from the spirit house to load them on the ship. News of the event spread to other villages which then followed suit when the *Stella Maris* arrived. At Tambari village, the elders even interrupted an initiation ceremony so that the youths could load the objects and carry them to the landing place (Anonymous Missionary 1932–33; Höltker 1940–41:40; Höltker 1941:214; Lommel 1953:3; Worsley 1957:101; Allen 1976:175).

1935/36: At Kambot, on the Keram River, an eminent head-hunter broke his bamboo spear and threw it away, signaling the end of his opposition to the mission (Schwab 1935–36; Höltker 1940–41:42; Höltker 1941:214, n. 2).

1935: In the Uligan area, rumors spread that the Bishop of Alexishafen intended to destroy the native people in an earthquake. There was rumored to be a spirit in the hinterland mountains with a skin of iron and stone and many hands who was known as "king." It was said that he had ordered the natives to settle on the river courses, observe certain food taboos, and abstain from making the sign of the cross lest a fire ignite one's face and burn (Bader, Otto 1935–36; Höltker 1940–41:57; Höltker 1941:212–213; Lommel 1953:32; Worsley 1957:101; Steinbauer 1971:41–42; see Allen 1976:175).

1937/38: The sorcerer, Yerumot, of Kambot, who had previously given his spirit masks and shields to the missionary, began to call himself the "Cook of the Devil" and proselytized in the area to promote a return to old "heathen beliefs." Although he refused all medical assistance from the missionary when he became ill, he did turn to Christianity shortly before his death (Schwab 1937–38; Höltker 1940–41:42–43; Höltker 1941:210; Lommel 1953:35; Worsley 1957:104).

It is not known, of course, how many other such incidents were simply not reported by missionaries in the *Steyler Missionsbote*. At least two, mentioned by Margaret Mead and Bryant Allen, appear to have taken hold in unmissionized inland areas in the early 1930s, and although both involved building special houses and preparing for a time of darkness that would herald a new era, they were not reported to have included an overt missionary component. Because of the time in which they occurred, however, both Mead and Allen suggest that they may have been off-shoots of The Four Black Kings movement (or, as Mead calls it, "The Wewak Messiah Cult"), transmitted inland from the coastal villages to the north. In areas where missionaries were present, there may also have been situations where missionaries simply did not recognize that changes in the intensity of native interest in the mission might be signs of phenomena of a similar kind (Lawrence 1964:84–85).

Indeed, given the undeniable variety of attitudes, scope, and consequence of the seven incidents mentioned above, it is understandable that missionaries in the field, who had to respond to them, might be more interested in their particularities than in the links that later scholars attempted to draw. It may also be noted that even some of the analysts preferred a "splitting" to a "lumping" approach. Höltker, for example, distinguished between cargo cults proper, which threatened both the administration and the mission; movements of renewal, which were generally friendly toward the mission and the administration, but which were sometimes characterized by a fanaticism that the mission could not support; and more clearly bounded moments of spontaneous religiosity (as in the "Christian awakening" of 1932 on the Sepik River) that Höltker was reluctant to call "cults" or "movements" at all (1941:213–214).

Mambu

By virtually anyone's criteria, both The Four Black Kings movement of 1931 in the coastal region of the Sepik, and the Mambu movement of 1937 to 1938, in the neighboring SVD jurisdiction of Alexishafen, would be classified as cargo cults of the classic type. Before returning to the Sepik, and the Wewak area in particular, it is worth reviewing the Mambu movement, because it is the only early cargo cult in SVD territory that is sufficiently well documented (Höltker 1941) and analyzed (Burridge 1960) to permit a modest illustration of the ways in which the situation of the mission and its missionaries affected their knowledge of, and involvement in, such incidents.

Because Georg Höltker was an SVD missionary (albeit an ethnologist on temporary assignment and not a regular member of the mission staff), his article is especially valuable in this regard. Höltker was able not only to witness the final period in the life of this movement, but also to interview and receive written reports from missionaries who had been involved earlier with the cult and its leader. In particular, Höltker acknowledges a short report dictated to him by Father Wilhelm Tranell of the Banara mission in May 1938, and a long report by Father Gerrit Koster, also of the Banara mission. The latter included information from Father Cornelius Van Baar of the Tangu mission, who had been the first missionary to deal with Mambu after his activities had achieved success. Father Höltker's article is divided into three main parts. It begins with an account of the background and personality of Mambu, his teachings, the course of events, and the reaction of the whites; it continues with a more analytical treatment of the prophet, his followers, and his teachings and methods; and, finally, attempts to place this movement in the context of others in the Territory of New Guinea and in wider Melanesia.

Mambu, the cult's leader, was from one of the small Apangan villages, lying some four to five hours inland from Bogia, in which missionaries from the Bogia station had maintained a "foothold" since around 1915. Born around 1907, Mambu was a baptized Catholic who first brought attention to himself when, not long after his return from several years of contract labor in the Rabaul area, he began to frequent the Bogia mission station. There, he made a sufficiently favorable impression that one missionary intended to send him as a mission aide to Uligan, a station further east along the coast. In late 1937, however, Mambu was involved in some peculiar incidents. He was found in the station church when the missionaries came in for 5 A.M. prayers, having already prepared the altar, a task normally performed by one of the mission sisters. Later, when one of the missionaries attempted to speak to him about this, Mambu listened impassively and left for home. Just as he was approaching the church, the evening bells rang; instead of standing respectfully to pray (as was the custom), Mambu fell down dramatically on both knees. Although he was not actually seen at the station again, he was the prime suspect in another peculiar incident in which a native intruded upon a mission sister while she slept at night, held her hand, and then ran away when she awoke.

Mambu's teachings, fully developed, included several of the elements that have characterized other "classic" cults: the notion that whites had unjustly appropriated goods ("cargo") that had been made by the ancestors for their descendants; the notion that a new era would soon arrive in which these wrongs would be righted and in which people would be free from daily toil; the notion that the new age must be prepared for immediately; and the warning that those who resist will be excluded from its benefits, if not actually killed or destroyed. Like other movements, too, Mambu's included a program of action. He prayed at the graves of the ancestors, introduced a kind of "baptism" for his followers, and ceremonially buried the people's traditional items of dress and enjoined them to wear only clothing imported by Europeans and sold in trade stores. People were told to harvest their gardens and to slaughter their pigs immediately, special houses or "temples" were built, and use was made of European symbols such as the flag, the crucifix, and the sign of the cross. In a gesture redolent of Christian scripture, Mambu distributed rice and fish to his people as a symbol of his special relationship to the ancestors themselves.

From the beginning, according to Höltker, Mambu preached noncompliance with the government. People were urged to refuse to maintain local paths and roads, and to refuse the officers' requests for carriers while on patrol. Mambu told his followers to pay *him* their head tax and to tell any government officer who might come through that they had already paid tax to the "black king." Opposition to the mission came only later, after Mambu's first tentative successes led to a confrontation with the priest at Tangu. Shortly after being informed of Mambu's activities by villagers who sought his advice, the priest met Mambu by chance in the bush, and made him hand over the tax money that he had collected from the village people. Mambu soon left the area, but henceforward told people in the new areas through which he traveled to have nothing to do with the mission. Those who continued to send their children to mission school would be excluded from the golden age to come, and those who went to church would be trapped by a fire at the church doors.

For some time, Mambu's movement continued to grow unimpeded by European intervention. Its center, to the east of Tangu and south of the coastal mission station at Banara, was in difficult country where the little hamlets of some half-dozen villages lay dispersed among the hills. Because of its isolated location and small population, the missionary from Banara went there only occasionally. The area, moreover, was one in which a white recruiter had been killed approximately ten years before, leaving a strong distrust of Europeans in its wake. Mambu himself carefully avoided any further confrontation with Europeans. To complicate matters, the missionary at Banara became ill, preventing his either learning much about the movement or initiating a patrol to investigate the occasional rumors himself. Virtually no other Europeans took these rumors seriously. The administrative officers and planters found the stories about Mambu amusing, and the traders on the coast were far too busy selling clothing to the converts to ask questions. For the missionaries in other areas to which the cult spread, it was quite otherwise. Their trips to the bush villages made it clear that something had changed—some of their own catechists had become involved, and their churches and schools were empty. Missionaries were met with coldness and antipathy by natives who had previously treated them with respect, and erstwhile Catholics reacted to the missionaries' admonishments with maddening passivity.

Clearly, there was little that missionaries could do once they had lost the confidence of villagers in the area. Höltker does not tell us whether the mission was a factor in provoking the government to take action, but eventually the administration found, arrested, and tried Mambu, and imprisoned him in Madang. It was some time, however, before the movement waned among his followers. In the Banara area, it even gained strength when a new missionary was sent to replace the old priest, who had to return to Europe for medical care. According to Höltker, the change of priests received a special interpretation by Mambu's followers, although exactly what the interpretation was is not clear. The cult eventually lost steam, partly, Höltker thinks, because of the patience of missionaries who received the Catholic members back into the fold, but principally because of the loss of its leader, and his followers' chagrin at the gradual realization that the millennium Mambu had prophesied would not soon come to pass. Even while Höltker was writing, however, reports had filtered back to Germany that a new cult had begun in a nearby area. Burridge, who worked among the Tangu in the early 1950s, reports that Mambu himself left a lasting impression embodied in lore and manifest in the proclivity of the Tangu to participate in one of the more ephemeral cults that passed through later on (Burridge 1960).

Cargo Cults and the Triangle

Höltker's analysis of Mambu and the movement he inspired considers whether Mambu himself was sincere, as well as whether the cult was essentially political or religious in content and thrust. Neither question is answered unambiguously, however, and it is to Höltker's credit that he offers some of the reasons why they are not. He notes, for example, that Mambu may have drawn upon traditional patterns of leadership, in which secret knowledge relating to religious and magical power was the key to political power as well. Furthermore, Mambu won influence by using indigenous means that European administrators and missionaries either could not, or would not, use. Mambu traveled from one village to another, sat down with small groups of men, chewed betel nut with them, and talked in general terms about many things to feel the ground for his ideas. Of special interest to Höltker from a missiological as well as an ethnological point of view, was Mambu's tolerance of ambiguity. Mambu was successful only in areas where he had to rely on Pidgin. The limited distribution of Pidgin at that time, however, precluded direct communication with the village elders and women over whom he achieved great influence, but over whose understanding of his ideas he had little control.

Although these factors presented the possibility that Mambu might have been a demagogue in search of personal power alone, Höltker did not find sufficient evidence for such an indictment. He suggests that perhaps Mambu's stance against Europeans was genuine, rooted in bitter personal experience while working as a laborer near Rabaul. Perhaps the intensity of religious feeling that he had displayed at the mission when he had first come home, along with the many religious elements—ancestors, prayers, baptism, temples, blessings—that he introduced into cult routine, are evidence that he should be judged not as a political leader (whether demagogue or liberator), but as the prophet of a new religion. On the question of whether Mambu might have been a true or a false prophet (that is, whether or not he believed in the religious aspect of his teaching), Höltker refuses to judge. He proposes as one possibility, however, that even had Mambu not believed at the start, he may have been moved to belief by the acceptance he won from the people, just as the people were moved to belief by Mambu himself.

Why were the people moved by Mambu? Höltker notes Mambu's courage in traveling to villages in which he was a stranger; the intense interest that people in more distant villages exhibited in the person, style, and stories of returned laborers; the fact that Mambu's stories articulated doubts and desires that the villagers had not yet coherently expressed; that in at least part of the area Mambu was the beneficiary of rumors concerning the bishop's evil designs and concerning a "king" in the mountains that had circulated some years before (the incident in Uligan in 1935). As Burridge has pointed out in his analysis, too, Mambu offered a way out of the triangle of power in which villagers felt trapped, by repudiating the type of Europeans with whom they were most familiar—administrative officers and missionaries (1960:141).

We may note that in doing so Mambu appropriated some of their most distinctive attributes to himself. Mambu collected taxes and called himself king; Mambu also taught new doctrine, built churches ("temples"), and deployed Christian symbols in officiating at ritual events. Just as the "cargo" that Europeans now controlled was understood to belong in reality to native New Guineans, so the dignity and power that these Europeans appeared to command was transferred to Mambu, and through him, to his followers themselves.

It is precisely in the prophet's role as a model of the "new man" that Burridge locates the significance of cargo cults and suggests a relation between such "classic" movements as that led by Mambu and some of the peculiar incidents reported prior to Mambu's movement in the *Steyler Missionsbote*. According to Burridge, the most pressing problems raised by colonialism appeared as *moral* problems, which villagers tended to explain in "myth-dreams" that traced the differences between Europeans and themselves, especially in regard to command over material resources, to their own primeval guilt. Burridge sees "the most significant theme in Cargo . . . to be moral regeneration: the creation of a new man, the creation of new unities, the creation of a new society" (1960:247). The prophet, then, offers this synthesis, transcending the divisions that the people perceived as signs, so to speak, of a fall from grace. The "new society" and the "new man" are keys to redemption for the moral problems posed by the arrival of Europeans with their guns and their goods, but most critically from the "moral surrender" which administrators and missionaries demanded as the price of access to the power which they controlled (1960:246–247).

The problem of reclaiming dignities that were lost when Europeans arrived and that were denied by Europeans as they pressed for acceptance of their political hegemony and religious expertise could be addressed in a number of ways, however. Lawrence's history of "cargo" in the Southern Madang district (1964), identifies a sequence of strategies that developed as New Guineans' experience with Europeans matured. Straightforward strategies such as attempts to gain access through simple exchange gave way to attempts to resist European encroachments on native autonomy first through active, and then passive, resistance. When it became clear that autonomy could not be won in these ways, some people gave wholesale cooperation a try, frequently with a subtext of cargo that administrators and missionaries generally failed to read. When this strategy in turn led to disillusionment, peculiar incidents occurred such as some of those noted in the *Steyler Missionsbote,* and perhaps to cults like Mambu's later on (Lawrence 1964:62–92).

The Four Black Kings

It is not necessary to hypothesize exactly the same sequence in the Sepik to suggest that the ground had been prepared for the incidents reported in the 1930s by previous moments in an "interpretive" or "redemptive" process akin to that proposed by Lawrence and Burridge in the neighboring district of Madang. As previously noted, colonial history along the north coast of the Sepik (or Aitape) District was marked by attempts at both active and passive resistance. During the 1920s, the coastal area around Wewak appears to have been quiescent from an administrative point of view, perhaps marking a period of calculated cooperation. If this sequence had the same undertones of cargo as Lawrence has suggested for the region to the southeast, it was condensed into a shorter period of time, for Europeans came twenty years later to the Sepik than to the east. The first full-fledged cult reported in the Sepik appeared approximately eight years before Mambu left the mission station at Bogia to take up the role filled earlier in the Sepik by the prophets known as the "four black kings."

The gist of what is known about The Four Black Kings movement already has appeared in the summaries of *Steyler Missionsbote* reports. Although this movement appears to have been preceded by the "God Father" incident at Suain, the "four black kings" appear to have inspired the first major disruption evident to Europeans in the triangle of power relations between missionaries, administrators, and natives since the arrival of the Australians during World War I. Like Mambu later on, these prophets articulated the idea that ancestors had made the cargo that Europeans were deflecting from the rightful recipients. Although some incidents and movements have dealt with the moral problems of the triangle by attempting a return to tradition (see the summaries above, The "Cook of the Devil," 1937 and 1938), the "four black kings," like Mambu, buried traditional items and envisioned a millennium marked by access to cargo, free of the present order's constraints. Some movements have sought to transcend the triangle by collapsing it into a "one-to-one" relation between villagers and either the administration or the mission (as perhaps, in such cooperative incidents as the gift of artifacts to Father Kirschbaum in 1932). However, The Four Black Kings, again like Mambu, sought to expel both in one blow (Burridge 1960:146, 246).

According to Brother Bartholomaus's brief report, relations between the mission and the people in the vicinity of Wewak appear to have broken down completely during the brief reign of the "four kings." The mission's catechists had to close schools "in Possau, Sassoya and other places (1932–33; 1980:89), and the "kings" would not even talk to Father Dingels, when he followed a "pilgrimage" of "multitudes," who travelled to see them:

> They met him on the track marching in single file. They were mumbling, God knows what, into their beards. The expression on their faces did not inspire confidence, it was terrible [1932–33; 1980:88].

Later, when the prophets had been arrested, and were waiting trial in Wewak, Brother Bartholomaus himself attempted to speak to those who had come to "pay for [their] freedom."

> I told them that it was all nonsense but they replied, 'The sea will yet engulf the place of the Government (Wewak) and all will be drowned.' They admonished me not to speak against the four. 'Don't talk against them,' they said, 'for they hear everything, and all the worse for you. Your face shall be turned round overnight' . . . [1932–33; 1980:89].

The strategies adopted by the mission and the administration in response to The Four Black Kings, as in the Mambu situation later on, reflected both the kinds of action each was best positioned to take, as well as the likelihood these actions had of achieving the desired results. According to the government's report to the League of Nations for 1930/31:

> The Roman Catholic Mission . . . did everything possible through its native teachers to refute the claims of these four natives, and to discredit their advice to other natives. Reports, however, of the supposed supernatural powers of these men spread rapidly along the Aitape coast, and had a disturbing effect on the native inhabitants, who are most superstitious. Action was subsequently taken by the Administration to remove the four natives to another part of the Territory for a period, and this resulted in the restoration of order in the district [Commonwealth of Australia 1932:96].

Clearly, the government's power of force, mobilized when followers of the "kings" refused to pay taxes, was more decisive than the mission's power of persuasion in quelling the disruption in colonial relations that this movement entailed. If Burridge's conclusions about the Mambu movement can also be applied to that instigated by The Four Black Kings, it is no surprise that neither missionaries (Father Dingels or Brother Bartholomaus, for example) nor native mission teachers were successful in discrediting the prophets and stemming the momentum of the cult. Apart from the fact that these mission teachers (that is, catechists) often became participants in cargo cults, they were, by their association with the mission, representatives of the very people whose power the leaders and their followers were claiming for themselves.

The mission's vulnerability to cooptation was evident from another source as well. Not only did cults like The Four Black Kings involve native claims on the missionaries' access to sources of power, but they were frequently followed by claims on mission prerogatives from other Europeans. As already noted in the last chapter, cargo cults were viewed as cases of misfired missionization by colonials, who were quick to note both the religious elements in cult ideology and the frequent participation of native mission converts and aides. The first piece in the *Pacific Islands Monthly* reporting the movement begun by the "four black kings" was headlined "Fanaticism" (1932), and the second was "A Plea for Better Regulation of Mission Activities in New Guinea" (Thomas 1935).

WORLD WAR II

The mission's situation became even less secure during the mid to late 1930s when the political climate in Europe was worsening. In his 1936 letter home, Father Angelus, the new mission procurator, wrote not only about a new government ordinance that restricted the validity of marriages conducted by clergy, but also about the problems posed for the mission by Hitler's recent moves to restrict the outflow of cash and goods from Germany. The Sepik mission's personnel were 75 percent German, and owing to the division of mission territory, plantation income covered only a third of the money required for annual expenditures. Once the door closed to German supplies and donations, Father Angelus warned, "nothing remains but to reduce our activities by about 50%"(1936). The mission's prospects were dampened not only by events in Europe, but also by reactions to these events by Australian authorities in Canberra and Rabaul. On the local level, Townsend attempted to ease the burden of regulations, issued in 1939, for the registration of aliens (1968:243). He could do little, however, about the general climate of suspicion among fellow colonials who referred to the missionaries as the "Kamarad Squad" (Marshall 1938:224) or among those who "ran about discovering plots under every church and coconut palm" (McCarthy 1963:179).

The Triangle Undone

The "four black kings," it turned out, had been partially right. It took a cataclysm of major proportions to end the old order and to usher in a new one, albeit not of the kind they had imagined. In the end, of course, the agency of destruction was neither supernatural, as the prophets had proposed, nor German, as the Australians had feared. Defense plans for New Guinea had been minimal (Townsend 1968:246–252). In January 1942, Japanese troops took Rabaul, and by March they were in control of all major ports and towns in the east. With the exception of some missionaries and a few hardy souls, who remained hidden in the hills as "coastwatchers" to report the movements of Japanese ships and personnel, the European population dispersed and fled. Native laborers on contract assignments in the Bismarck Archipelago were impressed into agricultural service for the Japanese occupation force, or into military service as carriers in the Japanese drive towards the south (Allen 1976:90). Workers in the goldfields of Morobe Province had some time to escape, and many from the Sepik trekked for months through the bush to return home. As the Japanese advanced westward towards Wewak, the few remaining government officials also had time to escape, and several managed to reach safety in the highlands after arduous treks through the mountains of the central cordillera. Only the Catholic missionaries remained on the coast, but in a few months they, too, were gone.

Approximately two thousand Japanese soldiers and accompanying war materiel were landed on the beach near Wewak on the night of 18 December 1942. In the next few days, the missionaries and schoolchildren were evicted from their main residence at Wirui, and the Japanese moved in. Despite the fears of some Australians in the late 1930s, the Japanese did not find collaborators among the predominantly German missionaries, nor did the Japanese treat them as allies. In fact, the Japanese suspected the missionaries of opposite sympathies from the start. At Christmas, troops dispersed a party gathered by the mission sisters at Wirui for fear that their phonograph was transmitting information to the Allies. The "fighting bishop" came in from mission headquarters on Kairiru Island, but his assurances of neutrality were offered in vain. A series of incidents continued to raise Japanese suspicions, and when a submarine finally attacked Japanese ships nearby in February 1943, the decision was made to send the missionaries to a prison camp in Rabaul.[6]

On 15 March 1943, the Japanese ship *Akikaze* left Kairiru Island with thirty-nine Catholic missionaries, two Chinese infants who had been placed in care of the nuns, and a native woman who refused to stay behind. At Manus Island, far to the north, twenty other foreigners were boarded, including a number of Lutheran missionaries and six additional Catholics. Somewhere en route, however, the captain of the *Akikaze* received word that the foreigners were not to be taken to Rabaul. A gallows was raised on board from which to hang the victims by their arms, and one by one the passengers were strung up, shot, and dumped unceremoniously into the sea. Bishop Loerks was the first to die, and the two Chinese children and a European infant from Manus were thrown overboard alive.[7]

Missionaries based at Alexishafen began their severest trials nearly a year later on 5 February 1944, when they boarded the *Yorishime Maru*, en route to a Japanese military base in Hollandia. Because they were refused permission to take shelter in the hold, the missionaries remained on deck and were subjected to the full force of allied fire as American bombers strafed the ship, unaware of who was on board. Fifty-nine people died during the worst strike and forty others were badly wounded. When the ship landed at Wewak, the few able survivors were permitted to bury the dead and to do what they could to ease the suffering of the rest. The passengers finally reached a camp near Hollandia where, for the next two months, they lived as best they could while their wounded, including Bishop Wolf, continued to sicken and die. It was not until April 1944 that the ravaged party was rescued by American troops and sent to Australia for care (Wantok 1974).[8]

These survivors, along with missionaries who had been stationed in the highlands and the few who had escaped from lowland stations before they could be found by the Japanese, were all who remained from the old days to return after the war. Indeed, of the 230 priests, Brothers, and Sisters "active in New Guinea before World War II, 122, or 53 percent, lost their lives during the war" (Divine Word Missionaries 1969:55). If my figures are correct, only about forty of the Divine Word missionaries, who were in New Guinea when the war began, survived.

The Japanese Occupation

For natives in the coastal region of the Sepik, the old colonial triangle was superseded early on by a direct, one-to-one relationship with the Japanese occupying force. With Europeans gone, the Japanese created their own administrative system, stationing small groups of soldiers in villages on the offshore islands and along the mainland coast—a novel arrangement combining the capacities for force and intimacy that had been previously split between the government and the mission. Young children were taught to count in Japanese, to sing Japanese songs, and to speak a little Japanese. Older youngsters received instruction in the use of firearms; adults collected firewood, carried cargo, and gathered food for the soldiers garrisoned in their villages (Somare 1975a:2–6). A system of village administration was also introduced, and some men appear to have been given what they interpreted as rank in the Japanese army (Allen 1976:86; Somare 1975a:5). Later in 1943, this system was extended geographically when Japanese losses to the south forced them to withdraw the 18th Army to the Sepik itself and to establish new units in villages farther west of Wewak along the coast.

The Japanese presented themselves to natives in the Sepik as allies against the whites who had previously exploited and brutalized them. Although this image may have hit a responsive chord among those who had been involved in cargo cults, the Japanese dealt severely with individuals who did not comply with their demands, and with those who clung to millenarian visions that did not flatter the Japanese. Cargo cult leaders on Kairiru Island were beheaded, perhaps for not accepting the claim that the Japanese themselves were agents of the new millennium. A captured Japanese document addressed to villagers in the area clearly stated the Japanese position:

> *Just now times are hard, but as soon as we have finished off the whites . . . we will send many ships laden with cargo and you will all*

have clothes, shoes, blankets, and firearms, canned food in abun-
dance, and all the utensils you desire. The white skins are cowardly,
they ground you down and exploited you, but we will treat you as
men. We are mighty and we are your friends and your ancestors
[APR 1943–44, in Allen 1976:87].

As the year went on, however, the Japanese began to desire not only
compliance in the villages but labor at their major installations on
Kairiru Island and in Wewak. Allen reports that inlanders from the
Dreikikir area, far to the west of Wewak, were "required to work for
periods of up to three weeks at a time at the coastal bases" (1976:88).
People from the offshore island of Koil, however, northeast of Wewak,
recall working in longer shifts. The Japanese would come and recruit one
group to work in Wewak growing vegetables, preparing sago, or cutting
timber for several months at a time. This group would then be returned
to the island, and a second group would return on the same ship to one of
the camps near Wewak or on Kairiru to continue the effort. Local villagers near Wewak previously had sought refuge in bush villages, but
laborers had to hide where they could when the Allies staged air raids,
and for villagers, laborers, and Japanese troops alike, food became
scarce as the war progressed (Smith 1978:31–32).

Japanese fortunes in the Sepik worsened when Americans landed in
Aitape in the spring of 1944 and began to work the hinterland areas to
collect information on the location of Japanese troops and to prevent the
villagers from providing aid to the enemy. As supply lines were cut when
Australian troops advanced eastward from Aitape in the fall of 1944,
many units of the Japanese force (then believed to number 35,000 men),
moved inland. Increasingly desperate, these men lived off the land where
they could, and in their hardest moments cannibalized villagers who had
been shot in the line of retreat, and even their own dead. General Adachi
dug in at Wewak, placing his men in caves carved into the sides of Wewak
Point. Yet, despite the heavy losses that reduced his troops to perhaps
13,000 men, Adachi did not surrender until 13 September 1945, nearly
two weeks after Emperor Hirohito had capitulated in Japan (Long
1963:271–387; 559).

The Triangle Reformed

It was several months before the triangle of relations between administrators, missionaries, and native New Guineans began to reform. The Sepik
came first into the hands of the Australian New Guinea Administration
Unit (ANGAU), which had administered whatever territory was not held
by the Japanese throughout the war. It was faced with the initial task of
cleaning up the mess, physical and political, left by the Japanese occupation and the military action of the final campaign. Certainly, the largest

issue addressed by ANGAU was the question of native loyalty. Along the north coast in the Madang and Sepik districts, many villagers had cooperated with the Japanese. ANGAU was concerned with punishing the principal offenders, discovering the causes of disaffection, and reestablishing Australian prestige and control.

It should be no surprise that the missions—especially those missions with predominantly German personnel—were singled out as scapegoats in the discussions occasioned by the question of native disloyalty. ANGAU, for example, was in possession of documents such as one written by Captain D.M. Feinberg in October 1944, describing the conditions that he discovered during a patrol to rout the Japanese inland from Aitape and to regain the support of villagers earlier in that year (APR 1943–1944). In a long section entitled "Native Disaffection and the Missions," Feinberg voiced the opinion that it was no coincidence that most of the principal collaborators with the Japanese had been Catholic catechists, and that the principal Japanese strongholds had been under strong mission influence for forty years.

Feinberg's argument about the catechists rested on the premise that the missionaries had taught them to view the administration as a rival and as a "tool to be adroitly used." Because the natives were unable, in Feinberg's opinion, to distinguish the different sectors of European society, they actually were loyal to none and viewed all with the same opportunistic attitude that the missionaries had encouraged them to apply to government. When the missionaries had gone and the Japanese had arrived, then, the catechists had simply allied themselves with the new power, not caring that the Japanese were as much against Christianity as they were against the Australian regime.

Feinberg's argument about the complicity of Catholic villages was also grounded in the belief that natives were unable to distinguish between the mission and the administration. According to Feinberg, the villagers' disaffection with the mission stemmed from the mission's insistence on rights to land alienated two generations before and with the mission's attempt to interfere with native marriage practices. The villagers, he argued, had been led to believe that the administration backed the mission on these matters, and he saw village cooperation with the Japanese as an outlet for their frustration. Feinberg considers neither the possibility that villagers might have had legitimate grounds for frustration with the administration itself, nor what the costs of "loyalty," that is, failure to cooperate with the Japanese, would have been.

Apparently aware that the charges that he had formulated could be interpreted to apply to *all* missionaries in areas formerly occupied by Japan, Feinberg added a special diatribe against the "intolerant German mind" of the majority of the SVDs, and added a comparison to make his point. At Vanimo (near the Dutch border), he explained, Catholic natives had offered no serious problems to the Allied forces, and there the natives had been the "spiritual sheep of an easy-going American [SVD] priest . . . who once confided to me his disapproval of his Teutonic co-workers." While Feinberg concluded his report with several suggestions for placing missions more firmly under government control, he also recommended replacing "aliens" with "British subjects" as mission personnel.

Such communiqués added substance to the general anti-German climate in Australian policy circles. Although twenty-eight non-German SVDs were permitted to return to Madang in late September and early October 1945, there was grave doubt about whether their German confreres also would be permitted to come. Australia's intransigence on this matter soon became an issue of international concern. In Catholic circles, Francis Spellman, archbishop of New York, complained to President Truman, and there were other points of pressure on Canberra, as well. Finally, on 12 February 1946, "the Secretary of the Australian Department of External Territories . . . inform[ed] the Apostolic Delegate in North Sydney that German missionaries . . . may return to New Guinea" (Divine Word Missionaries 1969:55). The German missionaries of the SVD were back in the Territory within a week, arriving just after the civil administration took over from ANGAU on 1 January 1946.

From this new beginning, however, the postwar triangle reformed with a somewhat different configuration of power than that of the old triangle from before the war (Burridge 1960:22). The complacent, old-fashioned, mercantilist colonialism of the preceding half-century was irrevocably destroyed, to be replaced by a government more willing and able to involve itself in "native affairs," and by a native populace more willing and able to use the new colonial order for its own ends. If one is especially concerned with the triangle as it reformed along the north coast, and in the Sepik in particular, one also must consider the devastation wrought by the war on the Catholic mission. More than half of its personnel had been lost, its stations were in ruins, and it had been discredited, justifiably or not, by the cargo cults, and by the so-called collaboration of Catholic New Guineans with the Japanese. As the triangle reformed after the war, the missionaries now found themselves situated between a much stronger administration and people whose war-time experience had made them increasingly determined to seek solutions to the problems of participation posed by the European presence.

CHAPTER 6

The Flying Bishop
Technical Ministries
and the Cultural Frontier

Ministry has come to be a churchy word, usually coupled with the sorts of things ecclesiastical leaders do; preaching, performing liturgical activities, guiding a church community. In reality it is a far broader ideal and has conceptual roots in diakonia, *service.*

—WILLIAM R. BURROWS

To the outsider the concept of a poor missionary flying about the countryside seems contradictory. But it is not. It is the only practical and economic way he has to get where he wants to go in a land where you can still count the highways on one hand.

—FRANCIS MIHALIC

It was argued earlier that the Catholic mission's experience in New Guinea before World War II developed in a milieu lacking both vigorous administrative and commercial development, and a "principle of unity" among the region's native people. However, the mission's experience following the war occurred in an atmosphere of both expanding government involvement in social and economic life, and mounting determination by New Guineans to participate more equitably in a new order of affairs. If earlier conditions had placed in question the mission's conventional ideals concerning the division of missionary labor and the centering of their religious community, new conditions fostered changes in the mission's conventional ideas concerning the practice of ministry itself.

As the SVD missiologist, William Burrows, observes in his study on *New Ministries* (1980), quoted above, "ministry" (and its conceptual root of "service") is an inherently *historical* concept. If such conventional theological glosses concerning the aims of ministry as "redemption" or

---

The epigraphs at the head of this chapter are from:
William R. Burrows's *New Ministries: The Global Context* (Maryknoll: Orbis Books, 1980), 55.
Francis Mihalic's *"On a Wing and a Prayer: Papua New Guinea's Flying Bishop"* in *Paradise* (In-flight magazine of Air Niugini), No. 3 (January 1977), 29.

"salvation from sin" have archaic ancestry, "it should be stressed that the very nature of the boundaries imposed by sin differs from culture to culture and epoch to epoch" (1980:58). Earlier missionaries in the Sepik inscribed warfare, headhunting, infanticide, spirit worship, sorcery, and so forth into their maps of the local "boundaries imposed by sin." Catholic missionaries enmeshed in the triangle as it formed after the war had to survey these boundaries anew, keeping in mind the aspirations expressed by the people with whom they worked for "cargo," in both the material and the moral sense of the term.

In this chapter, I will argue that missionaries in the Sepik identified a new frontier for mission work in the years after World War II. Its defining feature was neither the region's poor economic infrastructure, nor preexisting divisions among the region's people, but a "cultural gap" that appeared to limit the people's capacity to participate fully in the church and in the modern world. With this shift in focus, new roads were opened for ministry that had not been seen before. Spiritual work diversified to include a variety of social and technical services, and older images of missionary work became outmoded, as the opening quotation from Father Mihalic implies. It is significant that the bishop, presiding over a period of mission history that can be defined by its concern with a "cultural gap," was neither a developer of plantations nor a boat captain, but a frontier pilot, instead.

THE FLYING BISHOP

If Hagspiel began his account of the Catholic mission in the 1920s with a boat, virtually all accounts of the mission in the post-World War II era focus on the airplane. This is not to say that boats no longer were used in mission work. Indeed, on the island circuit from Wewak, missionaries in the mid-1970s still captained a coastal vessel named the *Gabriel.* The plane, however, has superseded the boat both in practical importance to the missionaries and in its symbolic role. Not only was Leo Arkfeld, bishop of the Sepik mission from 1948 to the late 1970s, an airplane pilot, honored for his service to the country with an O.B.E. (Officer [of the Order] of the British Empire), but planes differ from boats in ways that have enabled missionaries to both act on and define a new kind of frontier. Hagspiel's *Gabriel* could follow only existing waterways and, of course, the nature of a boat passage is to focus attention on the transit rather than on the points that mark a trip's beginning and journey's end. As captain of the *Gabriel,* Joseph Loerks had to wind his way through the infamous bends and twists of the Sepik River, but the flying bishop can soar over all the ambiguous and limiting elements that still symbolize a frontier.

Aviation Stories

Aviation has contributed greatly to the postwar missionary experience. The Wirui Airstrip, adjoining the grounds of the mission's postwar headquarters in Wewak, was closed only in 1976. Thus, for nearly thirty years the arrival and departure of the mission's own planes were part of daily life for the missionaries in Wewak, as well as for those who depended on them for supplies and transport to their stations in the bush. As Father Mihalic notes in his article, written for the general readership of the national airline's passenger magazine, Leo Arkfeld was already a pilot when appointed bishop of the Vicariate in July 1948, and "no sooner arrived in Wewak with his mitre and crozier and Auster aircraft than word got out that henceforth all mission stations were to be built adjacent to possible airstrip sites" (1977a:30). This set the scene for the future of aviation in the mission's Sepik territory and not, incidentally, for a new kind of folklore—the harrowing aviation tale. As Father Ivo Ruiter, one of the diocese's missionary pilots, has pointed out:

> . . . sometimes [the bishop] was desperate and picked sites that very little imitated an airstrip . . . we had to establish strips wherever we could. Consequently we are still operating off very subnormal strips, subnormal in width, subnormal in length. Some are tilted, some are pitched to a high gradient, and surprisingly, over the years we have had very few accidents [Ruiter 1976][1]

To be sure, aviation stories are not a genre exclusive to Catholic missionaries in the Sepik. Like journeys by ships and boats in an earlier day, trips by air now provide material for all travelers in New Guinea who wish to sum up their experience in more or less concise anecdotal form. Missionaries, like other frequent air travelers in the country, exchange such stories in casual conversation with each other and with outsiders. In most communities of people who travel much in the country by plane, aviation stories belong to a genre of oral literature that seldom finds its way into print. In the Diocese of Wewak, however, some stories are published for purposes of fund raising or public relations (as with Mihalic's article, cited above). Indeed, the bishop's secretary let me copy several pages of aviation stories transcribed from a tape dictated by Father Ruiter for exactly such purposes. These stories trace the history of Wirui Air Services from its beginning in 1948 until 1976, when the Wirui strip was finally closed (Appendix A).

The narrative thread of Father Ruiter's account is straightforward. We learn that Wirui Airstrip was used during World War II as a landing ground for the Japanese. After it was repaired for damage it suffered during the bombing, it served as the major landing field in Wewak, while the larger strip built by the Allies at Boram, a few miles away, was itself being repaired. The mission joined a few small commercial airlines at the

Wirui strip after Bishop Arkfeld arrived in 1948 with his Tiger Moth, a plane soon replaced by a single engine Auster that served the mission until 1952. The mission's fleet grew slowly with the addition of a Cessna 170 in that year, a Cessna 180 in 1954, and a second 180 in 1956. By the mid-1960s the mission was "doing as many as 14 departures a day" from their end of Wirui strip, and their planes were flying "to practically all corners" of Papua and New Guinea (Ruiter 1976:5). The bishop and his pilots flew to Lae and Port Moresby to pick up visitors and conduct diocesan business, and to Aitape, Vanimo, and Irian Jaya, where they helped the Dutch Franciscans set up their own air services (Ruiter 1976).

After this heady period, as civil aviation in the territory improved, and as other dioceses developed their own air services, mission flights from Wirui seldom went so far afield. However, as aviation meanwhile had enabled the opening and supply of a great many new stations in the interior, there was more than enough business to keep up the demand for mission flights. Indeed, it was not only "tradition" that made the government's decision to close the strip at Wirui so distressing to the missionaries, but the very great inconvenience that flying from Boram—four miles from the mission headquarters and warehouses—was expected to entail.

Father Ruiter's narrative is interesting not only for its outline of the history of aviation in the diocese, but also because it is told primarily through stories that convey the ethos of mission flying, and, by careful association of aviation with the mission's spiritual goals, the ethos of mission work itself. Frontier aviation (that is, missionization) does not exactly lend itself to official rules and regulations, but requires ingenuity, flexibility, and God's blessings for success. As Mihalic summed it up in his public relations piece, the bishop "flies on a wing and a prayer. This formula has always brought him back home unscathed—even when the wing was flapping a bit" (1977a:30). Not surprisingly, the largest single group of stories told by Father Ruiter concerns the pilots who have flown the mission's planes, and many focus on their close calls.

A brief glance at these stories affords the interesting observation that although most of the pilots who have flown for the mission have not been missionaries themselves, only four of these twenty-eight pilots figure in only five of Ruiter's stories, while the diocese's two principal missionary pilots—Father Ruiter and the Bishop—figure in approximately fifteen. A closer reading also reveals a significant difference in the relation of these two types of pilots to the circumstances in which they fly. In particular, we may note that the stories about "outside" pilots are tales of daring and indiscretion, of men who have created difficulties by their style rather than transcending them as the missionary pilots generally do. One of the hired pilots, for example, made a bet with a patrol officer while "under the influence of a few beers," and proceeded to take-off and land on a hazardous strip in the moonlight, having had no previous experience in flying at night (Ruiter 1976). Another pilot "buzzed" a European family at the strip near their timber mill, coming so close that they had to dive for the ground (Ruiter 1976), while a third was in the habit of performing dangerous airdrops, and sometimes terrified his passengers by shutting off his engine above Mt. Turu (4,000 ft.) to glide in the winds (Ruiter 1976).

Of course, a missionary is liable to lapses in judgment too. Father Ruiter tells one story "on himself" in which he showed off for a photographer, and came so close that he actually knocked the fellow down (1976). Yet all of the other stories about the bishop and about Father Ruiter (who has been flying the diocese almost as long), represent the situation in which they fly as difficult *prior to* any action on their own part—it is a situation to which they must respond, not one which they create. Their close calls are not caused by foolish exuberance (usually), but are generated by the situation itself—as in the following tale that Father Ruiter tells:

> *Oftentimes the airstrip was very busy with MAL and Gibbes [two private firms] who were operating at full strength the same time we also were operating at full strength. Had no tower, no radios, and no contact with one another, so we had to do everything by visual. Although the strip is quite flat, when there's one plane at each end, the other seems to disappear behind the horizon. Just had to line up and have a good look before we dashed off into the wild blue yonder lest we meet someone on the way. And actually this is what happened in the case of the bishop and the MAL pilot Wally Pavlovich. Wally had taken a good look and the bishop had taken a good look but they didn't spy each other and got off to a flying run down the strip when they sighted one another. But it was too late for either of them to abort so as they became airborne they gave way to the right. Wally claims, when asked what he did, that he took off his hat and said "Good day, Bishop." It was quite a close call [Ruiter 1976].*

This contrast between the stories about temporary pilots and missionary pilots suggest that the latter predominate in this collection only in part because of their longer periods of service. I was told that Father Ruiter dictated his history of Wirui Air Serivces primarily for a fund-raising group at home that supports the mission's air operations. The "Friends of Wewak" contribute their time and money not because they are small-plane enthusiasts or arm-chair bush pilots, but because they are Catholics supporting a mission of the church. The narrative is thus about *mission* aviation in particular, and the anecdotes are mostly about pilots whose close identification with the mission can lend their exploits metaphorical weight. These stories are not just about missionaries in the air, but are about missionaries on the ground, as well.

The Imagery of Aviation

Consider some of the principal themes that aviation imagery allows; the heroism of the lone pilot; the pilot's virtually unmediated capacity to get where he wants to go; his ability to overcome external resistance, to "devour space" and to bridge time (Barthes 1972:71). Descriptions of difficult flight conditions, treacherous terrain, and precarious air strips frame stories about mission pilots, and evoke a primitive country steeped in nature, over which the plane and pilot, harbingers of culture, can prevail. The fact that the bishop himself is a pilot, responsible historically for the growth of mission aviation in the diocese and for the mission's continuing effort to constitute a local Catholic church, makes a metonymic extension all the more compelling for storytellers and audience alike. And while metonymy (expressions linking elements of the same domain) has often been maligned as aesthetically inferior to metaphor (expressions linking elements from two different domains), it is clear that metonymy of the kind that substitutes part for whole—synecdoche—can have metaphorical force.[2]

In fact, most explications of mission aviation "take off" from the presumption that aviation and mission work are usually assumed to be distinct domains and then proceed to show why they are not. The bishop himself told me that the plane had made it possible for mission stations to be situated near major population centers in the interior, and aviation is frequently credited as responsible for the numbers as well as the location of the stations that the mission is able to maintain. The plane is also placed in the context of other values important to the mission community. There is, for example, the virtue of vitality; Ruiter and Mihalic (who presumably used the Ruiter tape in preparing his article for the Air Niugini magazine), both tell how, in its heyday, the strip at Wirui was rumored to be the busiest strip in the Southern hemisphere (Ruiter 1976; Mihalic 1977a:30). Naturally these were small planes, and not all of these flights resulted from the Catholic mission's operations, but they evoke an image of an active church, in the thick of things, in tune with the tempo of change at the time. There is also the value of efficiency:

Generally speaking a small plane can travel in one minute what it takes the best hiker an hour to walk. Besides, it can carry up to half a tonne of supplies which would require a couple of dozen carriers who would also need their own food and wages and spend days on trek [Mihalic 1977a:29].

Closely related to efficiency is the value of service. Because of its speed, the plane is an emergency vehicle which, when a sick or injured person requires medical care, simply cannot be beat.

Because these virtues could be obtained in a mission air service manned solely by "outside" pilots, Father Ruiter notes in an article entitled "Airborne Apostles," published in a magazine for lay Catholics at home, that "people often ask why priests are used as pilots" (1969:118). Not only can a priest who is a pilot say mass at a station temporarily without a priest, Ruiter explains (bringing technical expertise into close relation with conventionally defined spiritual work), but "many missionary areas are visited infrequently, and the missionaries there need to talk from time to time with someone who understands their problems, who can advise them and attend to their spiritual needs" (1969:118). Thus the old problem of isolation that so concerned Bruno Hagspiel in the 1920s is ameliorated by the pilot-priest, and indeed, in the dioceses served by Leo Arkfeld in 1977, the problem of central authority is, too. As Father Mihalic puts it, "there is no diocese in the world where personnel get to see their bishop as often as they do in the Wewak and Madang areas" (1977a:30).[3]

In denying the apparent contradiction between aviation and mission values through these kinds of associations, missionaries are employing what Roy Wagner calls "collectivizing symbolization"—that is, they are asserting aviation's "explicit conformity with some collectively held ideal. . . . That is, [they are] controlling [its interpretation] in accordance with a kind of model that signifies the 'holding together' of society and morality, building consistency and social cohesion" (1981:46). The most powerful images of the planes' complicity in this regard have to do with the planes' capacity to induce contiguity. Father Ruiter, for example, mentions six people under the category of "passengers" that illustrate the two principal worlds mediated by mission aviation (and, by extension, the mission itself). On the one hand there was Cardinal Gilroy of Sydney, Bishop Thomas of Ballarat, and Cardinal Manning of Los Angeles—clearly representatives of world Catholicism, while the others are representatives of the most needy in the mission's own sphere—the native sorcery victim evacuated to Wewak from Telefomin in the West Sepik; "the time the bishop brought in a man who was just skin and bone . . . afraid to eat because the *sanguma man* [sorcerer] had threatened his life;" "the man afflicted with yaws" from Nuku, also in the West Sepik, and from whose face "most of the flesh . . . was almost gone" (Ruiter 1976).

Although these images of contiguity can be adequately expressed in words, the photograph heading Father Mihalic's article is clearly the most economical expression of the juxtapositions in space and time that the speed of aviation allows. Here we see the "The Flying Bishop," on an airstrip somewhere in the bush, dressed in tropical whites with natives in traditional costume posed around him and his small, single-engined plane (Figure 6). From here to there, and from then to now, with nothing in between; as Barthes has said of the pilot-hero, "speed" is an experience

Figure 6. The Flying Bishop. Photo by Brother Salvius, courtesy of Father Francis Mihalic.

of "space devoured" (1972:71). In these mission representations. I would argue, the space devoured is the "cultural gap," and the time flying by is that which separates "them" from "us."

THE CULTURAL FRONTIER

Mission aviation, like mission plantations and the mission ship *Gabriel* in earlier years, provides an image in which the concept of "local efficacy" has been given concrete signification. Yet, the change in technological terms is significant because each image articulates historically specific situations in which the mission's efficacy has been placed in question, and these situations are what I have been calling "frontiers." In all three cases, the image resolves an opposition between official values and the avenues available for achieving them in the circumstances that prevailed (Merton 1976:11). The plantation image "resolves" problems posed for the mission by the region's poverty ("poor, poor New Guinea"); the *Gabriel* image "resolves" problems posed by political fragmentation and cultural diversity among the region's people (their "lack of any universal binding characteristic"), while the imagery of aviation "resolves" problems posed by the cultural distance between New Guineans and the West.

The Postwar Situation

Clearly, Leo Arkfeld's contribution to the mission as a pilot can encompass themes appropriate to earlier mission frontiers. Yet, the postwar frontier in which problems of material support and community cohesion were worked out was not the empty frontier of Eberhard Limbrock's time, nor even the rustic frontier of Joseph Loerks. Whereas in earlier years, the colonial government had been largely ineffective in creating an economic infrastructure and in stimulating commercial activity within the region, the government after the war became far more energetic in the field of public works. Expatriate commerce never prospered in the Sepik to the extent that it did in other districts, but, businessmen at least responded to the growth stimulated by government initiative with increasing activity in the region, providing improved services in shipping, transport, wholesale and retail trade, and construction. Thus, although the private expatriate sector never amounted to much in the way of production for export in the Sepik, the conditions that would permit organic solidarity between the political, economic, and religious sectors of colonial society were developing at the same time the Catholic mission was reconstituting its own system after its destruction in the war.

There can be little doubt that the increasing role played by the government both in stimulating economic growth and in the field of native affairs was one of the most important changes wrought by World War II in New Guinea (which, after the war, was administered jointly with Papua as a Trust Territory of the United Nations). Among the reasons behind this growth in government responsibility were 1) the generally heightened awareness of Papua and New Guinea among the Australian public and its leaders, owing to the fact that the Japanese advance to the south had come "perilously close to Australia"; 2) the willingness of Labor government leaders in Australia to "encourage new developments" and "to take account of ideas raised outside the traditional organs of government or within groups of experts temporarily drawn into government for the duration of the war," and 3) "the feeling that Australia owed something to the indigenes of Papua and New Guinea" for their service to Australia, and for their suffering in a war in which they had been victims of political events in which they themselves had never been actively involved (Hudson 1974:34–35).

Among the many experts whose ideas contributed to the climate in which Australia's postwar colonial policy took shape was the anthropologist Stanley Elkin, whose influential statement of 1943, entitled "Wanted—A Charter for the Native People of the Southwest Pacific," embraced the proposition that the objective of government in Pacific territories should be the "welfare and future progress of the native population" (Hudson 1974:39). The legislation introduced to reestablish civil administration in Papua and New Guinea in 1945 by E.J. Ward, then minister for External Territories, remained true to the spirit of Elkin's proposals by advocating a far greater role for the government in the fields of native health and education, by proposing that the role of European industry in economic development should no longer be regulated solely by market conditions but by the government's assessment of "the welfare of natives generally," and by suggesting that government actively seek to facilitate "a greater participation by the natives in the wealth of their country and eventually in its government" (Hudson 1974:42–43).

It was clear to all concerned colonials that Ward's policy aimed to alter radically the prewar balance of power among government, the commercial community, and the missions by having government assume control of the pace and pattern of "industrial" expansion in the territory, and of "education in its broadest sense" (Hudson 1974:43). Although Ward's program was watered down considerably in 1949 when the Labor government was replaced by a Liberal-Country Party coalition, the groundwork for increased government involvement in both areas had been irretrievably laid. During the long "era" (1951–1963) in which Australian colonial policy remained firmly in the hands of Paul Hasluck, the minister of External Territories, the government remained committed to the goal of native development. This government differed from its predecessor, however, by taking a more conciliatory stance towards the interests of private enterprise and the missions, and in its view that native development should be "gradual" and "uniform" throughout the country (Hudson 1974:51–62).

Given the history of the Sepik as a labor frontier, the paucity of infrastructure inherited from the past, and the damage inflicted in the final campaigns of World War II, development in this region of the kind envisioned by Canberra long remained an elusive goal. Only one of the district's prewar plantations had escaped significant damage, and expatriate planting, like gold mining in the rivers inland, never really revived. A glance at Table 4, on the value of exports in 1957 from the territory's major ports, illustrates how poor the Sepik remained in comparison with other districts. With the lack of opportunity at home, the Sepik soon regained its old place as the principal supplier of labor to other parts of the country. This was a dubious distinction, held until the late 1950s, for a supposedly developing region (Curtain 1977:6).

Nonetheless, there were significant changes in *local* patterns of development within the Sepik that affected the mission in the formative postwar years. Reconstruction in the area around Wewak, where both the government and the mission located their postwar headquarters, proceeded apace, employing skilled and unskilled native labor as well as

TABLE 4
Exports from Territory Ports, 1955–1956

Port	Territory Produce (£)	Re-exports (£)	Total (£)
Rabaul	5,326,647	262,711	5,326,648
Lae	2,277,620	297,342	2,574,962
Port Moresby	1,892,505	385,906	2,278,411
Samarai	1,073,054	13,070	1,086,124
Madang	994,969	68,704	1,063,673
Kavieng	742,349	8,322	750,671
Lorengau	136,132	24,218	160,350
Wewak	4,029	5,290	9,319

Source: *Pacific Islands Monthly* 1956b:49.

a growing population of Europeans, and creating a new market for goods and services. Ships called more frequently in Wewak than they had before; shops opened at the foot of Wewak Point. A phone system was installed in the town in 1955, and in the same year, the *Pacific Islands Monthly* was able to report the surprise and pleasure of natives, missionaries, and other isolated Europeans, when two landrovers passed by on the newly opened road from Wewak to Maprik (*Pacific Islands Monthly* 1955a,1955b).[4] Although the mission continued to provide for many of its own needs, the conditions fostered by reconstruction and by government-supported construction projects made it unnecessary for the mission to design its new material base for total self-sufficiency, while radio systems (at first adapted from salvaged war material), airplanes, and later, the roads, made communication within the mission more frequent and reliable than had been possible in the years before the war.

The missionaries' postwar frontier was not, in short, either an economic or a political frontier of the kind that had concerned the pioneer bishop, Eberhard Limbrock, or the official observer, Bruno Hagspiel, after World War I. The mission's biggest challenges no longer concerned their capacity to maintain *themselves* materially or spiritually in New Guinea, but their capacity to reassemble old congregations and to form new ones. Although these tasks were somewhat eased by the transfer to the Australian Franciscans of the old SVD territory from Aitape on west, the Wewak-based mission now faced in its own district new areas that were being opened to them by aviation and the roads.

As was argued in the last chapter, however, the mission's capacity for "outreach" has never been a simple function of its ability to position its missionaries advantageously and to maintain a sense of community among them. The "triangle," as it formed after the war, was complicated for the Catholic missionaries by the fact that the government now had more to offer native New Guineans, by the arrival of other groups of missionaries to the district (mainly evangelical missions and the Seventh-Day Adventists), and by the fact that the indigenous people were more vocal than ever about their own aspirations. The Catholic missionaries not only had a new cadre of personnel working in previously unmissionized areas in the Sepik, but even the experienced missionaries, who had been able to return, found it difficult to recognize those whom they thought they had known so well.

"Bisnis" and Cargo

By the end of World War II, New Guineans in the coastal region of the Sepik had witnessed the arrival of four successive colonial governments—German, Australian, Japanese, and Australian again. Each government had entered amidst promises that its regime would be more beneficent than the last, and the new Australian government was no exception. Indeed, promises were being made long before the Japanese had suffered decisive military defeat in the territory, and many of those who heard these promises were native police and members of the native military battalions, some of whom became prominent leaders of their people after the war. Few historians would deny that the wartime experience of these men significantly shaped their aspirations, vision, and capacity for the leadership roles they subsequently assumed (Barrett 1969). Not only did they often enjoy close relationships with European soldiers and earn respect by their initiative, courage, and bushcraft, but a number of them were trained in Australia, where they were shown things that gave substance to the propaganda they so often heard.

Peter Lawrence notes that Yali, who became one of the most widely known of these postwar leaders, recalled hearing the following address when he joined the armed forces in 1943:

> In the past, you natives have been kept backward. But now, if you help us win the war . . . we Europeans will help you. We will help you get houses with galvanized iron roofs, plank walls and floors, electric light, and motor vehicles, boats, good clothes, and good food. Life will be very different for you after the war [Lawrence 1964:124].

For Yali, such promises conjured up images of European culture with which he was familiar from New Guinea, and of which he had been "made more aware" during his trip to Queensland for jungle combat training in 1942: "the emphasis on cleanliness and hygiene; the houses in well-kept gardens neatly ordered along the streets; and the care with which the houses were furnished . . . (Lawrence 1964:123). Shown Australian farms and factories, as well as towns and cities, Yali also realized that "whatever the ultimate secret of all this wealth . . . the Europeans had to work and organize their labour supply to obtain it" (Lawrence 1964:123). When Yali returned to his home in the southern Madang Province after the war, he was determined to promote such changes, and with the encouragement of the administration, began what was known as the Rai Coast Rehabilitation Scheme. Emphasizing cooperation with the administration, Yali's program called for people to make "a real effort to live decent, clean, and orderly lives" (Lawrence 1964:144, see 141–165).

Men with comparable experience and vision also returned to their homes in the Sepik after the war. Among the most widely known and energetic of these men was Pita Simogun, who quickly gained prominence by promoting cooperative cash cropping as a means to participation in the new order, and who later achieved a national reputation as a native member of the territory's first legislative council. Like Yali, Simogun was sought out by administrative officers, eager to find men who could gain the confidence of villagers for the government's new program in a region where village loyalties were still suspect. Simogun, like Yali, had to work within a context framed by cargo expectations among many of the people but, unlike Yali, Simogun never became implicated in a full-fledged cargo movement and indeed, believed that Yali and others who did were wrong (Allen 1976:188,432).

Simogun believed not only that cargo cults were futile, but also that the contract labor system was poorly conceived: people should work for themselves to make their villages and their country strong. He was much impressed with the idea of agricultural cooperatives, which he had heard about in Australia and which were part of the new government's development program in New Guinea. Simogun came to believe that New Guineans could become "strong" only through "coming together." Recalling one of his first speeches after the war during an interview in the mid-1970s, Simogun told Bryant Allen:

> I held a meeting only. I did not start anything then. I took the frond of a coconut. I stood up and I broke the twigs one at a time. I said, look, if you don't come together this will happen. You have seen the way of the Japanese, the Americans, Australians, New Zealanders, and Englishmen. The Japanese came and took your land. If the Australians had not had the help of the Americans to drive out the Japanese, they might still be here . . . But you were lucky. They came and helped you. . . . Now the same thing. You, yourselves must come together. If you see a European, don't call him masta. It doesn't matter about the colour of his skin, black or white. All must come together. And I held the coconut twigs and said. Look, one at a time they are easy to break. Five together they bend, ten together they are too strong. Australia, America, New Zealand, England, they all

came together in this way. So they won this war. They came here,
joined with us, and made us strong. So it must be now. We must all
come together with them [Allen 1976:425].

Simogun requested and received a European advisor and manager for his cooperative in Dagua—the first to be organized in the Sepik—but, as so often has happened in New Guinea, Europeans found it difficult to gain control (Allen 1976:426). In fact, Simogun was an active proselytizer, and encouraged other former policemen to go into the bush and along the coast and teach people to plant coconuts, rice, or peanuts, to pool their money, and to organize cooperative ventures for themselves. People came to the coast for training at Simogun's coastal plantations, and went out again as "boss boys" with the message "you go back to your village and do what we are doing here" (Allen 1976:429). Indeed, this happened so quickly and with such success that patrol officers in the hinterland, hoping to persuade villages to try such ventures, were occasionally surprised to find rice fields planted and cooperatives in place when they arrived (Roscoe 1983:1; Allen 1976:198–200).

Both Bryant Allen, who worked in the Dreikikir area behind the coast to the west, and Paul Roscoe, who worked in the Yangoru area behind the coast to the east, believe that *bisnis,* like other items that passed from north to south through traditional trade routes, was changed in the process of transition, being seen in these hinterland areas, at least, as an answer to the secret of power and wealth. Allen, in particular, argues that the distinction between *bisnis* and *kago* (cargo), though apparently maintained by Simogun, could elsewhere collapse with relative ease. In his area of study, Allen argues:

> Bisnis *must not be equated with Western concepts of business. Bisnis*
> *is a broad concept manifested in a number of ways, which include*
> *producing crops for sale, and investing money in enterprises which it*
> *is believed will cause large amounts of money to accrue to the indi-*
> *vidual. The processes by which the money is generated are poorly*
> *understood, if understood at all, by many people. When* bisnis *was*
> *first introduced people believed it was the form of behaviour which*
> *Europeans used to gain access to wealth and power, and because of*
> *this they adopted rice growing enthusiastically. . . . When people*
> *found rice growing was not bringing about the changes they believed*
> *it would, they ceased planting [Allen 1976:251—252].*

The time was obviously right for *bisnis* in the first several years after the war, for other leaders were attempting to follow a similar course. Although some of these men achieved wider renown than others, few had purely local aspirations. Michael Somare, the first prime minister of independent Papua New Guinea, for example, recalled his father,

Ludwig Somare Sana, from the Murik Lakes area near the mouth of the Sepik River, as a moderately successful leader of the type:

> My father retired from the police force in 1947. The death of his brother . . . forced him to come home. He remained with his people leading an active life until his death. He had taught himself to read and write in the police force, and he felt that he could do something for the village. He began to organize the Karaus, the Mendams, and the Muriks into small cooperatives. He tried to encourage them to trade. At first they were reluctant to follow his advice. Then he began to trade himself. He began to make carvings, which he sold in Wewak; he collected oysters; he dried and smoked fish and took them to Wewak to market. He bought a small dinghy to carry out his trade.
>
> When he found the people in Murik not active enough, he moved to Angoram [on the Sepik River]. There he founded the Angoram Cooperative Society and was its chairman from 1961 to 1967. This was one of the most successful cooperative movements in the whole area [Somare 1975a:19].

Pita Simogun, like Ludwig Somare Sana, was a frequent visitor to Wewak. Yet, the major figure in Wewak and its immediate hinterland in the first years after the war appears to have been Yauiga—another former policeman who was also a war hero, and whose decoration ceremony in 1948 was witnessed by "some 30 Europeans and 8,000 natives from near and far" (*Pacific Islands Monthly* 1948:78). Yauiga, from one of the Wewak-Boiken-speaking villages inland from Wewak, combined his advocacy of *bisnis* with a campaign for the reform of village society. Writing in 1952, Father Andreas Gerstner, then serving as the priest for villages in the general Wewak vicinity, described how

> this unusual man . . . undertook a war against the old heathen spirit cult and has had up to now wide success. Beginning in 1947 and then up to February 1948, he has already undertaken one reform expedition to his own people, two in the Wewak region, one in the Boiken region, and one on the island of Kairiru. On each of these trips he stayed three to four weeks. Delegates from many different villages accompanied him. After arrival in a new village, Yauiga would first give a speech. He asked all the men to give up their spiritual and magical paraphernalia and whatever other things were known as causes of conflict and feud. He said in one such speech to his own people something like the following: 'So long as you keep the old things, you think only of them. You threaten with sorcery, quarrels, and fighting. A new time has come for us. We will better ourselves and follow the whites of the Administration and the Mission.' The men who heard him speak were quite ready to give up their religious and magical items. They brought him their spirit masks, war spears,

magical stones, and potions for good and bad magic, etc. All of these things were buried in a two-to-three meter deep hole on the edge of the village. Only the old men opposed him here and there. . . . But Yauiga made the refractory ones stay the whole day long in the hot sun until by evening they showed some pliancy [Gerstner 1952a:799–800].

Clearly, Yauiga's reform expedition made use of elements, like the surrender of certain traditional items and their formal burial, that are reminiscent of Mambu's cargo ritual in the Bogia hinterland some years before. But to the missionaries, his advocacy of *bisnis* placed him firmly in a different class. Gerstner tells us that Yauiga himself had employed "ten young men in each of four different places, who 'wash gold' in the rivers after the model of the white gold prospectors," that he was building a road inland with the aid of several villages, that he owned a truck, and that, from a settlement he established at Boram near Wewak, his people were extracting salt from seawater (1952a:799). Yauiga's base at Boram, in fact, was one of the first large migrant settlements in Wewak (not counting the administration's camps for reconstruction workers). Apparently based on a military camp model, Yauiga encouraged inland people to come and work for him on a variety of projects including, besides salt extraction, a coconut plantation cooperative, and a sago-processing operation. He is also reported to have purchased a sawmill from the government, and organized a school in Wewak in which inland people could be trained in the ways and means of *bisnis* (WPR 1958–59)

Yauiga was not the only advocate of *bisnis* to encourage settlement in Wewak. Indeed, the history of migrant settlement in this town indicates that enthusiasm for *bisnis* played hand-in-hand with local styles of "big man" politics. Many people from the island desired access to flat, coastal land for cash cropping, and many from distant coastal villages desired access to land near the roads and markets in the town. Yet, leaders from villages in the immediate Wewak vicinity appear to have interpreted the situation as an opportunity rather than a problem, for they themselves needed men and labor to participate in *bisnis*. By 1958, there were already twenty migrant settlements in the Wewak area built on village-owned land, and sixteen or seventeen of these originated through agreements between village and migrant leaders to cooperate in commercial enterprises (WPR 1958–59). Peligo settlement, for example, was planned by a former police sergeant from an inland village, acting in concert with the *luluai* of the coastal village of Moem.[5] The inland migrants were to live on Moem land and plant it with peanuts and coconuts; half the proceeds from the sale of the crop were to go to the former sergeant, and half to the *luluai,* presumably for redistribution to their respective groups. Yauiga was likewise "helped" by "big men" from Kreer village who, impressed with his plans for progress, had given him permission to settle his followers on the Boram land (Huber 1979a).

To the missionaries returning after the war, *bisnis* in all its many manifestations—from rice fields in the bush, to rural-urban migration, to articulate leaders like Simogun, Sana, and Yauiga—was a surprise. Father Gerstner introduced Yauiga in his article as "a modern type who in the old days would not have been conceivable at all" (1952a:799). As opposed to Father Höltker's highly ambivalent assessment of the cargo leader, Mambu, Father Gerstner was unreserved in Yauiga's praise: "a man with a sympathetic, respectable character, with sound judgement, astonishing farsightedness and quite unusual initiative" (1952a:799).

That the mission was not generally considered an adversary by early *bisnis* leaders surely heightened their stature in missionaries' eyes. Although Father Gerstner prefaced his complimentary remarks about Yauiga by noting that he was "still a pagan," Yauiga was, in fact, undergoing instruction to become a Catholic at that time (1952a:799). Ludwig Somare Sana remained a staunch Catholic until his death (Somare 1975a:22), and Pita Simogun was also a Catholic, dating his conversion to the time when he had seen the Bishop of Rabaul walk into "the fire and smoke" of a volcanic eruption and became convinced that "the Catholic mission must be strong" (Allen 1976:433). Even Yali, at the beginning of his postwar career, was not opposed to the Catholic mission. Though he never became a Catholic himself, Yali was instrumental in gaining the mission a foothold in previously Lutheran territory along the Rai Coast (favoring Catholics for their tolerant attitude towards traditional dancing and ceremony), and encouraged his people to send their children to mission schools (Lawrence 1964:144).

The mission could hardly ignore men like Simogun, Yauiga, or Yali, who had such great influence among the people at that time. The dangers of the situation, however, became evident when the attempt by Catholic missionaries at Alexishafen to use Yali for their own purposes came to grief. As Lawrence relates the incident, Yali's Rehabilitation Scheme was already being undermined in 1947 by former mission helpers who, acting as his secretaries, "were spreading cargo doctrine in his name." Unaware of this, the administration was still supporting Yali's work. Impressed "especially [with] its contribution to the improvement of race relations," the administration sent Yali from his home area to Bogia, where "the people were still openly hostile to the Administration and Europeans in general," hoping that Yali could convince them "that the Japanese had gone for ever and that the Australian Government was now finally in control. . . ." Yali was also asked to appoint former servicemen in the area as "boss boys" to assist the *luluais* and *tultuls* "help supervise the work of reconstruction, and generally guide the people towards cooperation with European officials" (Lawrence 1964:150).

En route to Bogia, however, Yali was invited to stop at the Catholic mission headquarters in Alexishafen, where "one of the high dignitaries" urged him to speak favorably at Bogia about the mission and "to persuade the natives to show a greater interest in Christianity, and particularly to give up polygyny." When Yali got to Bogia, the priest there seconded these suggestions, and Yali complied (Lawrence 1964:151). Unfortunately, when Yali left the region several weeks later, the "boss boys" whom he had appointed, "together with a renegade catechist . . . deliberately translated his instructions into cargo propaganda and claimed him as their authority for doing so." Yali's advocacy of monogamy had even worse results—"There were several cases of suicide, and one woman died as the result of the physical injuries she suffered when her husband evicted her." The administration sent Yali back to Bogia to rescind his instructions concerning marriage, and severely reprimanded him for his role in the debacle. Henceforward, Yali withdrew his support from the Catholic mission (Lawrence 1964:151–152).

I have found no record of such an incident in the Sepik, but there, as well, the boundaries between *bisnis, kago,* and Christianity proved porous, making the postwar years a vertiginous time. For example, on the offshore island of Koil, which had previously been all Catholic, a cargo cult in the late 1940s, generally considered an offshoot of Yali's movement (Gesch 1985:121), gave way to enthusiasm by half the island's population for the newly arrived Seventh-Day Adventists. In other places, typically inland from the coast, *bisnis* went into temporary eclipse when it failed to produce the results desired by the people, and was followed by periodic bursts of enthusiasm for trying out other "roads," including cargo ritual in its classic forms (Allen 1976; Roscoe 1983).

Indeed, the Catholic church itself was sometimes perceived as such a "road." Although missionaries found some of their old congregations truculent, elsewhere they were invited to build new stations, and sometimes their hosts had cargo expectations that were beyond the mission's capacity to fulfill. The mission could deal well enough with "rice Christians" in the hope that faith would eventually deepen among those at first attracted by the social or material advantages that a missionary and mission station might bring (Burridge 1978:14). Those who hoped to find in Christianity the secret to cargo, however, were bound to suffer disappointment and could, as we have seen, cause difficult problems for missionaries later on.

The most interesting case on record, which Gesch calls the Morman-Godfrey movement, after the priest Father Wilbert Morman) and catechist (Godfrey Wehuiemungu) involved, illustrates how ambiguous the situation could become. Morman, an American priest with "a reputation for being freewheeling, ready to adjust to a great variety of circumstances," was posted to the Negrie and Sassoya area southwest of Wewak shortly after coming to New Guinea in 1948. According to his own account, Morman decided that village people needed to contribute more directly to the church, and after a four-year absence, returned in 1959 with a "programme to announce."

> *Since there was no money to contribute, the baptized Catholics of each village should come in turns to work for a week at the Yangoru [mission] station. . . . People cooperated with this, and out of these groups, a leading core of loyalists emerged, called* bosboi *(boss boy, overseer). The* bosboi *played roles as church leaders and church elders: they organized work gangs and school attendance, but they also went to pray for the sick and Godfrey was their leader. Godfrey showed a genuine competence as a prayer leader; and once, accepted Morman's request for someone to denounce an initiation enclosure [Gesch 1985:123].*

Morman also encouraged village Catholics to build chapels in their villages, and from this, beginning in around 1960, a movement emerged that centered on the opening of twenty-six village chapels. The ceremonies included a ritual renunciation of sorcery (reminiscent of Yauiga's crusade in the years just after the war), a renunciation of polygamy, and a circular dance, the name of which signified "'We are just bush people,'—but we have initiated this work for ourselves!" (Gesch 1985:124). Morman told Gesch that approximately 5,000 villagers enrolled as catechumens after these ceremonies. Catholic life in the villages became intense:

> *The churches were used morning and night for prayers under the guidance of Legion of Mary members. These Legion of Mary men and women were stalwart leaders of prayer and village spokesmen on behalf of the Church, but their activities included a secret weekly meeting with money collection, and this left them prey to a cargo cult aura [Gesch 1985:124].*

As Gesch argues, Morman's program could be seen simply as successful evangelism (as Morman himself appeared to view it), but "it was also something else" (1985:124). He notes that Godfrey appeared to have "some cargo notions behind his activities also," and that the villagers recall this period in their history as an attempt to make something happen that failed. They recall thinking that through their prayers, Jesus would come back, "to the black man, and the 'good time' would ensue" (Gesch 1985:124). Yet, the expectations for what the 'good time' would entail were excessive; disappointed, people turned to other activities, including the Peli Movement, a classic cargo cult in the early seventies, instead.

It is not surprising in view of the ambiance created by *bisnis* and cargo in the period following World War II, that missionaries began to identify the poor integration of New Guinea villagers with western culture as the essence of a new mission frontier. *Bisnis,* with its emphasis on rational (that is, western) styles of enterprise, was a form of self-help with which missionaries could easily sympathize, but which was all too vulnerable to failure owing to the people's lack of experience, undercapitalization, inadequate infrastructure, fluctuating world markets, and so forth. Cargo, on the other hand, with its emphasis on irrational (that is, nonwestern) ritual means, was generally interpreted by the missionaries as resulting from natives' misunderstanding of European culture, and as expressing the mistaken assumption that the material benefits of civilization could be obtained without hard work. Leo Arkfeld himself explained in an open letter to friends of the mission at home how "in the process of evolution from a primitive to a higher culture, it seems Cargo Cults are a part of the developing process" (Arkfeld n.d. 4). Though written in the mid-1970s in relation to the Peli Movement, it reflects a perception developed in the earlier postwar years, that the mission's major challenge was to help New Guineans bridge this cultural gap.[6]

It is one thing to recognize cultural differences and another to try to bridge a cultural gap. Earlier missionaries had expended much effort on linguistic and ethnographic studies to both document the diversity of native cultures in the area and better communicate their message and bring people into the church. After the war, however, missionaries began to understand that the challenge was not simply in the "otherness" of the native cultures that shaped the lives and characters of the people with whom they had to deal, but in the *relation* between the native and western cultures. To be sure, missionaries still had to deal with customary practices like sorcery, which troubled the lives of their parishioners, or which, like polygamy or certain kinds of "cousin marriage," were considered contradictory to church law. However, cargo cults, *bisnis,* and even Seventh-Day Adventism, were recognized to be phenomena of a different nature than the traditional customs and behavior with which missionaries had been primarily concerned before World War II. They were phenomena that severely challenged conventional means of ministry. Missionary priests continued to fulfill the sacramental duties of their office, of course, but many also turned to the task of addressing the new set of problems posed by the poor adjustment of indigenous communities to the modern world. Spiritual work, previously conceived as a Catholic version of "preaching and teaching" now differentiated into a myriad of specialized ministries, just as material work had done long before.

TECHNICAL MINISTRIES

In concluding his article about "Papua New Guinea's Flying Bishop," Father Mihalic informs his readers that Leo Arkfeld was "recently awarded the OBE for services rendered to the country and its people. But that is life to him. That is why he came. Service is his business—and a pair of wings has been one of his best tools" (1977a:30). As we have seen, the conviction that the problems facing mission work in New Guinea could be alleviated by the use of technology has been a persistent theme in Catholic mission work along the north coast. It was only after the war, however, that mission technology was placed directly in the service of native people, and only after the war that the idea was applied to spiritual work itself.

To older members of the mission community, this marked a radical break with the mission's past. One elderly German priest proposed to me that American members of the Society were responsible for this new turn. A large number of American priests had arrived after the war, he explained, and the only things they would talk about were "tractors."[7] However that may be, it is clear that just as the new missionaries turned energetically to the task of leveling the ground for stations and air strips, many of them also began to direct whatever resources, tools, and expertise they could muster to fill in the "cultural gap". During the twenty years following World War II, mission stations throughout the district became minicenters for social services and economic development. Indeed, the 1966–1967 government report on the East Sepik District gave the Roman Catholic Mission special commendation for taking an "active part in community development projects and youth work."

"Building for Permanence"

It is important to recall that there was an enormous material burden of reconstruction facing the missionaries after the war. Even in Wewak, in the mid-1970s, water-filled bomb holes pocked stretches of land where the prewar plantation at Wirui once stood, and on the northern face of Mission Hill, one could still find remnants of the Japanese defense— rusted helmets, teapots, and artillery—half-hidden in the bush. The plain just below Mission Hill, where the station's main workshops stood during the mid-1970s, remained a jungle of craters, bush, and war materiel until the early 1960s. Father Liebert (an American, in fact), recalls driving a large diesel tractor himself in 1961 and 1962, to fill the holes and level the ground.

When the missionaries returned to Wewak in 1946 and 1947, of course, things were much worse.[8] Not only were there craters and tons of leftover war materiel everywhere, but temporary housing and offices had to be quickly built, and missionaries who were dispatched to other stations in the area found those, too, in a sorry state of disrepair. A government officer in 1945 reported that mission property at Marienberg, Karup Hill (?), and Murik had been "totally destroyed or looted" by the Japanese (WPR 1945–46), and the station at Boiken, "destroyed in the war," was reported to be still "dilapidated" in 1952 (WPR 1952–53).

TABLE 5
New Mission Stations in the Territory of the Diocese of Wewak,
1945–1976

Location (Deanery)	Before WWII	1940s	1950s	1960s	1970s	Total By 1976
Wewak	5	1	3	6	2	17
Maprik	1	3	6	8	0	18
Sepik	3	1	3	3	1	11
Whole Region	9	5	12	17	3	46

These numbers refer only to stations that persisted through time and were listed in the mission directory in 1976. Institutions like the teachers' college in Wewak, and the boys' high school and minor seminary on Kairiru Island are included among these "stations." I have excluded mission plantations and farms.

If reconstruction took time, this was partly because expansion was proceeding simultaneously, and at a rapid pace. Table 5 shows the number of mission stations built in each of the three subregions ("deaneries") of the mission's postwar territory, both before the war and in each decade thereafter. A glance at this table will show that five new stations were opened in the 1940s alone, even while work was continuing to refurbish the eight prewar stations left in the mission's territory after its separation from Aitape, where the Franciscans took over in 1952. In the 1950s, an additional thirteen stations were established, and in the 1960s, seventeen more (Figure 7).

Just as the date at which a station is opened marks the beginning of a more intense local ministry than would have been possible when the area was an outlying part of a larger territory into which a missionary from a distant base patrolled, so too the date at which a station is opened marks the beginning and not the end of its physicial construction. The processes are generally thought to parallel and interact with one another, so that while "spiritual progress" of a conventional type might be expressed officially in statistics, for example, giving numbers of catechumens, in practice it is far more common to use the concrete imagery of physical progress to suggest "spiritual progress" of a more substantial kind.

An authoritative case may be gleaned from an article by Adolph Noser who, at the time, was Archbishop of Madang. Writing for Catholic readers at home, Noser described how, since the war "the material side of the mission has undergone a complete transformation" with practically every station emerging "from the bush house stage to a complete

Figure 7. Diocese of Wewak, mid-1970s. (Based on a sketch map circulated by the Diocese of Wewak, with adjustments.)

set of permanent buildings: churches, schools, hospitals, rectories, convents, and teachers' residences." To bring the process into clear connection with the mission's wider goals, Noser ends this section with the "raising of the mission of Alexishafen to the Archdiocese of Madang . . . in a simple but interesting ceremony in the new cathedral on February 23, 1967" (1969:61). Although missionaries in the Diocese of Wewak distinguish the style of Bishop Arkfeld from that of Bishop Noser, "building for permanence" was highly valued in the Sepik area as well.

Consider the biography of Brother Joseph Czubik prepared by Father Mihalic in the spring of 1977 for the occasion of the fiftieth anniversary of his final vows. Brother Joe's career by then had spanned two periods of mission history. Bishop Loerks had met Brother Joe on a trip to Germany in 1934 and had arranged for this gifted craftsman to come with him to New Guinea instead of to the Philippines, where he had first been assigned. Though trained in cabinetmaking and woodworking, Brother Joe spent most of his mission career in construction. According to the celebratory biography:

> . . . the largest and sturdiest and most earthquake-proof buildings in
> the mission have been [Br. Joe's] handiwork. Before the war this was
> the gigantic mission house on the hill where Boystown now is; the
> various types of buildings from residences to schools to hospitals to

bulk stores that made up Bishop Loerks' headquarters in Bagaram, Kairiru. Only bombs managed to level them.

Fortunately, Brother Joe escaped the Japanese during the war, making an eight-week trek into the highlands with one other brother, a priest, and an Australian army lieutenant, who had come down from the highlands to the Sepik valley to scout and patrol. Returning to New Guinea in 1945, Brother Joe began again to build "another series of hitherto indestructible monuments:

> . . . the large house in Marienberg, the Wirui cathedral, the lay missionaries' house—which was the first permanent building in post war Wirui, the bishop's house . . . Brother Gonzaga's dentistry and clinic, the Rosary Sisters' convent. There is no doubt about it; when Brother Joe builds, it is a permanent building. . . . He builds sturdily, with mortise and tenon and wooden pegs instead of bolts. His build-ings give with earthquakes. He is adept at using what materials are to hand and improvising with them . . . such as iron mesh after the war and various types of scrap iron rods to use in reenforcing his concrete walls.

What is especially interesting here is that Brother Joe, a very resourceful builder of permanent structures in the literal sense of the term, was singled out to me as a model for the kind of work that other members of the mission staff would like to achieve within their own areas of responsi-bility. One priest, serving in the mid-1970s as the mission's specialist in radio systems, told me that he wondered, given how much he enjoyed his job, whether his true vocation might not have been that of a brother. Indeed, another priest proposed to me that the best exemplars of the SVD spirit today were undoubtedly the SVD Brothers, who, like Brother Joe, could devote themselves to the perfection of a craft.

Of course the priests (with a few exceptions) were also members of the SVD, and they evinced a spirit akin to Brother Joe's in their approach to spiritual work in the years after the war. Just as Bishop Arkfeld located new stations near land that would accommodate an airstrip site, so too did his priests shape ministries around problems that were amenable to craftsmanlike solutions. By the mid-1970s, the head station at Wirui was home for a number of priests with specialized roles in diocesan-level projects (as had always been the case at "headquarters"), but mission stations scattered throughout the region had also become local centers for a wide variety of specialized services and projects organized by their resident priests. What I am suggesting is that these ministries that pro-vided outlets for the SVD spirit of craftsmanship in turn inspired the missionaries' pastoral imagination in the difficult period following World War II.

Perfecting the Parish

It is important to recognize for the missionaries under discussion here, that the "craftsman" model of ministry, like the aviation model (which may be taken as a special case), combines technique and expertise with a certain improvisatory virtuosity—not exactly that of the amateur, but quiet definitely not that of advanced technology in a corporate setting, either. The craftsman model is profoundly individualistic, resonating well with the changes in mission polity that were discussed in Chapter 4. I asked one priest whether he believed that new priests coming to the diocese with frontier expectations were likely to be disappointed. He replied that, on the contrary, at least until very recently, they would have been satisfied, for self-reliance was at a premium owing to the relative difficulty of communication in the district, and the relatively large station areas for which a priest had responsibility. Unlike the Franciscans working in the old SVD territory of Aitape, who continue to stress "community" in their religious life, another priest explained, SVD spiritual training stresses exercises that enable individual resilience in relative isolation from their confreres at relatively isolated posts.

Far more common as expressions of identity than contrasts with other mission societies, however, are contrasts between dioceses among the territories in New Guinea that are entrusted to the SVD. Some of these contrasts concern differences in levels of development between districts and differences among the native inhabitants themselves. Thus, the highlands highway, for example, is said to make a different situation for priests in the dioceses of Goroka and Mt. Hagen than that of priests in the dioceses of Wewak and Madang, most of whom cannot so easily hop in a truck to pick up supplies when they run low. I was also told that missionaries in the highlands work more in local languages than missionaries in the Sepik, who more often work in New Guinea Pidgin because of the greater number of languages and dialects as one moves towards the coast.

Although such environmental factors are believed to shape different patterns of mission work among the various SVD dioceses, other differences of great importance to the missionaries result from variations in the character and style of their individual bishops. In this regard, the missionaries with whom I spoke in the Diocese of Wewak agreed that Leo Arkfeld had long been regarded as the most innovative bishop in New Guinea. Bishop Noser of Madang had been widely known for being, as one missionary put it, "very directive in pastoral and financial matters." Arkfeld, by contrast, supported individual experimentation and initiative among his staff. His philosophy was summed up as "the truth will out: what is good will last." To this end, I was told, he could be counted upon to support new projects, even if their promoters' confreres objected to them at the mission's periodic convocations.

One of the more interesting aspects of this situation concerns the question of status within the cadre of missionary priests. As one might expect, informants denied that assignment to a specialized ministry in Wewak was much desired, and claimed to prefer "real missionary work" at one of the outstations where, with few exceptions, priests are singly placed. Yet among those so placed, I was told, reputation was likely to depend on the success with which a priest was able to build up his station—that is to show the same innovative spirit and commitment to craftsmanship that the bishop himself exhibited at the level of the diocese as a whole. Those who did not exhibit the flexibility required for success were subjects of concern, as with new priests direct from the seminary, who have a tendency to "do too much" at first, or those who are simply incapable of learning from experience. There had recently been, for example, a priest with previous experience in India who had tried to run his parish in Wewak on a "tight Indian model." His inability to adapt to local conditions, which Sepik missionaries generally believe not to be amenable to such a style, resulted in illness, probably from stress, and the priest was transferred to the highlands where it was hoped "the weather" would be better for his health.

Clearly, Catholic mission culture after the war continued to provide a fairly wide latitude for individual missionaries, especially priests, to fashion what they considered to be locally responsive ministries, and in postwar conditions these tended to involve a fairly wide range of secular services. To be sure, some of these—particularly schools—had lengthy pedigrees in the mission's work and were subject to considerable outside pressure. As the "Hasluck era" began, the emphasis on "uniform development" led to a tremendous push by the administration to expand primary education to all areas of the country, and the Christian missions were pushed to expand their school systems and to improve and secularize curricula. With increasing government funding and oversight, the Catholic mission's system of primary education became more complex, requiring more buildings and more personnel at the stations—for which the station priest, of course, was responsible (Downs 1980:49-50, 100, 128).

To subsidize their schools and other services, missionaries frequently opened trade stores at their stations, although, in part, this also responded to demands from local people for whom the mission station was often the only accessible outpost. Missionaries offered aid and advice to villagers attempting to develop local sources of cash income as well. On the island circuit, for example, the missionaries bought copra from villagers and carried it to market on mission boats; in the Sepik River and Maprik areas, missionaries purchased artifacts made in the villages and resold them to buyers in Wewak; one missionary recalled efforts to stimulate logging among villagers in his area on one of the Sepik River tributaries. A record of all the economic development projects that Catholic missionaries either assisted or helped to organize in their station areas has yet to be made, but would range from cattle ranching to chicken raising, and from growing peanuts to making doughnuts for sale in the town.

Needless to say, such activities—particularly the trade stores and the art business—exposed the mission to familiar critiques from outsiders, who suspected that these projects were undertaken more by a desire for profit than by a desire to serve. Yet, the dynamics of the triangle should not be forgotten in assessing the general pattern of missionary involvement in the economies of many of the local areas in which they worked. For the most part, it is probably true that villagers welcomed the assistance of the local missionary in their attempts to enter the cash economy from a village base. Indeed, because the missionary still remained in a single area for a relatively long period of time, such assistance could place him firmly within a local system of reciprocity and moral obligation, with the missionary giving what he was best equipped to give.

Whether or not the missionary was aware of the political and moral effects that his projects had for his personal involvement in local social relations, the missionary tended to view his assistance as service in response to local needs. And, depending on the imagination that the priest might bring to his task, these services might include work relating to community development as well as economic development in the narrow sense of the term. These projects have included such staples as youth groups, women's clubs, and sports teams, as well as more ambitious plans. One missionary, for example, began a club for Papua New Guinean civil servants who wished to give up drinking, while another built up his mission station so that it was "really something," to stem the tide of urban migration and the consequent demoralization of village life.

Many more such projects could be listed here, because the organization of mission work, already described, encouraged missionaries to develop their pastoral imagination along such lines. It should also be recognized that as the postwar period progressed, the same improvements that enabled missionaries to expand into the interior and to maintain better communications through improved roadways and radio networks also made it possible for them to pursue projects at their stations with less support from the wider mission community. Aside from the bishop's encouragement, new sources of finance also facilitated this de facto autonomy for the modern missionary priest. Most still rely on diocesan and society funds, and most still receive funds for general purposes from organizations, congregations, and individuals at home, but since the war, international Catholic agencies have emerged, that can also be approached to help fund special economic or community development projects on a larger, as well as smaller, scale.

The Persistence of the Cultural Gap

Because of its longevity and wide geographical coverage, the technical ministries that proliferated and developed in the postwar years have given the Catholic mission a special place in many parts of the Sepik. Especially through its services in the fields of education, health, transportation, and communication, the mission has attained a special place in the region at large. In 1975, the diocese of Wewak maintained fifty-four primary schools, 2 high schools (one for boys, one for girls), three vocational centers, a teacher-training college serving four dioceses, and the country's only school for juvenile delinquent boys. Its medical institutions included one dental clinic, eleven community health subcenters in rural areas, one rural health center, and about twenty aid posts supervised by mission health workers. A directory of the Diocese of Wewak (1975) also listed four formally organized Young Catholic centers ("each . . . has its own by-laws"), and a Christian Living Center "for a small number of teenage students and working girls" in Wewak. The country's leading newspaper in New Guinea Pidgin, *Wantok,* was initiated in the diocese and published at the diocesan press until 1977 when it was moved to Port Moresby by its founder and editor, Father Francis Mihalic. It will be recalled that he is also the author of the biography of Brother Joe and the article on "The Flying Bishop" with which this chapter began.

Although these facts and figures should suggest the kind of presence that the mission was able to attain in the postwar climate of enthusiasm for social and economic development, there are other, less concrete, indicators as well. It may be noted that the flying bishop became not only a favorite image within the community of missionaries, but also a familiar and popular figure to the region's people. He was respected as the leader of the church, of course, but also genuinely liked for his accessibility, his generosity, and his low-key style. I was told that when Leo Arkfeld was appointed archbishop of Madang (a year or so before my arrival), crowds had gathered at mission headquaters to protest his leaving the diocese. Indeed, the leaders of the Peli Movement, the cargo cult that developed in the Yangoru area southwest of Wewak in the 1970s, persistently asked the bishop's blessings for their enterprise, which included among its teachings the familiar theme that the bishop and his priests possessed special power (*pawa*) that distinguished them from other emissaries of the outside world (Arkfeld n.d.:4; Knight 1975:16).[9]

Of course, such a dramatic and recent reminder as the Peli Movement that cargo thinking has persisted in the region, the public reminder that cargo thinkers may attribute to missionaries a privileged kind of knowledge and efficacy, and the possibility that missionaries can unwittingly be drawn into or contribute to a cargo ambiance, have all introduced a degree of caution into the missionaries' assessment of their own capacity to help people bridge the deeper aspects of the cultural gap. Aware of just such possibilities, for example, the bishop no longer likes to leave a particular priest in a particular place for a lifetime of service. As he explained it to me, he prefers to switch priests around after several years in one post. He would prefer people to become Catholic Christians, not "Fr. Joe or Fr. Ed Christians" instead.[10]

Yet, it has been not only in the context of cargo, per se, that missionaries have perceived a persisting cultural gap. If the schools, boats, planes, and projects that missionaries have placed at the people's service have contributed to the people's well-being, they also provide frames—as the photograph of the flying bishop illustrates—in which the concept of a cultural gap may be displayed. In discussing a string of failed projects initiated by both himself and villagers near his station, for example, a priest explained to me that they faltered because the people's pattern of life promoted neither commitment to sustained effort, nor the capacity for delayed gratification. The sports clubs had failed because people would not show up for regular practice; a chicken farm had been abandoned because the young man for whom it had been designed failed to devote himself responsibly to its care. These were, the priest said, manifestations of a "cultural gulf" that boded ill for the future, and which he feared his best efforts could not overcome.

CONCLUSION

The cultural frontier thus persists for Catholic missionaries in the Sepik, its very resistance motivating missionaries to continue their efforts. Events not yet discussed, however, have given these efforts inflections beyond the socioeconomic sphere. After the end of the Hasluck era in the Territory of Papua and New Guinea, a new emphasis on political development arose, and by the end of the 1960s the country began to rush headlong to self-government (1 December 1973) and independence (16 September 1975). At the very time that Hasluck was resigning, however, Vatican Council II was taking place in Rome. Although the theology of "integral salvation" that developed from this council placed a halo around the kinds of technical ministries discussed in this chapter, the Council also called for the missions to make new efforts to localize personnel, empower the laity, and articulate local culture with the church.

The implicit argument in the imagery of the flying bishop had been that, despite conventional wisdom, development ministries were consistent with the mission's broader ecclesiastical goals. Once the goals were reformulated to include "localization" in its broader sense, however, confidence that technical ministries and church formation were complementary pursuits slowly began to wane. As Burridge has argued, it is difficult, and perhaps impossible, to do both at once:

Traditionally, evangelical frustrations were overcome by attacking them in intellectual pursuits: recording and learning the languages and customs and reflecting on what was being discovered. . . . Today, however, most of the creative fire in that intellectual, spiritual, and moral effort is absorbed into the impersonal routines of bureaucracies and channeled into a variety of practical skills which, even in innocence, place a missionary in a position of power over his charges. They come to rely on his knowledge of bureaucracies and on his skills as a social worker and technical expert. They begin to enjoy advantages quite disproportionate to the contribution they have made themselves [1978:27].

Indeed, the next chapter suggests that by the mid-1970s, Catholic missionaries in the Sepik were on the verge of defining "localization" as a new frontier. Questions were already being raised about whether the structure of the church was compatible with Melanesian forms of cooperation and community, whether the "service station ministries" that developed after the war, were not outdated, and whether new forms of ministry should be sought (Burrows 1980). Although the flying bishop was still flying in the mid-1970s, he was also appearing on ceremonial occasions as a "feathered bishop," wearing a miter of Sepik craftsmanship on his head.

CHAPTER 7

The Catholic Mission and the Local Church

This evening your new chapel was blessed. It's made of modern materials and designed with modern methods, but its structure, its inspiring, is taken from the haus tambaran, *the spirit house of the past, and the point I was making to you was that we look at this chapel. If it was built in Rome, if it was built in Australia, if it was built elsewhere, the structure would be completely different. In the old time you wouldn't find a Maprik or Sepik design, and you wouldn't even see on . . . the bishop, who was wearing a robe this evening, a Maprik design at the back. But as I said, we are now changing. It's a changing pattern. We have to get what is best in the west and what is best in the Melanesian society and put them together.*

—MICHAEL SOMARE

Throughout this study, I have argued that problems facing all colonial agents along the north coast of New Guinea were experienced by Catholic missionaries in unique ways. The conditions that affected the missionaries' attempt to constitute a church also affected efforts by government and commercial agents to constitute their own projects in this region of the country. As I have shown in the last several chapters, however, the mission's division of labor, notions of community, position vis-à-vis other groups, and "spirit," defined special lines of pressure that have been reflected in the missionaries' imagery and in the specific directions taken by their work. As the postwar period proceeded, localization became another "problem" that virtually all introduced institutions had to face, and which the Catholic missionaries interpreted and pursued in unique ways.

Although the term "localization" has sometimes been used in the context of colonial and postcolonial societies to refer exclusively to the replacement of foreign by national personnel, it may also be used, as Michael Somare's statement above implies, to refer to the transformation

---

The epigraph at the head of this chapter is from
Michael Somare's Address to the Graduating Class
of St. Benedict's Teachers College, Wewak (1975).

of introduced institutions by the incorporation of local modes of organization, thought, and style (Ballard 1972). Whether localization should proceed slowly or quickly, what changes should be made to recruit and accommodate Papua New Guinean staff, and what areas of operation might be amenable to local "inspiring" without sacrificing the "best of the west," became questions that exercised the leadership in various branches of the public service, business firms, and churches, as well. Although the discourse on localization did not displace the discourse on development in the country at large, the two sat uneasily together for, despite Somare's politic optimism that blending was possible, the one asked Papua New Guinea to conform to western institutions, while the other asked these institutions to conform to Papua New Guinea, instead.

As noted in the last chapter, localization was not only a political imperative for the Catholic church in Papua New Guinea, but also, especially through Vatican II, an ecclesiastical imperative as well. This chapter reviews the ideological context in which questions were posed concerning localization in the Catholic mission in the Sepik, examines how missionaries approached the issues of recruiting and training local staff, and discusses the ambiguous position in which the new discourse placed the missionary priest. Indeed, it can be argued that priestly ministry itself was placed in question, as the missionaries sought ways to better integrate the church with the village world, and as they began to define the Sepik as a new, ecclesiastical, frontier.

THE ECCLESIASTICAL FRONTIER

Michel Foucault has noted that "establishing discontinuities is not an easy task even for history in general" (1973:50). While Foucault was writing specifically about the task of social historians, it is important to note that "establishing discontinuities" may be a problem for the actors in history themselves. There are times when people feel called upon to reconstruct their projects and to represent themselves in new ways. To be sure, Catholic missionaries had begun to make adjustments in their practice from the moment that Father Limbrock and his pioneer party settled on Tumleo Island in 1897. Yet, it was only in the light of the theological climate created by Vatican II and the political climate created by the country's rush towards independence, that the missionaries began to envision discontinuities in the nature of the project itself. For most of their history, the missionaries had used imagery drawn from the domain of western technology to represent the ways in which they had adapted to the Melanesian world. As I already have noted, however, their imagery in the era of localization was beginning to change—the bishop sometimes appeared in public with a feathered mitre, and sometimes, as Somare pointed out, in robes with a Maprik design on the back.

Vatican II and Independence

It was suggested earlier that the hierarchical nature of the Catholic Church should be taken seriously when considering the local history of Catholic mission work. Allowing for Vatican bureaucracy, Sahlins' argument that the history of heroic polities "shows an unusual capacity for sudden change or rupture" (1983:520–521), is applicable at the highest levels of the Roman Catholic Church as well. Certainly, the Second Vatican Council was widely considered by churchmen and churchwomen to mark such a rupture. For those concerned particularly with Roman Catholic missions, the Vatican Council's emphasis on community as opposed to the individual, on the local, as opposed to the universal, church, and on dialogue with other religions and cultures, represented a "definite turning point in the theology of mission within the Catholic church" (Arbuckle 1978:280–281).

That these changes in theological outlook were not limited solely to professional missiologists and theologians, but had, within a decade, become familiar and acceptable to missionaries in such faraway fields as Polynesia and Micronesia, is one of the principal lessons to be drawn from Gerald Arbuckle's "The Impact of Vatican II on the Marists in Oceania," and of Francis X. Hezel's "Indigenization as a Missionary Goal in the Caroline and Marshall Islands," both published in 1978. Arbuckle, for example, distributed a questionnaire to missionary priests of the Society of Mary in Polynesia and found that a large proportion of the respondents checked positions in accord with Vatican II or post-Vatican II thinking on a number of theological issues: salvation (58.6 percent), the relationship of mission to development or socioeconomic change (62.5 percent), the concept of church (80 percent), the theology of ministry (90.5 percent), and the purpose of missionary activity (91.6 percent).[1] Theological "orientation" does not necessarily translate into practice, however, and Arbuckle found little evidence in the eight small island dioceses in which these Marists worked of change "in the understanding and use of local customs and languages, for example, and in the relationship between missionary and lay people" (1978:285).

Hezel's review of post-Vatican II developments among Jesuit missionaries in the Caroline-Marshall Islands focuses less on doctrine than on mission policy, but here, it appears, the more radical implications of Vatican II were embraced.

> . . . the missionary thrust of the Catholic church in the Caroline and Marshall Islands has changed (if we may over-simplify a bit) from promoting material development as measured by Western standards—better houses and better schools—to helping people achieve a sense of self-confidence and mastery over their destiny. The ideal missionary is no longer the man who has erected edifices, whether concrete buildings or parish clubs. He is the man who has

given of himself so that his people might learn who they are and what they can do . . . [1978:268-269].

Nor did the Jesuit imagination stop within parish, or even church, boundaries. As Hezel puts it, the discussions held by these missionaries' Vicariate Pastoral Planning Council in June 1971, resulted in "a widespread appreciation among participants that one age had ended and another had begun in Micronesia" (1978:268).

The concern of Catholic missionaries has become more than indigenization of the church; it is indigenization of the society itself (if we may speak of such a thing) with all its political and economic structures [1978:269].

If it is fair to take the Marists in Oceania as an example of a more conservative mission group (Arbuckle 1978:290), and the Jesuits in Micronesia as an example of a missionary group on the more liberal end of the spectrum, the missionaries of the Society of the Divine Word working in the same general area of the world in the Vatican II period, certainly fell somewhere in between. The cultural frontier still persisted for missionaries in the Diocese of Wewak; although they applied themselves with more vigor than the Marists to the task of "indigenizing" the church, they had neither abandoned "better houses and better schools" as media for Christian ministry, nor embodied their ideals in the image of a "radical" priest.

Of course, neither Vatican II nor the response to it of missionaries around the world, occurred in a political vacuum. As Hezel notes, the "new theological currents . . . publicized and legitimized for Catholics during the 1960s in several documents issued by the Vatican II Council" were influenced by a "new consciousness of the Third World and its aspirations" that accompanied the "rise of nationalism in Africa and parts of Asia" (1978:264). Without prejudging the nature of the Marists' or the Jesuits' response to the different political conditions obtaining in Polynesia and Micronesia during the decade following Vatican II, the response of SVD missionaries along the north coast of New Guinea during that period was clearly in tune with the political temper in the country at the time.

The "rise of nationalism," it must be said, was ambiguous at best in the Territory of Papua and New Guinea during the mid-1960s when the Vatican II council disbanded. It is true that there had been increasing external pressures during the final years of the Hasluck era to set a timetable for self-government, and that when the new administration under C.E. Barnes took over in December 1963, "government policies could no longer be made on an assumption that Australian trusteeship had an indefinite time to run" (Downs 1980:273; see 214-266). Yet, in some respects, Barnes's administration was a step backwards, for although Hasluck's "concept of gradualist, balanced social development" had at least set the grounds for localization in government and the economy, Barnes's "concentration of effort on areas and projects of greatest economic promise," placed greater stress on economic efficiency and growth (Ward and Ballard 1976:442).

At the time when Barnes took control, the country had not yet fostered an ideologically sophisticated elite, and in the Sepik, as in most other parts of the territory, there was no discernible popular movement for political independence. Indeed, nationalist sentiment in the territory was officially regarded as a threat to the goal of independence, because economic development was seen as the essential first step:

> From the beginning, Barnes's commitment to the need for economic growth made him more sensitive than seemed necessary to any event or situation that might disturb political peace and thereby threaten a 'favourable climate for business' [Downs 1980:278].

To be sure, some situations developed that did threaten political peace, in particular the rise of separatist groups in New Britain and in Bougainville. However, most influential Papua New Guineans with nationalist aspirations during the mid to late 1960s, were "careful politicians," who exercised caution in phrasing the issues and in selecting the forums in which to voice their concerns (Downs 1980:460).

Australians who opposed Barnes's policies were less circumspect, and while the role played by the rising group of disaffected Papua New Guinean politicians and public servants should not be underestimated, most analysts maintain that the sudden impetus for rapid political change came more from abroad than at home. Indeed, the Australian government was virtually compelled to act in 1970 when the leader of the Opposition, Gough Whitlam, made a provocative tour of the territory

> proclaiming that if Labor was elected to govern Australia in 1972 he would give the Territory immediate self-government and that by 1976 he hoped Papua and New Guinea would have complete independence with continued Australian aid and assistance [Downs 1980:463].

Only six months later, the Australian Prime Minister John C. Groton arrived in the territory to announce a significant transfer of power from Canberra to Port Moresby that was to signify his party's commitment to early self-government as well (Downs 1980:469–479). Events moved so quickly thereafter that Whitlam, who became Prime Minister when Labor won the Australian elections of 1972, was placed in the awkward position of defending the pace of political development in Papua and

New Guinea from the charge that it was too fast, rather than too slow (Downs 1980:498).

Within the country itself there was a climate of confusion and fear. Between 1971 and 1973, the expatriate population fell by over 8,000 (from 53,132 to 44,437, or 16.4 percent) as the civil service was rapidly localized and as uncertainty about the status and safety of Europeans rose (Downs 1980:502–503). Regional interests were varied and divisive. Quite aside from secessionist sentiments in Papua, New Britain, and especially in Bougainville, there were "conservatives" in the highlands, who opposed early independence, fearing that power would be concentrated in the hands of people from districts that had a longer colonial history and, therefore, a larger corps of educated people to represent their interests in the House of Assembly and in the government departments.

Many Papua New Guineans were uncertain about the meaning of "self-government" and "independence." In the Sepik, there were areas where cargo expectations became focused on these terms (Scaglion 1983; Gesch 1985:60) and throughout the country, there were people who feared that independence would involve a complete severance from Australia with unknown consequences for the patterns of everyday life. Michael Somare, the chief minister prior to independence, and the country's first prime minister afterwards, spent much time on tour, trying to allay these fears, and to increase public support for independence by instilling pride in Melanesian traditions (kastam), and for the nation, above local or regional loyalties and concerns.

In this general political climate, it is not surprising that some of the more radical emphases emerging from Vatican II and post-Vatican II theology did not find voice among the Catholic missionaries in the Sepik. The mission's involvement in social and economic development was not only supported by the liberal stream in Vatican II theology, but was also consonant with government policy during both the Hasluck and Barnes administrations, and after independence as well. As the 1960s wore on, however, and it became clear that independence was imminent, the mission's concurrent efforts to localize personnel became more insistent and, in fact, were complicated by the political situation.

As we shall see, serious efforts to establish a local clergy had only gotten underway in the early to mid 1960s; among other problems, there were grave difficulties in keeping highly educated candidates for the priesthood in the service of the church. Although there was never a strong antimission movement in the country at large, highly educated young men were the ones most likely to engage in sophisticated critique of colonial institutions. And, as independence approached and the pace of localization in government increased, the opportunities to serve the country in positions of responsibility and power became greater in politics and public service than in the Roman Catholic Church.

Localizing Personnel

In November 1966, when the Vatican established the hierarchy of dioceses and bishops in the Territory of New Guinea, the political developments that would bring the country to independence nine years later were virtually inconceivable. It was realized that the country was on the "Threshold of Self-Government"—the title of an article in the 1969 edition of an SVD magazine that was devoted especially to celebrating the new status of the Society's New Guinea field. Yet the author of that piece had still been able to conclude:

> *"without authoritative guidance from some external source for perhaps another 50 years, [a hastily independent New Guinea] will revert to the turbulent disunity which was its condition when Western influence began to assert itself less than 80 years ago" (Franks 1969:28).*

As three of the other articles in the same issue show, however, the authority of western models for the church in New Guinea was already being questioned.

That two of these articles came from missionaries in the Diocese of Wewak is significant, because Leo Arkfeld was widely considered to be one of the most forward-looking of the SVD bishops in this regard as well. In 1951, Pope Pius XII's encyclical *Evangelii Praecones* had called attention to the need for local clergy in mission territories. By 1952, the Diocese of Wewak had opened its own minor seminary for boys who showed promise for the priesthood; in the same year Arkfeld had established the native Sisters of the Rosary in Wewak; and in the mid-1950s he had begun a Candidate School for young men who wished to become brothers. From today's perspective these seem sufficiently conventional innovations. William Burrows reminds us, however, that there was in Pius XII's encyclical "no recognition" of a possible form of Christianity at variance with the Roman, Latin model" (1985:2), and indeed, in the 1950s, there appear to have been some missionaries who felt that Arkfeld's attempt to introduce even these models for religious life in New Guinea was premature or quixotic at best. In writing about the origins of the indigenous brotherhood, Father William Liebert remarked: "it was a venture that not everyone believed in! But the Bishop had always been a farsighted man, and in addition has an unshakable trust in God" (1969:113).

By the time that Liebert was writing his article for the 1969 issue of *The Word in the World,* however, Vatican II had intervened. Although less imaginative in the area of "fellowship structures" than some missiologists would have liked, Vatican II did lead to a radical rethinking of the role and nature of brothers' and sisters' religious congregations. The issue that Liebert believed he had to address in the late 1960s was less whether native candidates for the brotherhood could "measure up" to western standards, than whether it was wise to introduce to New Guinea a way of life that was already being criticized as "moribund," or to begin another religious institute when the "Church herself has asked small congregations to merge" (1969:113).

Liebert's immediate answer was that the question itself was ill-founded, for "religious institute after institute has taken up the challenge of Vatican II and produced a revision of rules and a renewal of spiritual life that is unparalleled in the history of the Church" (1969:113). Clearly some sort of renewal was called for in the brother's institute that Liebert himself directed. As he explicitly notes, despite sufficient interest on the part of young men in the diocese, the brotherhood had not yet thrived. Nine years after its formal creation, the first ten novices had come and gone; only one of the second class had yet taken final vows, and the fate of the other eighteen members who were currently novices or in temporary vows—not to mention the thirty-six candidates in training at the minor seminary—was uncertain.

To be sure, Liebert noted several features of "The Cultural Problem" that made religious life, as conventionally conceived in the church, a difficult choice for young men from New Guinea to sustain (1969:114–116). The significance of Vatican II in this regard, however, was that it presented the possibility of modifying the institution itself rather than simply waiting for people to be "ready" to adapt. If, to Liebert, "the basic idea of the religious life, the giving of one's whole self to the service of the Church, as a witness of the life and service of Christ" (1969:114) was an unassailable core from which the values of hard work, discipline, humility, and celibacy were inseparable, he did see regions of religious life in which typically western expressions distort the basic idea of witness in New Guinea circumstances.

"Witness," of course, involves the way in which religious life is related to the everyday world, and Father Liebert was concerned with how the native brotherhood could separate them in a meaningful way. The attachment of the individual to his home community should not be devalued in New Guinea, according to Liebert, but should serve as a model for ties within the religious community to make it strong enough to motivate and to guide "apostolic activity" without turning in on itself, and thus away from the world. Food and dress, with the exception of the cassock for liturgical occasions, Liebert thought, should be similar to that of other, young, educated men. This naturally raised the question of the vow of poverty, however, and a serious problem of cultural translation around the meaning of wealth. Liebert insisted that a careful distinction between "destitution" and "religious poverty" would have to be drawn, because in New Guinea a young man with no money may be seen as a *rabisman* (from the English, "rubbish man"), a term implying moral, as well as social, turpitude. Current practice severely limited the cash available to brothers, but Liebert believed that "this problem" would have "to be examined carefully to learn whether such an arrangement is the best way to *fulfill* the witness role of poverty among the people" (1969:115).

If Liebert considered the insensitive extension of western models for religious life counterproductive in the New Guinea situation, his confrere, Leo Brouwer, writing about the situation of catechists, faulted an insensitive extension of the missionary model instead. "We must . . . get away from the idea that catechists, like us, are working for God, and should be content with whatever we give them as a gift (1969:122). In other countries, according to Brouwer, catechists were recruited from the ranks of fully-trained teachers, took religion as a higher course of study, and were paid extra to serve as catechists. The position elsewhere was one of trust and respect, whereas young men entering catechetical training in New Guinea preferred to be called "teachers of religion," because the designation "catechist" had come to be regarded as a derogatory term.

Brouwer noted that just eight years earlier, when he arrived as a missionary priest in 1961, the cadre of catechists could be "classified in several groups." The oldest were the few catechists left who had received their training before World War II, "by and large good characters and faithful to the mission" but who, as "experts in the old type of religious instruction: drilling of prayers, main truths of faith and answers to the catechism questions," were not sufficiently flexible to adapt to new methods or to the liturgical changes later authorized by Vatican II (1969:119). These elder catechists, however, contrasted favorably with the group that received its formal training beginning at Marienberg, on the Sepik River, in 1952. In the rush to reestablish the mission system after the war and to provide priests with help in their large station areas, men with little previous schooling had been trained, some of whom were not even baptized Catholics at the beginning of the course. The next cohort, trained on Kairiru Island, were better educated in reading and writing, but many priests, desperate for catechists to place in village schools, also recruited and trained their own men, including dropouts from the Kairiru primary school as well as relatively uneducated men from their own local areas (1969:119–120).

In the characteristically entrepreneurial spirit of his order, Brouwer had taken up, as a special ministry, the task of improving catechetical training in the diocese. Yet, he also realized that there were systemic factors beyond training that adversely affected the situation of catechists in the field (1969:120). When Brouwer's new catechetical course opened at Chambri, Bishop Arkfeld decided that the graduates should receive the same wages as the most highly qualified schoolteachers. Previously, catechists had been poorly paid, which had led to hardship for those with families, and had made it necessary for all to find other roads to respect from villagers whose social and economic expectations had been rapidly rising in the years after the war (1969:120,122).

If catechists had displayed a tendency to style themselves as "big men" in the villages to which they were assigned, to become involved with local women, or to lapse into the "pagan customs of their district," it was not, Brouwer argued, because of pride or perversity but, in large part, because they received such poor support from the mission itself. Their low status was not only publicly proclaimed by their low salaries, but they might, for example, see the priest for whom they worked only once or twice a year, and even then the occasion was less for collegial conference than to be "scolded for everything that went wrong in their village during [the priest's] absence" (1969:120).

The keynote to Brouwer's article is presented at the end, in the form of a quotation from the *Decree on the Missions, Vatican II:*

> *'In our time, when there are few clerics to preach the Gospel to such great multitudes and to exercise the pastoral ministry, the role of catechist is of maximum importance. Therefore, their training must be so thorough and so well adapted to cultural advances that, as powerful co-workers of the priestly order, they can perform their task as superbly as can be, even though it is weighted down with new and expanding burdens' [in Brouwer 1969:123].*

Father Liebert had observed in his article on the brothers that the post-Vatican II period "can be called the age of the laity" (1969:114). As Father Brouwer implied by citing the *Decree on the Missions,* the conventional relations of status and power within the mission had become not only counterproductive in practice, but also ecclesiastically anachronistic.

The Native Clergy

In moving from the articles on the brothers and the catechists to Patrick Murphy's article on native priests, it is important to note that unlike Father Liebert and Father Brouwer, Father Murphy was not attached to the Diocese of Wewak, nor to any of the other dioceses in Papua New Guinea, although he was a member of the SVD. The former authors had been sent to New Guinea to take up general mission work, and assumed their specific roles as novice master for the indigenous brothers at the bishop's request, and director of a catechetical school by personal inclination. Father Murphy, in contrast, had been sent to New Guinea specifically to establish and lead the region's first major (college-level) seminary.

This assignment in itself had been the result of some fairly high-level negotiations, because even before Vatican II, the question of the native clergy had been considered sufficiently important to override the traditional autonomy of the various bishops in favor of a cooperative arrangement for training native diocesan priests. Channel College, the regional minor (secondary school level) seminary had been founded in 1955 and entrusted to the Australian branch of the Missionaries of the Sacred Heart; when the time had come to establish the regional major seminary in the early 1960s, this new institution was entrusted to the SVD (Murphy 1969:86).

Murphy makes no apologies in his article for what appears to be a rather late start in the formation of a native clergy in New Guinea. In contrast to the situation of the catechists where low standards of training had been accepted, the high educational standards that the church maintained for priests had made the missions vulnerable to the generally low state of education in the territory at large. Indeed, Murphy informs us that when the minor seminary, Channel College, was founded in 1955, it became "the first organized attempt at a secondary school in the Territory of New Guinea" (1969:86); it may also be noted that when the major seminary opened its doors on 1 March 1963, it anticipated by three years the founding of the country's only full-fledged tertiary institution, the University of Papua New Guinea (Downs 1980:402–415). Two corollaries of this situation are worth noting: first, that only one priest from mainland New Guinea had reached major orders (the deaconate) by 1968, and second, that only a very small number of native priests from the entire region had been trained and ordained before Vatican II.

It is perhaps this latter fact that endows the rest of Murphy's piece with such a heady sense of possibility. Although the most serious impediments to forming a native clergy, such as the requirements that priests be male, celibate, and highly educated, were not negotiable on the local scene, in principle, at least, the new seminary was free to devise a program that would produce a leadership for the local church that was almost entirely formed under the enlightened guidelines of postconciliar thought. Within the Catholic community itself, for example, the new emphasis was on cooperation between bishops and between religious orders. However, although the SVD had been appointed to administer the regional seminary in the name of the regional bishops and the Vatican, rivalries lingered among the societies working in the territory's several dioceses. Indeed, the regional seminary had already been moved from Madang to Port Moresby, in part to join forces with a separate major seminary founded by the Missionaries of the Sacred Heart, and Murphy hoped to find a way in the future to involve all the orders working in the region in administering a common seminary study center. Ecumenism appears to be another example of the postconciliar developments that Murphy had in mind:

> It is by no means beyond the bounds of possibility that the major
> seminary complex . . . could develop into a center of higher religious

studies for the whole Territory with participation not only by Catholic laity as well as religious Brothers and Sisters, but also by non-Catholic students [Murphy 1969:88].

While hoping to bridge these old divisions through the administrative structure and clientele of the seminary, Murphy was also concerned about devising a program for his seminarians that did not foster new divisions. Another reason for the move from Madang to Port Moresby had been to take advantage of the virtues of the country's capital city, because "here the students could meet and mingle with people from all over the Territory in various stages of professional formation" (1969:87). Murphy felt strongly that a program identical to those in seminaries in Australia would be a disservice to the future church. It should be "equal to that of the best educated in New Guinea," and should use government standards for recruitment so that the seminarians' studies could be recognized by government authorities (1969:91). Cooperative programs with the new university would prevent the isolation of seminary students from the country's emerging secular elite, while "visits to centers of social work and social action, conversations with political leaders and public servants . . ." would enable them to "keep contact with the newly emerging modern life of the country" (1969:89).

Keeping students in contact with the village sector of society in the territory was quite another question for Murphy, far more subtle in its ramifications and far more resistant to administrative solutions. Murphy nodded perfunctorily towards the time-honored routine of having students raise their own gardens to keep "in touch with the life of the people:" he appears, however, to have dropped this practice as an empty symbol once the seminary moved away from Madang (1969:89). Compartmentalization in thought and understanding were far greater dangers to the church, Murphy suggested, than the physical separation of seminarians from the conditions of village life.

Pedagogical solutions might be attempted—teaching by induction rather than by lecture, for example, might encourage students to exercise their own modes of thought in grasping theology and discourage their tendency merely to memorize foreign materials. Indigenous styles of communication like storytelling and parables, should be stressed if these young men were ever to convey their spiritual knowledge to villagers unschooled in western "analytical methods of approaching God's Word " (1969:89–90). Flexibility on the part of the western seminary staff would also be necessary if students were to have the freedom to "make different emphases and see different meanings in familiar texts," that is, to develop their capacity to give these texts an indigenous interpretation (1969:90).

Summarizing a paper that had been presented at one of the several conferences that had been held in the region about the training of the local clergy, Murphy pointed out that "the whole question rests upon what the Church, i.e., God's people, expect of the native priest in New Guinea" (1969:91). As Murphy makes clear, one thing that western missionary priests expected was that indigenous priests would be *different* from themselves. First, the native clergy would be a secular clergy, that is to say, not divided from each other by the different spiritual traditions of the various religious orders (1969:91). Second, native priests would be close to the people and capable of communicating effectively with them. They would not be like "the missionary of whom it is said, 'He scratches where it doesn't hurt' " (1969:90). And third, although here the contrast is less with missionary priests than with a potential fostered by the structure of the church itself, the native clergy would take their priesthood "as attitude and service rather than status and right" (1969:89).

THE PLACE OF THE MISSIONARY PRIEST

In previous periods of mission history, the pair of terms "mission" and "church" were associated respectively with the locale, on the one hand, and with Rome on the other—the latter providing the criteria of authenticity by which the mission's work was to be judged. The thrust of Vatican II and post-Vatican II theology was, in effect, to reverse these signs. The term "foreign mission," which had traditionally connoted a mission *to* foreign lands, now tended to be thought of as a mission *from* foreign lands, while the term "church," which had traditionally emphasized the universal relevance of Roman Catholic forms, now came to connote (in some circles, at any rate) that institution as shaped by, and expressive of, local cultural styles (Arbuckle 1978:280; Murphy 1970:700–701). In the 1930s, Father Angelus wrote home that he hoped to live to see the day when the first native priests would be raised to the altar. However, Father Angelus, who took great delight in hearing Tumleo children sing the two-voice motets taught by missionary sisters, would not have expected the native priests to serve in a church that was arranged any differently from the model he had carried with him from home.

After Vatican II, this assumption of continuity had been changed. No one yet knew, of course, what an authentically localized Catholic Church in New Guinea would look like, but one thing was certain. Foreign missionaries, however important they remained in practice, were displaced by the discourse about it from their earlier role as direct precursors of the local church. In a 1970 paper, addressed to a general academic audience in Papua New Guinea, Patrick Murphy suggested that the Roman Catholic Church in that country was in fact only then in the transition from evangelization to formation and growth, while the process of "indigenization," wherein the local church assumes its "own characteristics of time, place, and culture," had not really begun (1970:700–701). Ideally, the agents of this transformation would be the native priests, brothers, sisters, and laity (including catechists) themselves. Yet, as the figures Murphy offered on personnel in all the region's dioceses show (Table 6), the number of indigenous priests, brothers, and sisters was still very low; and the laity, though large, was not yet well formed. The situation placed foreign missionaries throughout the country, especially priests, in the awkward position of having to guide the project towards ideals like "indigenization" and "laicization," for which, even given experiments like Liebert's with the brothers, or Brower's with catechists, there were no adequate models in hand.

The Mission Community in Wewak

"What you have to understand," a missionary priest told me when I first arrived in Wewak, "is that the ecclesiastical and order organizations are

TABLE 6

Catholic Church Statistics Papua New Guinea, c. 1970

	Indigenous priests	Overseas priests	Indigenous brothers	Indigenous sisters
Port Moresby	1	12		92 (for Papua)
Bereina	3	44	6	
Sideia	1	20	8	
Mendi		26		
Daru		13		
Madang		43	9	34
Wewak		62	18	42
Aitape		36	1	
Mt. Hagen		37		
Goroka	1	35		
Vanimo		10		
Lae		8		
Rabaul	4	60	6	97
Kavieng	3	19		
Bougainville	7	35	26	34
(MSC Indigenous brothers)			18	
(OLSH Indigenous sisters)				26

Source: Murphy 1970:704.

different, the latter like a branch, the former like a trunk." This simile may suggest a relation of precedence between the church and the mission that has always been formally correct, but it also suggests a center-periphery relation that until very recent years could not be said to have a basis in practice at all. To be sure, the offices of ecclesiastical leader and religious superior had been separated back in Limbrock's time, but all the bishops in territories entrusted to the SVD had been selected from SVD ranks, and certainly in the ecclesiastical territory in the Sepik, virtually all mission personnel (excepting, of course, catechists and other native assistants) had been SVD brothers, sisters, and priests until the period after World War II. Then, things began to change. By 1976, according to the directory of the Diocese of Wewak, only ninety-five of the 227 people counted as staff were SVD, and the proportion would be even lower if the total had included Papua New Guineans in various stages of preparation for the brotherhood or for the sister's congregation (Diocese of Wewak 1976).

The diversification of the mission community in regard to types and affiliations of personnel can be dated to the 1950s, when the expansion of the mission system was underway and when the first steps towards localization had taken place. The Papua New Guinea congregation of the Sisters of the Rosary had been founded in 1952. Lay missionaries from overseas first arrived in 1954, as did diocesan priests on temporary loan from dioceses in other countries. In 1957, Sisters of Mercy from Australia had come to begin work on a teacher's training institution, and to help staff the mission's primary schools and medical posts. The Congregation of the Sacred Heart for Papua New Guinea brothers had been formally established in 1959, and in the same year Marist Brothers from Australia came to teach at the high school for boys on Kairiru Island. Further additions followed with the founding of St. Benedict's Teacher's College (supported by four dioceses) in 1969; Christian Brothers from Australia were invited to take charge of teaching in this institution in 1969, and since then Franciscan Missionaries of Mary (sisters), Montfort Sisters, and Missionary Sisters of the Immaculate Conception have provided additional members of St. Benedict's staff (Diocese of Wewak 1975).

The numbers and nationalities of the various types and affiliations of personnel listed in the 1976 directory are shown in Table 7. Although these figures suggest that the diocese had indeed made progress towards forging an identity separate from that of its sponsoring mission society by the mid-1970s, they do not suggest great progress towards the new ecclesiastical goals. It was, for one thing, still very much a foreign community, only thirty-eight of its 227 members being Papua New Guineans[2], and it was still very closely tied with the SVD. Because of its special historical relationship with the diocese, the Society of the Divine Word still provided the bishop and his principal officers. Although it provided only fifteen of the diocese's seventy-one sisters, it provided twenty-five of the

TABLE 7

Status and Affiliation of Diocesan Personnel, by Country of Origin, 1976

	TOTAL	PNG	Australia	Germany	USA	Netherlands	Austria	Poland	Hungary	England	Canada	Philippines	Ireland	Czechoslovakia	Italy	Switzerland	New Zealand	Not Known
Priests	67	2	11	17	17	7	1	4	3	1	-	-	2	1	-	-	-	1
SVD	55	0	5	17	16	6	1	4	3	0	0	0	2	1	0	0	0	0
Non-SVD	12	2	6	-	1	1	-	-	-	1	-	-	-	-	-	-	-	1
Seminarians	11	7	-	-	-	-	-	-	-	-	-	-	-	-	-	-	-	4
Brothers	46	5	7	9	4	3	4	1	1	1	-	1	-	1	-	1	-	8
SVD	25	0	0	9	4	3	4	1	1	0	0	1	0	1	0	1	0	0
Marist	11	-	5	-	-	-	-	-	-	1	-	-	-	-	-	-	-	5
Christian	5	-	2	-	-	-	-	-	-	-	-	-	-	-	-	-	-	3
Sacred Heart	5	5	0	0	0	0	0	0	0	0	0	0	0	0	0	0	0	0
Sisters	71	24	20	7	1	2	1	1	-	-	-	2	1	-	-	-	-	12
SSHS	15	-	-	7	1	2	1	1	-	-	-	1	-	-	-	-	-	2
Mercy	26	-	20	-	-	-	-	-	-	-	-	-	1	-	-	-	-	5
Rosary	24	24	0	0	0	0	0	0	0	0	0	0	0	0	0	0	0	0
Other	6	-	-	-	-	-	-	-	-	-	-	-	1	-	-	-	-	5
Lay	32	-	10	1	1	2	6	-	-	1	3	-	-	-	2	-	1	5
Totals	227	38	48	34	23	14	12	6	4	3	3	3	3	2	2	1	1	30

Source: Numbers of Personnel, Diocese of Wewak 1976; Nationality, Bishop's Secretary, personal communication.

diocese's forty-six brothers, and fifty-five of the diocese's sixty-seven priests.

The mission's reliance on overseas personnel, and especially on members of the SVD, was of concern even to those who remained unmoved by the more liberal theological and political arguments of the day. As one can see from Table 8, showing the ages and nationalities of the diocese's SVD personnel, only 3 of the Sister Servants of the Holy Spirit (SSHS—the SVD sister's congregation) were under forty years of age in 1976, and nine were over fifty. At least fifteen of the twenty-five SVD brothers were over forty, as were at least thirty-eight of the fifty-five SVD priests. Indeed, even if the five priests whose ages I did not discover are counted among the younger men, the table shows that nearly 50 percent (twenty-seven out of fifty-five) of the SVD priests in 1976 were over fifty years of age. In an era when vocations for all religious orders had de-

TABLE 8
SVD Personnel in the Diocese of Wewak
by Status, Nationality, and Age, 1976

	Total	71+	61–70	51–60	41–50	31–40	21–30	N.K.
Priests								
Germany	17	2	5	4	2	4	0	0
USA	16	—	4	5	4	—	1	2
Netherlands	6	—	—	2	2	1	—	1
Australia	5	0	0	1	2	2	0	0
Poland	4	—	—	—	—	1	1	2
Hungary	3	0	1	1	1	0	0	0
Ireland	2	0	0	0	0	0	2	0
Austria	1	0	1	0	0	0	0	0
Czechoslovakia	1	0	1	0	0	0	0	0
Total Priests	55	2	12	13	11	8	4	5
Brothers								
Germany	9	1	—	2	3	1	—	2
USA	4	—	—	—	3	—	—	1
Austria	4	2	—	—	—	1	—	1
Netherlands	3	0	0	0	1	2	0	0
Poland	1	0	1	0	0	0	0	0
Hungary	1	—	—	—	—	—	—	1
Philippines	1	0	0	0	0	0	1	0
Czechoslovakia	1	0	1	0	0	0	0	0
Switzerland	1	1	0	0	0	0	0	0
Total Brothers	25	4	2	2	7	4	1	5
Sisters								
Germany	7	1	2	2	0	2	0	0
Netherlands	2	0	0	0	1	1	0	0
Philippines	1	0	0	1	0	0	0	0
Not Known	2	2	0	0	0	0	0	0
USA	1	0	0	1	0	0	0	0
Austria	1	0	0	0	1	0	0	0
Poland	1	0	0	0	0	1	0	0
Total Sisters	15	3	2	4	2	4	0	0
Total SVD	95	9	16	19	21	16	5	10

Source: Diocese of Wewak 1976.

clined in the home countries from which the Society had traditionally drawn its recruits, no one seriously entertained the illusion that all of these older members could be replaced, nor that those who did come would represent a mix of nationalities similar to that which currently pertained. One of the younger SVD brothers had come from the Philippines, for example, and it was widely believed that most future European priests would come from Poland, where the peculiar political situation made religious life a more attractive vocation than in other European countries.

To a certain extent, the Australian Sisters of Mercy and the Papua New Guinea Sisters of the Rosary were performing many of the general nursing, teaching, and pastoral tasks that traditionally had been the work of the SSHS. Some lay volunteers did teaching and clerical work in the diocese, and it was also this group that augmented the diocese's pool of technically skilled people, traditionally provided by the brothers of the SVD. Some of the traditional functions of priests in the diocese had been taken over by the Marist Brothers and the Christian Brothers, who specialized in high school and college teaching, and by the Papua New Guinea Sacred Heart Brothers, who had taken on special responsibility for running Boy's Town—at the time, the country's only reformatory for delinquent boys.

Diocesan priests on loan from dioceses abroad helped more directly to alleviate the current shortage of priests. However, for those who were looking for a local cadre of clerics to help avert the crisis of numbers that was imminent in the next ten to twenty years, as well as for those who were relying on local priests to imbue Catholicism in the Sepik with a structure and spirit more attuned to the region's culture, the picture looked a bit grim. In 1976 there was only one local priest in the diocese, and he was on temporary leave to serve as the acting premier of the East Sepik Province. By mid-1977, a second young man had been ordained a priest, and a third had been raised to major orders as a deacon. Other seminarians were in the "pipeline," but while they were cherished, their day was in the future and their numbers were few.

In the meantime, as Table 9 shows, the SVD's ninety-five members—although less than half of the total staff—provided the largest single subgroup of the diocese's personnel, far outnumbering any of the others. This general numerical predominance had combined with the history of the diocese, the composition of the clerical staff, and the continuing power and prestige of the priesthood, to produce what was widely recognized within the community as its defining social fact. Despite the arrival of other overseas groups, despite the increasing number of Papua New Guinea sisters, brothers, and priests, and despite the changes expected in the relatively near future, the spirit of "the SVD mob" (as one of the Australian Marist Brothers called them) still dominated the diocesan staff.

TABLE 9
Personnel in the Diocese of Wewak, 1976

SVD (Priests, Brothers, Sisters)	95	41.9%
Lay Volunteers	32	14.1%
Sisters of Mercy	26	11.5%
Rosary Sisters	24	10.6%
Non-SVD Priests	12	5.3%
Seminarians	11	4.8%
Marist Brothers	11	4.8%
Christian Brothers	5	2.2%
Sacred Heart Brothers	5	2.2%
Franciscan Sisters	5	2.2%
Montfort Sisters	1	.4%
Total	227	100.0%

Source: Diocese of Wewak 1976.

The Ambiguities of Localization

If the mission's efforts to localize personnel had not yet penetrated the higher levels of the mission's staff by the mid-1970s, this does not mean that mission activity itself had remained unchanged during the past ten years. It does mean, however, that these changes had been driven by foreign missionaries, and not by local people themselves. At least in the assessment of Father Cherubim Dambui, the diocese's first local priest, the results so far were ambiguous, as one might expect.[3]

Many of the changes that had occurred since Vatican II, according to Father Dambui, had exacerbated rather than bridged the old division between the people and the church. Changes in the form of the mass, the introduction of indigenous elements into church ceremonies, and the "swing in [religious] teaching" were neither much appreciated nor well understood. For example, devotion to Mary had been stressed by earlier missionaries, but was no longer receiving much attention from younger missionaries who now favored a more Christ-centered religion. These changes, in Father Dambui's opinion, had upset older Catholic traditions that "had started to take root." Both traditional religion and traditional Catholicism had, he explained, associated secrecy with power. When the language of the Mass was changed from Latin to Pidgin, the people finally understood what it meant—it didn't mean anything.[4]

Father Dambui suggested that there had been other parallels between traditional Catholicism and indigenous religion that earlier missionaries had not even tried to relate, thus excluding the potential for meaningful syncretism. In the face of missionaries' indifference to, if not outright denunciation of, indigenous religious traditions, many people had given up the latter to try Catholicism in correct (that is, missionary) form. Now, when the mission was trying to incorporate these traditional forms into the church itself, people were resisting because they continued to view Christianity and *kastom* (custom) as two separate roads. "You told us before," they argue, "that these things were bad."[5]

I asked Father Dambui if he thought the connection with Rome might be a contributing factor to the mission's problems in localization, but he replied that in fact, it was less so than it used to be, citing the national Bishops' Conference, which, according to Church lawyers, was supposed to give the country's bishops "rather alot of power." The Bishops' Conference should have no interference in terms of administrative policies for organization on the local level and in terms of functions of the church, because these things are not basic to questions of faith and morals. For example, the structure of a diocese and the relationship of the bishop to the priests can be defined locally. The problem, therefore, lay not in Rome but in Papua New Guinea itself. The country's bishops, he said, have been delegated responsibility, but owing to their upbringing and past relationship with Rome, are not quite sure whether to go ahead and decide matters.

A number of features of local mission practice that the bishops could change had, in Father Dambui's opinion, outlived their time. The idea of self-reliance, for example, which lies behind many of the bishops' activities, had led the missions to do much outside of the people's interests. Because most of the decisions in regard to these activities have been made by expatriate clerics, the people tended to see the mission as something apart from, not affecting, their lives. People use mission services, of course, but these are seen as something done at a distance from themselves, as an establishment. Father Dambui thought the objections raised by some local politicians ("stop doing business and get to your preaching") were based on "well-grounded observations." He appreciated the fact that the mission was responsible for opening many areas of the district, but regretted that education had not kept pace with mission expansion, leaving the mission with a big expatriate staff and only minimal participation in policy decisions by Papua New Guineans themselves.

Father Dambui pointed out that Wirui—the mission headquarters in Wewak—is one of the biggest establishments in Wewak, on a big piece of land. Yet, despite pressing urban problems, it is still geared to servicing outstations, and especially to providing services to priests and mission personnel. A look at the residential plan at Wirui reveals housing for the Europeans clustered in the central section of the mission, and housing for the Papua New Guinean staff located in the peripheries. Father Dambui then proceeded to draw for me a new ground plan for Wirui with the houses arranged in an oval pattern, with the priests, brothers, and local staff dwelling on the sides, and the bishop at one end. One might also, he suggested, bring in people from the community at large if empty houses were available—perhaps for those with personal religious feelings, or for whatever reason they might wish to come. Implicit in this idea, it must be noted, is not only the effacement of distinctions that expatriate missionaries make among types of mission workers, but also the distinction between the races that had become embedded in this division, just as class distinctions among foreign missionaries were before.

Father Dambui himself had frequently been troubled by signs of racism and paternalism that should have died long ago, and he was inclined to believe that the conditions for the reproduction of colonialist attitudes would continue as long as the mission remained dominated by overseas personnel. The current shortage of priests from overseas had caused difficulties in the mission, but the positive side effect was that it increased the likelihood that Papua New Guinean staff would take over some of the priests' traditional functions, and presumably guide localization as well.

Obstacles to Localization

Although no one knew what a church guided by Papua New Guineans would be like, it must be noted from the observations made by Father Dambui that some of the mission's more "old fashioned," or exotic, features were appreciated by the very people who were theoretically to be the agents for changing them in an "indigenous" direction. If we can assume that few Papua New Guineans any longer condoned the more obvious signs of racism and paternalism that they occasionally encountered from overseas personnel, there were still aspects of mission practice—quite outside the contested realm of religious teaching and liturgical reform—that maintained the simple appeal of continuity in a rather dizzying time of change, and that engaged the people's own aspirations and leadership styles.

If Father Dambui and others criticized mission services as an expatriate establishment, these same services, especially in the fields of transportation, communication, health care, education, and economic development were nonetheless appreciated by many government officials and the public at large. Indeed, this was the theme of my first meeting in Wewak—with the Provincial Commissioner, then the highest government authority at the local (provincial) level. Having just flown in from Port Moresby where the general tone in the academic community was hostile not only to colonial institutions but also to anthropologists, I was apprehensive about presenting myself to this New Guinean official. However, I received a cordial welcome both as an anthropologist and as a student of the church. In this official's opinion, moreover, the Catholic mission was a worthy institution, contributing much to the general welfare. In fact, he insisted that *all* missions active in the province focus on social and economic development. He explained that there are cargo cults in some areas because the people involved received religious teaching without understanding money.[6] Government officials were not the only ones who would be reluctant to see mission services cut back. Amid much talk among New Guineans that the level of service provided by the government had declined with localization, the services provided by Catholic missionaries remained as efficient and accessible as they had been before.

The question of access, of course, involves consideration of both social organization and style. It should be helpful here to draw on Robert Gordon's recent reassessment (1983; Gordon and Meggitt 1985) of the role of the colonial *kiap* (the government patrol officer), and some of Stephen Reed's observations on colonial relations in the years just before World War II (1943). Gordon's paper takes as its immediate problem the resurgence of tribal fighting since the early 1970s in the Enga Province of the New Guinea Highlands, and attempts to explicate its relation to changes in colonial and postcolonial administration. Beginning in the early 1960s, these changes had brought about the "decline of the Kiapdom," under the influence of which the region had been pacified in earlier years. In assessing the reasons for the success of the colonial *kiaps,* Gordon proposes three critical factors:

> (1) As an organization of one, [the kiap] had a vested interest in seeing that decisions made in one of his capacities were carried out in his other capacities [p. 220].

> (2) Colonial kiaps were comparatively isolated from the villagers: their police and interpreters served to keep the villagers at a distance . . . [p. 220].

> (3) . . . the colonial kiaps could see 'inside' Enga and make decisions which the people accepted, because they were independent of them. Their relatively high salaries and life style made them virtually unbribable and hence impenetrable. . . . They were relatively good magistrates because they were neither desperate for, nor needed, Enga approval [p. 221].

Although I emphasized differences between the positions of government agents and missionary priests in Chapter 5, it makes sense to note some of the general similarities in evaluating the situation of the mission at a time when the public service had been radically altered by bureaucratization and localization. Analogous changes had simply not occurred within the mission. In most parishes or station areas of the diocese, the priest still remained a generalist rather than a specialist, and still retained the quality—at least in most aspects of his work—of an "organization of one" (chapters 3 and 6). Although the relative longevity of their stay in one area, along with the very nature of evangelical and pastoral work, had always made priests less isolated from village life than *kiaps,* other factors continued to prevent accessibility from crossing certain bounds. Quite aside from the presence of government and quite aside from a missionary's own proclivities, the very size of the mission's station areas still made it necessary for a priest to rely on catechists for regular contact with villagers living far from the mission station, and still tended to not only minimize the priest's interference in day-to-day affairs, but also allow the villagers and catechists to look after local religious life on their own. Finally, if the missionary's situation has made him more dependent on the people's approval than the *kiap,* the same kinds of cultural factors mentioned by Gordon continued to lend the missionary of the 1960s and 1970s that impenetrable quality enjoyed by his predecessors and by colonial *kiaps* as well. In short, within the relatively broad areas of their competence, missionaries could still get things done, could be petitioned *or* avoided, and, moreover, had an aura of mystery and power that even (or especially) in the postcolonial era, continued in many practical respects to serve them well.

This is not to say that people in the East Sepik Province have always *liked* the missionary in their area, but that the bases for their authority had some elements in common with both the colonial *kiaps* and the indigenous leadership. Stephen Reed, writing about colonial relations during the late 1930s, insisted on the importance in "culture contact" of the individual and his style (1943:212–216):

> . . . *natives are quick to distinguish in Europeans those personality traits which they respect or admire, as well as those which they dislike or do not trust. On the Sepik River, where the native cultures set a high value on aggressive and truculent behavior, one government official, known by the natives to be in constant fear of attack, received little co-operation, either from his native police boys or from the villagers in his district. The other* kiap *on the river, known as a stern disciplinarian, was much more successful in his dealings with these people. They preferred to take their court cases to him, even though his post was several days' journey farther away from that of his less admired colleague. Corvees, moreover, were always more readily undertaken by the villagers in his district [Reed 1943:214].*

Although Reed admits to knowing little about the individual styles of the Catholic missionaries in the area in the mid-1930s, having never worked with "strongly missionized natives," he offers the example of Father Kirschbaum of Marienberg, whose "fame in the Sepik District spread far beyond the area of white contact" as evidence that "a tolerant and understanding missionary may gain the . . . respect and love of the natives" (1943:215). He was also able to "gather" that some missionaries were "regarded as too strict in what they expect the natives to learn in the way of dogma; others are thought to be especially exacting in matters of morality" (1943:215). I may also note in this context, that when Father Andreas Gerstner (the ethnographer of the Wewak-Boiken people) died, an obituary printed by the mission noted that he had enjoyed the reputation of being an especially gifted confessor! (Louisson c. 1963).

It should not be surprising to discover that the importance of individual style continued to shape relations between missionaries and parishioners in the mid-1970s. Certainly, the individual characteristics of missionaries were of considerable interest to people with whom I spoke in Wewak. Given the changes in ministry that I discussed in the last chapter, however, it should also not be surprising to find that people commented more frequently on styles of technical service than on styles of conducting more conventional kinds of spiritual work. Koil Islanders, for example, fondly recall the boat-captain priest who would never decline to overload his boat with passengers on his island route. They recall, especially, how he used to anchor west of Wewak to let out the excess number and then travel into the main harbor, cool and innocent, under the watchful eye of the harbor master. His most recent successor was disliked in equal measure for he abode by the rules, leaving passengers behind when the *Gabriel*'s meager limit was filled, and leaving cargo behind when people ran late in loading. This was not a situation which the Koil Islanders cared to leave to fate. Their appeal to the bishop to replace this rather dour and intractable missionary with the newly ordained native priest from a neighboring island was, in fact, calculated to assert a modicum of control. The bishop, however, who well understood local political culture, apparently refused, for the new priest received a special ministry in Wewak as his first assignment—keeping up, as much as possible in the case of a local priest, the tradition of clerical independence from the village scene.

MODELS FOR LAY LEADERSHIP

Communicating the concept of the church never has been an easy task for Catholic missionaries along the north coast of New Guinea, partly because they have not considered indigenous forms of cooperation and leadership appropriate models for teaching by analogy or for use as raw material for integrating village Christianity with the church. If it has often been necessary for Catholicism to be nurtured at the village level with only occasional guidance from a priest, missionaries nonetheless continued to view the church as separate from the village scene. In a region with hundreds of autonomous village communities in which the most visible leaders appeared to be "big men," whose ascendancy was based on coalitions almost as ephemeral as the cults and other waves of enthusiasm that periodically swept the region, missionaries intent on "building for permanence" had focused their efforts on building new structures for conducting religious life, rather than attempting to adapt the old.

The emerging discourse on localization clearly required a reevaluation of indigenous social and cultural forms as part of the effort to involve indigenous people more actively in the official life of the church. Of course, it also made village Christianity more visible to the missionaries and questioned its "traditional" separation from the clerically dominated church. As one missionary put it, "we have made our people stupid," leaving little room for them to gain the experience necessary to run the local church. The priest in charge of the diocese's new Pastoral Training Center for catechists and other lay leaders told me about a speech in which the mission's most distinguished catechist had elegantly phrased the current dilemma: Before was the *taim bilong lo;* Now it is *taim bilong fri'* (time of law/ time of freedom). You young men will have a much harder time of things. Before we carried trees just as we were told, like laborers, but now it is different. We can no longer look to the priests to tell us what to do; we have to work for ourselves to make the church strong.

Creating Christian Communities in Wewak

Few anthropologists have studied village-level Christianity in Papua New Guinea, and in the Sepik region I know of only one—Michael Smith, who worked from 1975 to 1976 in Koragur village on Kairiru Island (1978; 1980; 1982a; 1982b). Although Smith found an attitude of skepticism toward Christianity growing among Koragur villagers in the mid-1970s, he attributed much of the "continuing vitality of Catholic religious life" in Koragur not to their proximity to a mission station nor to a particularly efficacious priest, but "to the presence of an exceptional [village] leader" (Smith 1978:183). Whatever may be the pattern of Catholic life in villages elsewhere in the region, it is certainly true that by the mid-1970s, those missionaries who had taken the challenge of localization most seriously had also identified the development of lay leadership at the village level as a critical first step.[7]

The novelty of this move should not be obscured by its seeming common sense. As we have seen, missionaries in the fairly recent past had considered the center of church life to be the station, and had regarded those upon whom the church relied at the village level with some ambivalence. After all, from the priests' point of view, village catechists were prone to "lapse" in the long absences of the priest; those who most clearly adopted local leadership styles sometimes engendered, by their self-confidence and willingness to take things into their own hands, excesses of religious enthusiasm that could embarrass or annoy the priest. It was only in the new context created by Vatican II, Independence, and recent trends in clerical demography that missionaries had begun to change their ideas about where to locate the center of Christian life in the region, and about the potential value of fostering a strong cadre of village-level church leaders.

The shortcomings of the older system were probably more apparent in the new urban areas than in the rural areas for which, after all, the station system had been designed. Wewak, for example, had grown from a small European settlement with several villages in its immediate environment and a migrant population (not counting those in institutional housing) of under 2,000 in 1958 to a sprawling urban area with a population estimated at 20,300 for June 1977 (WPR 1958–59; Bureau of Statistics, 1976). The station priest in Wirui immediately after World War II had an area to patrol that was not much different from others in the mission's territory at that time (WPR 1949–50). By the late 1960s, however, the town had grown large enough to be divided into four parishes, none of which included villages far from the boundaries of the urban area itself. Even at that, it was difficult for an urban priest to keep up. Although Wewak has been called a "settled" town in comparison with others in Papua New Guinea (Curtain and May, 1979:66), there is still a great deal of coming and going from home village to urban settlement, in part because more than three-quarters of the town's indigenous residents come from the East Sepik Province and contiguous parts of the West Sepik Province, to which transportation by car, truck, or boat is relatively easy to find and relatively cheap.

The fact that so many people living in Wewak come from its home and neighboring provinces bears on other aspects of religious sociology as well. The 1966 census indicated that 6,148 of the 7,967 indigenous residents of Wewak (that is, 75.6 percent) claimed to be Catholic (Bureau of Statistics 1966:44). Although this proportion surely decreased as people from more distant areas came to settle in town, it was probably still quite large in the mid-1970s, as so many still came from areas in which the Catholic mission traditionally had been strong (Curtain and May 1979:66). On the other hand, the very pattern of movement that was made possible by the local origins of so many urban residents meant that people might be less motivated to participate in parish life in the town than in the villages from which they came and to which they periodically returned. Indeed, they might expect a visit from the station priest of their home area when he came to Wewak to attend a meeting or to purchase supplies. Certainly the Koil Islanders, at whose settlement I lived while in town, went more frequently to Wirui to inquire of their own island circuit priest about boat schedules than they went to attend church during their typically short stays in the town.[8] Indeed, those Catholics in Wewak who were probably at the greatest disadvantage were residents of the villages that the growing town had engulfed to some extent, for they had no station priest of their own. At Kreer, for example, I was told that "the old fathers used to come around and help us when we were sick, and talk, but now we're not even sure who the father who should be looking after us is."

Although many missionaries were inclined to view urban life as sharply distinct from village life and to interpret such comments and behavior as signs of the religious apathy and materialism that theoretically accompany urbanization, others disagreed. The SVD anthropologist, William Siefert, for example, based at The Melanesian Institute, a Christian study center in the highlands, argued that missionaries must be aware of the many significant continuities between urban and rural life in Papua New Guinea if they wished to develop successful ministries in the towns (1978:28). It is also true, however, that there were significant continuities in mission practice as well. In particular, ministries in Wewak were just as liable to have differences in focus as rural areas, owing to differences in temperament and style among the individual priests. In the 1960s and 1970s, of course, these differences were visible not only in the kinds of development projects priests undertook, but also in the ways in which localization goals were pursued.

Consider the neighboring parishes in Wewak of Kaindi and Wirui. Priests in both these parishes have believed their people troubled by "spiritual hunger" (as the priest at Kaindi put it), and have identified social problems as contributing to their parishioners' distress. The American priest at Kaindi, however, was a rather typical "cultural frontiersman," who had identified unemployed youth as the most troubled people in his parish. This priest had devoted his considerable skills to organizing a series of small business projects for these youth—cash cropping peanuts, for example, and making doughnuts for sale in the town. He had, moreover, received a loan from the bishop to build a modern hall for his Young Catholics organization, where sporting events and dances could be held. He also sponsored adult literacy and bible study groups. In short, he was developing a station-centered ministry that in most practical respects was indistinguishable from the bush model with which he had become familiar during his earlier years of service in the diocese.

The Dutch priest who was assigned to Wirui parish at the time when it was split from the other parishes in the town could be classified as an "ecclesiastical" frontiersman instead. This priest had identified community structure rather than youth unemployment as a principal factor behind the spiritual problems of his parishioners in Wewak. When the government decided to move a large group of "squatters" off the site that eventually became the town's playing field, this priest was instrumental in setting up a new settlement for them at Nuigo, on mission land near the Wirui Air Strip. Believing that spiritual life must be supported by a strong sense of community, the priest helped to design the new settlement with "blocks" laid aside for people from the same home areas, and believing that religious life must be supported by strong leadership, he had a man selected as a church leader from each of these blocks as well. Eventually, church leaders were selected from most of the other settlements within the compass of Wirui parish, and in the mid-1970s, when I was in Wewak, these church leaders were meeting weekly with the new parish priest.

This new parish priest, a German, fit neither category of frontiersman very well. He claimed to be from the old school, and thus more comfortable with more conventional kinds of spiritual work. Indeed, he was not thrilled to be posted to an urban area, and hoped to return after his next leave to one of the newer mission stations on a Sepik River tributary where he had been posted before. Nonetheless, he kept up with the church leaders' meetings, which were run on a sort of modified Robert's Rules basis in the parish office every Wednesday night. Various topics were entered for discussion at these meetings: repairs to the houses of the teachers and the catechist in the Catholic primary school compound; arrangements for cutting the grass in the cemetery at Wirui; concern over a former church leader from Nuigo who had taken a second wife; a complaint about a priest who had refused to invite one of the church leaders into his house, while extending an invitation to the church leader's white companion; what to do about the trash left outside the Cathedral on Friday nights when the bishop showed free movies on the outside screen to anyone in town who wished to come; and news about the church leaders' own communities, especially news about the small projects they wished to undertake, or had undertaken, with funds contributed by the Catholic residents in their communities. All of this was very useful, the parish priest said, but neither he nor the church leaders themselves were very sure of what it was they were really supposed to be leading, or how they were supposed to define their role.

Pastoral Power

Western sociologists have often distinguished between the sacramental, or magical, aspect of the priestly role and the "religious" or pastoral duties assumed by priests in some traditions. In his article on "The Priesthood in Sociological Theory," Bill McSweeney argues that most sociologists of religion, including Max Weber himself, have underplayed the magical element in discussing Roman Catholic priests, thereby missing the key to understanding "the peculiar way in which priest/laity relations operate in everyday life" (1974:6). Indeed, McSweeney goes further, to argue that emphasis on the "religious" or pastoral element causes sociologists to misunderstand the Catholic Church itself: "Both theologically and socially the objective [magical] element has always taken primacy over the subjective [religious] in the Roman Catholic church" (1974:13). A somewhat different view of the issue is presented by the anthropologist

Lawrence Taylor, who argues that the distinction be applied historically to analyze change within the church. In mid-nineteenth century Ireland, Taylor notes, the old type of priest whose position in the community depended on "magicoreligious" power was replaced by a new "better educated and more indoctrinated type" for whom, as Weber (1963:75) had argued, " 'pastoral care in all its forms is . . . the real instrument of power' " (Taylor 1985:703).

There was, of course, no way in which the Catholic mission could delegate to the laity the sacramental, or magical, power of the priest.[9] Through the offices of catechist, church leader, and prayer leader, however, the mission did hope to bring laymen and laywomen into pastoral roles that could be recognized by the church. Yet, as we have seen in the case of the church leaders in Wirui parish, attaining pastoral power in urban settlements under the close watch of a priest could be an elusive task. And, even in the villages, those catechists able to attain positions of power often did so in ways that the missionaries found suspect. As Smith has argued, the authority of catechists, like those who fill village-based government positions, ultimately derives from institutions with roots outside the village; however, as is true of indigenous leaders, none can operate without taking part in "intravillage social relationships of a strongly reciprocal nature" (1982:511). The missionaries hoped that laymen (and laywomen) would be able to assume priestly pastoral roles in the new, localized, church, and in the Diocese of Wewak, but the missionaries also realized that to be effective, the new lay leaders would have to have strong local ties. It was a matter of great importance to the mission, therefore, to be sure that these church leaders understand the difference between pastoral power and power of other kinds.

For Papua New Guineans in many parts of the Sepik, the activities of "big men" provide the most familiar model of efficacious leadership. Although the specific contexts in which big men operate vary with the region or village of the Province, usually they are men who achieve recognition for their ability to manage reciprocal relationships successfully enough to mobilize people and resources for communal events and competitive display. The long yam festivals of the Abelam in the Maprik area, or the taro and pig exchanges on Vokeo and Koil Islands, provide traditional examples that continue today. In the urban context of Wewak, big men were instrumental in shaping the first migrant settlements; leaders in the coastal villages in the late 1940s and 1950s "invited" inland leaders, like the reformer Yauiga, to settle with their followers on village-owned land near Wewak to cooperate in *bisnis* (Huber 1979a). Leaders in Wewak during the mid-1970s tended to be involved in such activities on a somewhat larger scale, supplementing contributions from followers with small business development grants, for example; and their political activity more often involved government office than before. Nonetheless, they were still men who could make things happen—men with notable gifts for management and persuasion. Big men sometimes engendered resentment, but they were valued for they could create and sustain morale.

The model of religious leadership most familiar to Catholic missionaries is that of Jesus Christ. Indeed, their vocation is patterned after Christ's ministry, and is centered on its central element—personal sacrifice. The vows of poverty, chastity, and obedience, which the "religious" among them have taken, are glosses on that central term. If their actual patterns of ministry have contained elements that can be interpreted in terms of the big man model—the material goods with which they have been able to surround themselves, the projects they have brought to fruition, the services they have provided via radio, plane, ship, and so forth—the value of personal abnegation that underlies their notion of service, and indeed their very presence in New Guinea, is essentially foreign to the land to which they have come.[10]

Consider, for example, the following attempt by a Papua New Guinean catechist in Wewak to elucidate the passage from the Gospel of John about "the good shepherd who lays down his life for the sheep" (John 10:14–18):

> It is true that we have no sheep in this country, and many of us do not understand. . . . But the meaning of Jesus as a shepherd—I think we can grasp if we think about how we look after pigs. A man who has a village pig is just like a shepherd and knows well how to look after his pig. If something happens to injure the pig, he must go to help. . . . If another man comes along and calls, the pig will run—but wait! the pig will find out that this is not the man or woman who looks after it and will return [Tangugo Pastoral Center, 1976].

Clearly, looking after a pig in New Guinea lends itself to different emphasis than looking after biblical sheep. The Christian notion of sacrifice (the pure gift) is submitted to the logic of reciprocity in the catechist's version, and to the Christian notion of ministry is added the idea of creating a personal followership, which tends to make western missionaries somewhat uneasy. The bishop, who was at the same ceremony, and who spoke later on, urged people to understand the story in a somewhat different way:

> We must all become shepherds like Jesus. . . . Jesus has taught us much about this. He said that he himself was the good shepherd, and Jesus said that a good shepherd worries about his sheep. If one goes and falls down into a ditch, he leaves the other ones and goes to get the one who has fallen. He holds it in his hands and is happy. He returns and everyone is happy because the sheep that was lost has come back. . . . I think that in this story, Jesus was showing us that we must think about each one, "personal apostolate, ah?" We shouldn't think that making everyone in the village Catholic will

make it good—although it's fine if you can. But I think the work involves reaching out to individuals. You must take the time to sit down with them one by one in their homes, each family, or with one man alone, and talk to them, meet with them, win them over one by one. Many times, Jesus worked like this, he worked with one at a time [Tangugo Pastoral Center, 1976].

If Jesus Christ and the biblical stories in which his ministry is recounted provide the most authoritative texts against which different conceptions of church leadership can be aired and negotiated among the missionaries and laity in the diocese of Wewak, the most concrete text available for such discourse is the ministry of the missionary priests themselves. The catechist at the official opening of the Tangugo Pastoral Center made this clear by noting that it was now time "for all of us catechists to work just like priests." And in his own speech, the bishop did not exactly disagree: "This idea of mine, "—to build the new pastoral center for the laity— "came from the Vatican Council of Rome when I read about ways they suggested to make the Church become strong. Their idea—that God works through many roads (i.e. through the laity as well as the priests) made me happy." Of course, what is at issue here is the nature of the priest's pastoral power.

It is clear that the bishop addressing the group of catechists and dignitaries assembled for the opening of the new center for training lay religious leaders in Wewak was concerned with explicating what the church meant by pastoral care ("personal apostolate, ah?"). Through the use of the term "apostolate," the bishop wanted people to understand the spirit of sacrifice that the role theoretically implied, and he attempted to translate the idea by stressing the object of ministry rather than the subject. The layman should attempt to work in private with one person at a time, rather than as a public personality. While the adequacy of this translation could be questioned, the bishop's point was that pastoral power should not be exercised for political or material gain.

Yet, the question of the magical power of the priest could not be altogether ignored. In a historical context marked strongly for the missionaries by cargo cults, there was concern that the nature of the lay leader's legitimate pastoral power might be misunderstood. It may be recalled that priests had often been attributed a special power, implied by the Pidgin term *pawa,* over forces that fostered material as well as moral well-being. Other speeches at the ceremony thus attempted to explain that the lay pastor not only should pursue an apostolate without thoughts of personal reward from his "flock," but also without any expectation of reward from God, either. As the new head of the Pastoral Center (a Dutch priest), explained to those present:

Sometimes I worried about where to find money, how this center would be built, but always, always, always, something came

through and I felt the hand of God. I felt it was God helping and that
[this building] was completed because it was God's wish. It is not
because we worked or because we were good and God rewarded us.
No, it is something God wanted and which he made happen. He uses
us, that's all; men are in his hands [Tangugo Pastoral Center, 1976].

Papua New Guineans, as this priest well realized, do not so easily discount the network of obligations among men that are required to bring a
project to a successful conclusion, nor do they so easily discount reciprocity in the cosmic scheme (Knight 1982:399–400;407–408). Yet, from
the missionaries' point of view, it was precisely the separation of the person from his ministry that Papua New Guineans had to understand if
they were to be trusted to share in the pastoral power of the priest. The
separation of person from ministry that the missionaries were attempting
to communicate on the occasion of the dedication of the new pastoral
center, thus served not only the logic of ritual, enabling the project to be
dedicated to God, but as an edifying device, aimed at encouraging the
proper placement of the powers of the religious leader—lay or priest.

I close with another passage from the speech of the bishop at this
occasion, in which he made the point humorously—much to the delight
of a most unconvinced crowd:

I am happy today because we all know, this is a work of God. Many
things have contributed to this center. The little help I gave, I think is
really nothing—it's just my work. . . . I have been just a servant (boi
nating in Pidgin) in starting this center. I went all over to find money.
I had tried Austria first many years before, but that didn't work.
Later though some Austrians came to visit—Monseigneur Wagner
and some priests travelled around and I took them in my car to show
them this site here. We tried to drive in but the car slipped and be-
came stuck in a ditch. Then we walked down the road and found
some men to come free the car. I think these Austrians must have
thought about this and felt sorry. And they gave us the money
[Tangugo Pastoral Center, 1976].

It is in the gap between the innumerable little contributions that men can
make to an effort and the enormity of the result, the bishop was saying,
that we find the hand of God. The priest, in this respect, is no different
from anyone else. God "uses us, that's all; men are in his hands."

CHAPTER 8

The Bishops' Progress
Summary and Conclusions

This study has been organized around several images that Catholic missionaries have used to represent themselves in successive periods of mission history—the pioneer years from 1896 to World War I, the interwar years, the period following World War II, and the period initiated by Vatican II and the move towards national independence. I have focused especially on images that represent the mission's ecclesiastical superiors, or bishops, through a set of practical skills. These skills have provided the means by which the concept of "local efficacy" has been given concrete signification, but each image also articulates an historically specific situation in which the mission's local efficacy has been placed in question—situations that I call "frontiers." Using episcopal imagery as an entree to Catholic missionary history, I have explored how these missionaries have defined their frontiers, how they have acted upon them, and how agents whose mission was defined in terms of cultural reproduction ("planting the church"), responded to the inevitability of cultural change.

The outline of mission history that I have presented, however, is a record not only of successive mission frontiers, but also of progress towards the constitution of a distinctive regional church. This is not to say that missionaries alone have been responsible for this progress, that it has been uncontested, nor that it is yet complete. For most of mission history, fashioning a distinctive Sepik church was less a goal of missionary activity than its unanticipated result. Nonetheless, Catholic missionaries in the Sepik have had to adjust their projects to the circumstances in which they worked; consequently, the mission church they established acquired special inflections in function and form. If one can examine "literary encounters with the exotic" for a "poetics of displacement" (Clifford 1984:683), one can examine the history of these encounters for a sociology of displacement as well.

THE SOCIOLOGY OF DISPLACEMENT

I begin with a "parable" of sorts—another "missionary story" about a group mentioned in the introduction, the congregationalist Brethren working in New Guinea under the auspices of Christian Missions in Many Lands (the CMML). The year was 1976, and I was in the midst of my fieldwork on the Catholic mission in Wewak. The CMML was not very active in the coastal region of the East Sepik Province. However, because Wewak was the largest town in the northwest, the CMML did maintain some offices there—a publishing firm and bookstore, a hostel for traveling missionaries, and a home for the missionaries' children, so that they could attend the region's only Australian curriculum school. When I discovered that I had met the current manager of these operations several years earlier during my first trip to Papua New Guinea, I decided to pay my respects.

In the course of our conversation, I told this missionary that I was in Wewak to study the Roman Catholic Church. "Why would you want to do that?" he asked. I said I was interested in how the church was organized in the Sepik, and in how the organization worked. And then, on sudden inspiration, I asked him to tell me how his church was organized. He stared at me for a long time, thought carefully about my question, and finally replied: "But we aren't organized at all!" Amazed, I noted the enterprise in Wewak that he was running, not to mention the mission's outlying stations, hospital, stores, and schools. "Oh the CMML, of course, it's organized," he said, relieved, "I thought you said our church."

If I had returned to Papua New Guinea to study the Brethren missionaries of the CMML, I might have ended up writing about the ironies of missionary experience, but would, no doubt, have had to deal with a different set of contradictions than I have here. In the case of the Brethren, I might have started by looking at the problems that arose for congregationalists who had to pursue their goals in the context of a supralocal organization, the CMML. As it was, I went to study missionaries who had been adjusting their practice to conditions that required more "localism" than appeared to be consistent with official views of their church.

Clearly the forms taken by the various mission churches in Papua New Guinea today reflect the principles of church polity that their missionaries have had in mind. The church established by the Brethren is protected from the organizational imperatives of mission work by its formal separation from the CMML. The Evangelical Lutheran Church of New Guinea has its synods; the Roman Catholic Church has its full complement of dioceses and archdioceses and its national bishops' conference. To what extent, however, do mission churches in Papua New Guinea also reflect a history of "connivance"—a bending of principles in the conditions missionaries found in the field?[1]

The church historian, Sidney Mead, has argued that basic features of organized religion in America today such as freedom of religion and a tendency towards localism, are less the result of a successful planting of early Americans' religious ideals than "in a real sense the elevation of connivance forced by necessity to the eminence of a principle of action" (1956:210). In regard to lesser aspects of American religious practice, connivance also appears to have been a guiding force. Mead cites the case, for example, of one Reverend Jonas Michaelius of New Amsterdam (New York) who, in explaining to "some of his brethren back home in 1628 some of the irregularities attending the formation of his church and why he departed from its accepted norms . . . noted simply that 'one cannot observe strictly all the usual formalities in making a beginning under such circumstances' " (1956:210).

The letters of Father Limbrock in New Guinea to his Superior at home (Chapter 3), and the remarks of Father Hagspiel and Father Angelus about the New Guinea mission in the 1920s and 1930s (Chapter 4), read like an extended footnote to Reverend Michaelius' remarks. In the passages that Father Wiltgen quotes from Father Limbrock's communication, we hear time and again how economic circumstances along the north coast made it necessary for the missionaries to do "everything" for themselves, thus obscuring their distinction between spiritual and material work. Father Hagspiel notes that circumstances in the region weakened community bonds, while Father Angelus, writing home to his seminary colleagues, characterizes New Guinea as a place where normal hierarchical relations within the mission community become inverted or confused.

Certainly, the circumstances faced by Catholic missionaries along the north coast before World War II were found to some extent in other areas of New Guinea. Other missionary groups in the country during the same period of time faced similar pressures towards displacement, and responded with "connivance" as well. Rowley, for example, notes that among the various mission groups that began work early in New Guinea's colonial history (London Missionary Society, Methodists, Catholics,

Lutherans, Anglicans) one could see "a broad but suggestive similarity of technique largely made inevitable by the nature of the tasks" (1965:138). Thus, virtually all missions, regardless of denomination, were

> soon immersed in work which demanded scholarship, administrative ability and competence in all kinds of practical tasks. The Europeans had to learn the vernaculars, create written languages, translate the scriptures across cultural as well as linguistic barriers. They had to establish systems of schooling to teach converts to read, write and count; and train New Guinean teachers to extend these systems. Primary, technical, and teacher-training schools had to be developed. School texts had to be prepared, and printers trained to print them. Tradesmen had to be trained to build in new ways to serve purposes hitherto unknown in village life . . . One result was to facilitate the emergence of new leadership with a wider range of acceptance; and this was exercised by the European and indigenous mission hierarchy. Through this hierarchy the missionary in control exerted his authority, under conditions where very often there could be no very definite distinction between the spiritual and the secular (1965:144–145).

These commonalities may have provoked different tensions among missionary groups committed to different ecclesiastical ideals, but they also provided a set of common themes to which governments and villagers responded.

Power

"Connivance" in the face of circumstance is a factor that must be taken into account in considering how organized Christianity in Papua New Guinea has developed, but it is not the only one. Power relations between the different parties in the field must also be considered. Seventeenth century clergy in the American colonies, for example, were thrown firmly into the hands of the laity they served and this, according to Mead, was the origin of "the tendency in all transplanted churches of whatever polity to gravitate toward an actual 'congregationalism' or localism" (1956:212). As noted in Chapter 5, however, power was quite differently structured in colonial New Guinea. Missionaries were not able to shape their projects precisely according to the image they had in mind, but their position as white men in a colonial country, along with their resources and technical expertise, made them quite capable of maintaining a firm distinction between leaders and laity as their churches took form. Indeed, missionaries were further separated from "the people" than clergy at comparable levels had been at home. In contrast to Mead's ministers in America, then, missionaries in New Guinea faced special problems in bridging the distance between themselves and the people.

From Beidelman's point of view, the bureaucratic structure that mission churches developed in colonial situations is "the most important theoretical aspect of mission studies" (1974:246). The roles this structure opened to the cadre of native church workers are especially important, because their power as medial personnel could complicate and even qualify the exercise of power by the missionaries themselves. The ambiguous position of catechists in the Catholic mission in the Sepik stems partly from the missionaries'—and government officials'—recognition of this potentiality. As observed in the case of cargo cults, missionaries might instruct their catechists to denounce the prophets, but might also find themselves abandoned not only by villagers, but by the catechists as well. Even in normal times, of course, missionaries could be embarrassed or perplexed by catechists and other native church leaders on whom (officially) organized Catholicism in the villages relied.

The social and cultural distance between the expatriate leaders and the indigenous membership of mission churches has often been singled out as one of the most characteristic and sociologically significant features of Christianity in Melanesia over the years. Certainly, some of the more exotic developments among native Christians have been attributed to this distance by missionaries themselves. The proclivity of Sepik people to seek in cargo cults, *bisnis,* and even Catholicism a secret key to participation in modern times was interpreted by missionaries as evidence of a gap in knowledge, opportunity, and technique. As I have argued in Chapter 6, this concept of a "cultural gap" framed possibilities for innovative technical ministries that shifted the spiritual focus of mission work from sacrament to service in the years after World War II.

Paradoxically, however, missionaries have often found that their efforts to serve the people with whom they work have complicated some of their ecclesiastical goals—in particular, the transfer of power in the mission church to the people themselves. The problems for a clerical organization like the Roman Catholic Church in New Guinea have been especially difficult. Missionaries here have had little control over the criteria and conditions that severely limited the number of indigenous candidates to the priesthood, nor could they transfer to the laity the "magical" powers of the priest. The ecclesiastical frontier for these missionaries has amounted to a search for ways to displace the priests from their central role in other functions of the church. Although missionaries could, and did, attempt to improve the status of indigenous mission personnel, to involve the laity in pastoral work, and to endow the church with a local spirit and style, localization has remained an effort primarily directed by, and subject to the creativity of, missionaries themselves.

As I have argued in Chapter 7, missionaries' distance from the people they evangelize may have hampered their capacity to meaningfully involve local people in running the church. It may also have been a critical component of the missionaries' mystique, and the power accorded to the religion they preached (Guiart 1970; Rowley 1965:128–159; Gordon and Meggitt 1985). The extent to which village people have actively collaborated in maintaining this distance is a question that deserves to be raised. Certainly, many village Catholics in the Sepik appear to be suspicious of modern missionaries who attempt to demystify Catholic practice by softening the exotic elements that earlier missionaries had introduced. Perhaps, too, there is something in the basic structure of societies in this part of the world that gives "strangers" and their products some special potency and value that people are reluctant to give up (Simmel 1950). However that may be, it is clear that distance contributes not only to the stranger's aura of power, but to people's autonomy from strangers as well.

Because Sepik villagers, like most Melanesians, have had ample opportunity to interpret and develop Christianity according to their own lights, Catholicism in the Sepik cannot be fully understood without careful attention to the village world. My objectives in this study, however, have been limited to exploring, first, the development of a mission-church (which is not the same thing as local Christianity), and second, the experience of the missionaries themselves. I have been concerned, in other words, with agents at the highest levels of Catholic organization in the Sepik region of Papua New Guinea, and have sought to understand some of the distinctive features of their practice in terms of the tension between local imperatives and metropolitan ideals. I have, of course, attempted to specify what some of these local imperatives were, how they entered into the missionaries' discourse, and how they shaped missionary practice in the field. That Sepik people have played a major role in shaping the local imperatives to which missionaries have responded should be obvious. Yet, it should also be obvious that one cannot understand the missionaries' response without an understanding of missionary culture and society as well.

IRONIC SELF-REPRESENTATION

As Sperber and Wilson have noted, "the connection of irony with implications of failure to reach a certain standard" has long been recognized (1981:312). Certainly, critics of missionaries, including anthropologists, have never been slow to use irony to imply that missionaries have failed. Yet, part of my argument in this book has been that such critiques can themselves be treated ironically, reversing the implication from failure to success. By so doing, the challenge can be acknowledged but at the same time denied validity and force. I have attempted to show that Catholic missionaries in the Sepik have not only used irony to render their experience intelligible, but also as an argument for their project's viability in face of the odds.

Missionary Experience

The missionary stories I tell in this book bear a family resemblance to those anthropologists casually tell, but they differ from them most fundamentally by being based on stories that missionaries tell about themselves. Indeed, some of the stories I heard from missionaries in Wewak are little ironic vignettes, virtually indistinguishable from outsiders' missionary tales. "The funniest confession story I ever heard," for example, turned on a linguistic problem: a newly arrived priest without full command of New Guinea Pidgin, wondered what his colleagues were teaching about sin when a penitent told him in confession, "mi silip nating, pater". The young priest thought the poor fellow was worried about sleeping naked. In fact, he was confessing to omitting his prayers, of not remembering God.[2]

As Fussell has shown so elegantly in his study of the literature of World War I, however, irony can provide coherence to more serious stories as well. Noting the vivid images that soldiers remember from war, Fussell comments: "The very enormity of the proceedings, their absurd remove from the usages of the normal world, will guarantee that a structure of irony sufficient for ready narrative recall will attach to them" (1975:326). Although missionary work in New Guinea provided nothing as extreme (except, perhaps, during the Japanese invasion in World War II), it did provide a setting that challenged expectations for the missionaries' project based on the "the usages" of the world from which the missionaries had come. The critical difference between Fussell's images of war and the images of mission discussed in this book, however, lies in the larger story these images have been used to tell. Fussell argues that the military memory has been aided by a narrative "educing the pattern: innocence savaged and destroyed" (1975:335). I have argued that the missionary memory has been shaped by and, in turn, has given local meaning to a master narrative of the project's historical progress "from mission to church."

The extracts from missionary letters and reports that I have been able to use for the earlier periods of mission history differ little in this regard from those of other Europeans who traveled and worked in the Sepik in the years before World War II. It was quite common for writers of whatever persuasion to communicate the character of their experience through anecdotes and images that showed how extraordinary ordinary routines could become. Sometimes the contrast was made explicit: "Everywhere else you can buy everything or almost everything with money; here they don't even know what money is" (Limbrock, in Wiltgen 1969a:339-340). Sometimes the contrast was made partially or only implied: "Perhaps the South Seas is the only place where you can see a bishop in shirt-sleeves" (Marshall 1938:221); "Plans seldom materialize in New Guinea" (Angelus 1936). Whether the contrasting case was mentioned explicitly or not, however, the formula was simple and the message clear: New Guinea is a place where business does not proceed as usual, or more pointedly, as imagined or planned.

This, of course, was a situation that invited innovative response ("connivance") from both the institutions and individuals involved. One could expect normal expectations to be violated (New Guinea as "the land of the unexpected"); the ideals were an inadequate guide for work in the situation at hand. Frontier life could be a liberating experience, but it could also be unsettling when it challenged the very nature of the task one had come, or been sent, to perform. To deal successfully in the circumstances in which they had been placed, missionaries—like other colonials—had to depart in practice from some of the ideals that defined their task. Irony provided a structure in which colonists could articulate, and act on, this situation.

The political possibilities of this common descriptive strategy should be apparent. It could be used, as Margaret Mead sometimes did in her letters (1977), to critique colonial society in the region as a sham (Chapter 3). G.W.L. Townsend, an administrative officer in the Sepik in the period between the two world wars, used irony in his memoirs as a weapon against the idiocies of excessive bureaucratic regulation on the administrative field staff. Indeed, Townsend "had the reputation of being an 'outside' man, who waged a life-long war . . . with headquarters" (McCarthy 1963:64). From several of Townsend's references to the Catholic mission in the 1920s and 1930s, one is led to infer that he found the mission's way of running its business in New Guinea more effective than the government's. Bishop Loerks, for example, could manage most of his affairs without orders emanating from afar—and his priests even had horses to ride. Townsend (in his own opinion, of course) was constantly bedeviled by rules and regulations and, owing to frugality in Rabaul, had to trudge along on foot patrols (1968:95,221–222). As we have seen, however, the missionaries had uses for irony of their own.

Like Townsend, the Catholic missionaries had discovered that effective work in New Guinea required some play with the formal expectations of their sending agency. Unlike Townsend, however, whose experience led him to question the sense of "headquarter's" bureaucratic regulations in such conditions, the missionaries could not question the validity of the church without also throwing into question the validity of their project as well. Nor, of course, could they accept Margaret Mead's solution (although other outsiders did at times), and see their own attempt to constitute the church in the Sepik as a sham. The problem posed by their experience, then, was to bring together two worlds that sometimes appeared radically incompatible—New Guinea and the Roman Catholic Church.

Episcopal images were admirably suited to this task, because of the identification of the episcopal office with the church. By representing the bishop through traits that were not conventionally associated with bishops but useful in the New Guinea situation, these images bring the two worlds into productive contact, while respecting the sense of distance that the figures ultimately mask. As Frederic Jameson has noted:

> in order to act on the real, [the literary or aesthetic gesture] cannot simply allow reality to persevere in its being outside of itself, inertly, at distance; it must draw the real into its own texture. . . . The symbolic act therefore begins by producing its own context in the same moment of emergence in which it steps back over against it, measuring with an eye to its own active project [1982:74].

The argument of these images, then, is ironic—what appears to be incompatible, is ultimately compatible. The boundaries between the two worlds are blurred, as the bishop becomes represented in a single image that combines his church office and the characteristics that define his competence in the mission field.[3]

The pioneer leader of the mission had viewed the frontier as preeminently economic in nature, and the "material upbuilding" with which he responded was eventually presented by the missionaries not as a deflection from the mission's more "spiritual" tasks, but rather as a condition and sign of the mission's capacities to perform them. Joseph Loerks, the "fighting bishop" of the interwar years, renowned for his secular expertise and individualistic style, was presented not as the negation, but as the guarantee, of the mission's capacity to maintain itself as a centered religious community. The challenge to mission efficacy posed after the war by the "cultural gap" was met in part by the development of technical service ministries that were represented in the image of the "flying bishop," not as a deflection from, but as a vital addition to, the mission's spiritual work.

Stable and Unstable Irony

The concept of irony has a long history both in literary criticism and in sociological analysis. In literary criticism, the object of analysis is usually intentional irony; in sociology, the irony is most often in the eyes of the analyst, as the dilemmas of social agents and the unintended consequences of their action are unveiled. When the agents themselves apprehend their situation ironically, however, the line between sociological analysis and literary criticism begins to blur. The "sociological" side of the inquiry may establish that there were indeed ironies of situation that the agents either recognized or ignored. If they actually used these ironies to represent themselves to others, the "literary" side of the inquiry must be called into play. What have the agents meant in these representations? Do they take a clear, that is, stable, stand, or is their irony unstable, leading to a series of negations that appear to have no end (Booth

1974:240-277). My position throughout this study has been that the missionaries used stable irony as a rhetorical strategy for containing the instabilities in their situation itself.

Clearly, the mission's episcopal images fall into the general class of "intentional" irony. The defining characteristic of intentional irony, according to Booth, is an "unequivocal invitation to reconstruct" (1974:233)—in this case, to reconstruct the conventional expectations about mission work that the image (or the situation it articulates) appears to violate. Commenting on the situation eventually embodied in the image of Limbrock as "The Man of Providence," the Superior General of the SVD counseled the missionaries themselves to reconsider their opposition to Limbrock's policies and to see "this physical work [as] an honor for the first missionaries . . ." (Wiltgen 1969a:352). Father Angelus invites his former seminary colleagues to reconstruct their notion of mission community by explicitly contrasting the conventional designation of his bishop as "the father of the mission" with the bishop's preferred designation, "the servant of the servants of God" (1936). Father Mihalic, writing about "the flying bishop" for the general public, also provides straightforward instruction: "To an outsider the concept of a poor missionary flying about the countryside seems contradictory, but it is not" (1977a:29). Although I have not seen the missionaries do this themselves with the emerging image of "the feathered bishop," Chapter 7 leads with a quotation from the independent country's first prime minister, in which he invites the congregation to read the items of Sepik "inspiration" in the new college chapel as a statement that what had before been considered incompatible, now is not.

As Booth points out, however, images like those I have been discussing hardly need such glosses to be recognized as ironic, for quite without external comment, they "assert an irony in things or events that the speaker has observed and wants to share" (1974:236). The missionaries' religious culture, of course, provided them with ready models, from hagiographical formulae to biblical verse. Indeed, as Booth notes, ironic reversals are often used to express the inadequacy of our worldly expectations in the context of God's larger plan:

> But he that is the greatest among you shall be your servant. And whosoever shall exalt himself shall be abased; and he that shall humble himself shall be exalted [Matthew 23:11-12].

It is not difficult to imagine that the missionaries' episcopal imagery, and indeed many of their other ironic comments on the missionary experience in New Guinea, were dignified for audiences sensitive to this tradition by their implicit quotation of hagiographic and biblical forms.

The stability of ironic expressions is a characteristic logically distinct from their degree of openness or the "scope of 'truth revealed' " (Booth

1974:234). The examples of irony discussed in this book have been quite overt, requiring little effort on the part of competent readers (that is, those familiar with the conventions of the church) for their identification. Owing to their resonance with religious expression generally, the missionaries' ironies had a sliding scale of truth revealed. Although they referred explicitly to a local situation, they could place this situation in a larger ironic context as well. In assessing the stability of irony, the relevant question is not whether there are hidden meanings, nor how far one should interpret the meaning one finds, but "How much reason does the reader have for thinking his immediate task completed once an asserted irony has been understood or a covert irony has been reconstructed?" (1974:234). In other words, does the author stand by the reconstruction that he or she invites?

One way to phrase this question in the case of the mission's episcopal imagery is to ask whether the missionaries believed in it, or found it convincing or compelling themselves. As one critic has noted, for example, I base my case, at least for the first two images, on a very small number of sources, and mostly published sources at that (Ranger 1987:183). Ranger correctly points out that had I been able to examine a wider range of sources, in particular correspondence, I might have found more evidence of dissension within the ranks, especially concerning bishops and their policies. As was apparent in the controversy surrounding Eberhard Limbrock, this is certainly a possibility and as I have suggested, following a lead from Townsend (1968:226), some of the "earnest young and not so young Fathers who hoped to convert the whole of the population by Easter at the latest" may have found Joseph Loerks' style less than satisfactory, at best. What Ranger is suggesting is that private experience may have diverged from public imagery, and that the latter may have masked lines of division within the community that actually shaped missionary experience every bit as much as boats and planes and material tasks.

My best, if somewhat evasive, answer to this critique has been that if these public images mask internal controversies and contradictions, they do so by mentioning them, and that is precisely their point. Father Janssen, Father Angelus, Father Mihalic, and even Prime Minister Somare, whose comments on the situations and images I have reproduced above, leave their audiences (missionaries in New Guinea; seminary colleagues at home; readers of Air Niugini magazine; guests at the graduation ceremonies of St. Benedict's Teachers College) no doubt about where they stand on the issues the images mention. They negate a negation (X appears to contradict Y, but it does not), and the intended irony stops here. The audience is left on solid ground. Whether or not they choose to stand with the author–speaker image is another question, but at least a "stable reconstruction can be made out of the ruins revealed through the irony" (Booth 1974:240).

"For the determined ironist," Booth writes, "any anomaly or incongruity is ironic, and almost any phenomenon can be seen as incongruous in some light or other . . ." (1974:236). For a determined ironist, I imagine, the concept of an anthropology of missionaries is itself ironic, at least in the context of conventional expectations about the kind of people anthropologists usually study, and conventional expectations about the kind of attitude that anthropologists are supposed to evince to their subjects in the field. Given the ambivalence, if not outright antipathy, with which anthropologists often speak about missionaries and the missionary project, the ironist might expect an anthropology of missionaries to violate such expectations and, therefore, its identity as anthropology as well.

Certainly anthropologists have been slow to study not only missionaries, but also Christianity itself (Schneider and Lindenbaum 1987:1–2). Although fewer anthropologists today appear to take seriously the ironist's position, I have some concern that these two subjects of study, which should be complementary, are in danger of being constructed as competitive, instead. Terence Ranger, a historian of Christianity in Africa, for example, has objected that missionaries themselves are not an appropriate focus for studies of Christian evangelism. The *real* story, he argues is the "concealed and mysterious manner" in which local Christianity evolves.[4] After all, Ranger argues, things did not turn out as missionaries hoped or feared, and thus to understand how things turned out as they did, one must look beyond the hopes and fears they have expressed in the written record of the missionary project, and in what missionaries do and say today (1987:182). Surely, however, Christian evangelism raises many questions besides who won and who lost, however subtly one construes the result. The question I want to raise in this section is simply what anthropology, and history, can gain from the study of missionaries in the field.

The Extrinsic Value of Mission Studies

The extrinsic value of mission studies is widely recognized in the anthropological community. Simply stated, this amounts to an appreciation that scholarly work on missionaries and missions may enhance our knowledge of the history of a particular region, and of the outsiders with whom the indigenous people of that region have had to deal. Anthropologists of the Sepik region of Papua New Guinea, for example, may find it valuable to know more about when the Catholic mission's various stations were established, the relative autonomy of the station priest, the languages used in mission work, the place of native catechists in the mission system, and a host of other features of mission practice that may have impinged on the lives of villagers. What anthropologist would not welcome a study of the kinds of instruction offered in the mission's primary schools, or accounts of the kinds of religious observances missionaries have urged villagers to follow over the years? Scholarship of this type can contribute greatly to the history of the region and its people, in the most straightforward sense of the term.

At a higher level of abstraction, we may also appreciate the fact that missionaries have been not only actors in regional history, but also recorders of that history and ethnographers as well. Clearly, studies of mission historiography and ethnography can illuminate the accounts that missionaries have written and the information they contain. One would like to know more, for example, about the generic conventions that have shaped missionary writing, and also more about the special biases associated with the place of such writing in missionaries' own agendas; the authors' training, experience, and position in the mission; the audiences for whom accounts of various kinds were intended, and the use to which the writers believed they might be put. Anthropologists claim some sophistication in their use of oral literature among the indigenous people with whom they usually work. Memoirs, letters, and reports written by travelers, patrol officers, and missionaries should, of course, receive no less care.

The most obvious way in which the study of missions already has contributed to anthropological concerns, involves analysis of the role of missionaries and other colonial agents in historical events or situations. This is the strategy used by Burridge (1960) to situate cargo cults among the Tangu and Manam Islanders in the context of the triangle of power from which the cults arose, and by Lawrence (1964) in his analysis of the movement led by Yali. Burridge asks explicitly what difference various kinds of organization made in the placement of administrative officers and missionaries vis-à-vis indigenous villagers. One might explore this question further by asking, as Gordon (1983) and Gordon and Meggitt (1985) have done for the colonial administration, how organizational changes over time have affected the ways in which missionaries interact with the people among whom they work.

It should not be assumed that mission studies are relevant only to the past. Many indigenous people work both for mission organizations and as missionaries in their own right. How mission communities are formed, how relations between indigenous and expatriate personnel are managed, how mission personnel interact with people in the communities near their stations, are all questions that bear on contemporary life in Papua New Guinea and in other countries where Christian missionaries are active today. The roles Christian missions continue to play in education, transportation, communications, health care, economic development, and politics at regional and national levels also may be mentioned as an area of inquiry of interest to anthropologists whose concerns transcend village-level society itself.

The Intrinsic Value of Mission Studies

The distinction I am making between the extrinsic and intrinsic value of mission studies is akin to that frequently made in symbolic anthropology between metonymy and metaphor. The extrinsic value of mission studies comes from their contribution to our understanding of the places where missionaries have worked, the people with whom they have interacted, the events in which they have participated, the services they provide, and so forth. Because missions have been part of the scene, knowledge of them can contribute to our knowledge of the whole. The intrinsic value of mission studies has less to do with contiguity than with similarity. What can be gained by exploring missionaries and mission communities in their own right? To what aspects of the broader human condition can mission studies speak?

The first answer is that the possibilities are limited only by the investigator's sociological imagination and by empirical facts. Virtually any topic of theoretical interest can be studied in any society, missionary or otherwise, given a basis for it in the facts. Even a topic like marriage among people who do not marry—that is, Catholic missionary priests, brothers, and nuns—could be productively pursued. How does the absence of marriage affect patterns of life in the community and the way in which its members are perceived by the people among whom they work? What are the missionaries' attitudes towards the marriage customs of indigenous people? How does the rule of celibacy affect the group's capacity to draw indigenous people into positions of respect and responsibility within its ranks? Among whom do missionaries fear that the rule is most likely to be broken—their women or their men?

Because missions tend to be " 'greedy institutions,' demanding total control rather than compartmentalized conduct" (Beidelman 1982a:21), the range of topics relating to their work is correspondingly large. Missionaries' attitudes towards wealth is another example of a topic that merits further exploration. The Catholic missionaries of the SVD take a vow of poverty, but the institution they built in New Guinea was opulent by the standards of other colonial institutions along the north coast. How did this affect the way in which they were viewed by other colonists and by indigenous people? What kinds of problems did the different resources (contributions from home) of the individual priests cause within the community? How has the rule of poverty affected their capacity to recruit indigenous sisters, brothers and priests? We have, for example, already seen that after Vatican II, these missionaries were beginning to publicly question whether conventional expressions of poverty could adequately serve as witness in a culture quite different from the missionaries' own.

Although I suspect that examining such topics as marriage, wealth, not to mention authority, concepts of time, language, and aesthetics, may prove the best way to explore the culture of any mission group, it is true that their significance still derives from the group's special calling and role. Clearly, mission studies themselves have a special calling to address the issues of cross–cultural communication, the structure of colonial societies, how institutions develop, and the sociology of reform (Beidelman 1974, 1982a; Burridge 1978). It is possible, however, to speak to issues of even more general import. Almost by definition, mission studies involve the question of how people encounter the exotic, how they tolerate ambiguity in the different regions of their lives, and how they manage the contradictions that arise from living and working in an unfamiliar world.

Marshall Sahlins has suggested that: "In their practical projects and social arrangements, informed by the received meanings of persons and things, people submit these cultural categories to empirical risks" (1985:ix). Although Sahlins' claim is that culture is both reproduced and changed in the course of everyday life, his most striking cases involve the unusual event or circumstance, that is, Hawaiians' encounters with Captain Cook and later Europeans, or Maori interpretations of, and action in regard to, European settlers in New Zealand. What I am suggesting is that mission studies can also contribute to our understanding of cultural stability and cultural change. In this case, of course, the focus is not how missionaries contributed to change among the people they evangelized, but the risks to which they put their own cultural categories in their "practical projects and social arrangements" in the field. In the particular case I have presented, we have seen missionaries expose such basic categories as spiritual and material labor, hierarchy and community, ministry, and authority to relatively severe risk.

Comparative Mission Research

In the introduction to this study, I discussed some of the implications of missionary groups' different ecclesiastical ideals. Many of the topics I have suggested above could be profitably pursued through comparative research. Some obvious strategies for comparison come immediately to mind. Different mission groups working in the same region provide the opportunity to explore how one locale may be differently viewed and occupied. Conversely, the "same" mission group could be studied in different locales, for example, the SVD dioceses in Wewak and Mount Hagen. Two broadly similar groups could also be compared: Catholic SVDs in the diocese of Wewak with Catholic Franciscans, who replaced the SVDs at Aitape after World War II. Missionary groups that appear to be diametrically opposed on some critical feature might prove especially informative—that is, the congregationalist CMML and the hierarchical Catholics, or a group such as the Seventh-Day Adventists with a largely indigenous staff and a group staffed primarily by expatriates.

I have proposed both implicitly and explicitly throughout this study that much can be learned by looking for similarities and differences between different groups of outsiders on the colonial or postcolonial scene. Let me conclude by recommending once again that we emulate the aging steward on the ship that brought so many people from Sydney to New Guinea during the 1920s and 1930s, and engage in further comparisons between missionaries, government officers, traders and planters, and visiting VIPs (Chapter 3). Perhaps we could include ourselves, anthropologists, among the VIPs, but as young Father Angelus's remarks on his fellow travelers aboard a coastal steamer suggest, anthropologists have more often been viewed by others as just another occupational type on the New Guinea scene.

APPENDIX A

Wirui Services Story

(The Wirui airstrip) existed during the war as a Japanese landing ground, and after the war was filled in again and became the main landing ground airfield for Wewak, while the longer airstrip, built by the allies at Boram, was being repaired. By the time we started to operate, there was very little military traffic, but it was used rather heavily by Mandated Airlines (MAL), Gibbes Sepik Airways. We ourselves began there when the Bishop first came to Wewak, when he landed to look at the diocese. He flew here from Lae. It was a colorful beginning. He came here. Everything went well, but he loitered a bit in getting away from Wewak; then he stopped at Awar, and finally took off for Madang. This is the time they brought the jeeps out from Madang town to act as landing lights on the airstrip. It was well after dark. The Tiger Moth had no landing lights. The bishop tells that it took seven attempts before he felt he was close enough to the ground to make a landing. A hair-raising beginning to his career as a flying bishop!

When the bishop got back from the U.S. after being consecrated, he immediately started flying with an Auster. He had come by this by trading an English Dragon airplane made of fabric and wood, a bit too large, so he opted for trading it for a single-engine Auster, and this he used in the early years—1948 to 1952.

In 1952, Father Ruiter came to the mission. Father Kelly about a year before had been doing the maintenance and a bit of flying, but he had an unfortunate accident at Maprik, gave up the flying, and concentrated on the maintenance.

This appendix is based on a transcript of a tape
dictated by Father Ivo Ruiter, c. 1976.

The two of us worked together, first on one Auster, then on another, to make the plane Father Kelly had damaged airworthy again. By the time I was ready to fly we had two Austers.

As time went on, the planes became more in demand; we had more stations. So the bishop on a trip to America came across the Cessna 170, which was faster and carried a bit more than the Auster. So he purchased the one called A.V. So we had PH AV. This went on until 1954 (one Auster, Cessna 170). The bishop again on a trip to America came across the Cessna 180, which was quite a step up from the 170 (145 h.p. went up to 230 h.p.), and this seemed to be ideal for us because it had more speed, picked up a bigger load, and consequently [we] were interested in this 180. So now we had the Auster, Cessna 170 and 180, got rid of the Auster. By 1954, we had one Cessna 170 and one Cessna 180. In 1956, we acquired another Cessna 180 and that was called A.V.V. The first one we liked to call Ave Maria, and the next one Ave Virgo, and we tried to keep these names because of our blue and white colors. The planes were always blessed and sort of dedicated to our Blessed Mother by our bishop.

Although eventually all the big planes were now going to Boram, one day the DC3 got into bad weather around Boram so to our surprise we had a great big DC3 parked in front of our hangar; it looked well out-of-place beside the small Cessnas. The DC3 was out of order in landing there, but the pilot justified himself by not having fuel to go back to Madang. But it enhanced the history of our airstrip, because after DC3s were no longer allowed to land, this one did land.

Oftentimes the airstrip was very busy with MAL and Gibbes, who were operating at full strength the same time we also were operating at full strength. Had no tower, no radios, and no contact with one another, so we had to do everything by visual. Although the strip is quite flat, when there's one plane at each end, the other seems to disappear behind the horizon. Just had to line up and have a good look before we dashed off into the wild blue yonder lest we meet someone on the way. And actually this is what happened in the case of the bishop and the MAL pilot Wally Pavlovich. Wally had taken a good look and the bishop had taken a good look, but they didn't spy each other and got off to a flying run down the strip, when they sighted one another. But it was too late for either of them to abort, so as they became airborne, they gave way to the right. Wally claims, when asked what he did, that he took off his hat and said "Good day, Bishop." It was quite a close call.

Another time, the bishop was flying in from an outstation, and at that time we had a very small tower built at Wirui. The bishop was coming in normally, making his approach. In the meantime, a plane from West Irian (MAF based up there) was coming across from Boram where he'd gone through customs, and he was just doing a flip over to Wewak to the MAF hangar. He had come from one side and the bishop from the other onto the same strip. They were approaching onto the strip, the bishop above, and neither had seen the other. Fortunately, the little tower was operating and the man in the tower shouted out to the bishop, "Alpha Victor Echo, climb away in your present position," so the bishop put on power, he was by now almost down to the ground, almost piggyback on the other. I was in the hangar and wondered why the bishop was on full power. He passed our hangar and started to make another circuit and approach. He hadn't seen the other plane, so as he made his circuit, he saw it on the ground below.

Many an incident such as this has given the airstrip a bit of color. At the height of operations at Wirui, 1965, 1966, 1967, we were doing as many as fourteen departures a day from our end of the strip, and on the other was MAL and Gibbes Sepik and eventually MAF, so oftentimes we had more movements there than on any other strip in the southern hemisphere, it was so claimed. Finally MAL and Gibbes moved to Boram and made it a bit easier, and eventually air traffic control came in and made it more safe off Wirui. During the heyday there was no tower, no clearance, and we did everything by visual check. I think we have to admire the pilots who were operating at this time. Incidents there were, but no accidents.

During this time, our planes went to practically all corners of PNG. The bishop used to go down to Lae to pick up passengers, who otherwise would have to wait some days for the next DC3 to Wewak. He'd go down in the little Auster and pick up the two or three passengers. This was quite frequent. He had to refuel on the way. We didn't call at Madang, we went right down the valley to Lae and stopped at a place called Nadzab. The bishop would refuel from one or two four-gallon tins of fuel, which would be just enough to get down to Lae. Fortunately for me, by the time I was eligible to make these long cross-country flights, we had the Cessna 170, which had enough fuel to go all the way.

We used to operate down to Moresby, up to West Irian (we helped the Dutch Franciscans to start their flying operations), Vanimo, Aitape, unitl these places finally got their own airplanes, until finally off of Wirui we were operating mainly to the Western Highlands and Sepik districts.

We used to be plagued with long grass, and we used to share the expense of keeping the grass cut, but in the rainy season the grass would get long and the cutter would break down, and oftentimes we were operating in grass up to two feet tall. But DCA were not so particular, or they couldn't be because they didn't have the personnel, so by running through the grass we flattened it enough for operations. The strip was so situated and so made that it never was closed due to strip conditions. It was made well out of very strong coral and formed a permanent surface. It had a good watershed on it. Other than a few potholes that developed over the years, it remained a good coral strip. The pilots became familiar with the potholes and just landed around them; no one came to serious grief on our airstrip. Once the District Commissioner was flying, the seat of the 170 slipped back, and he lost rudder control. The plane went up a little in the air, caught a wing, and fell back on the ground—only a small accident and that's the only accident. No, there was part of an accident to an MAL plane on takeoff. One of the brakes locked and the plane went off the side of the strip into a bomb hole. Bomb holes are all around the Wirui strip.

[There was] another incident that was quite humorous but could have been tragic. After MAL and Gibbes had left, the Dragon had some sort of engine failure on takeoff from Boram but was able to continue and land at Wirui, but the brakes were not too good. It headed down the strip towards Frank Breuer's house, stopping a couple of feet before the front porch. Mrs. Breuer heard this noise, came out, opened the door, and there was the big old Dragon right straight in front of her.

Another time a Norsman (of Gibbes), a larger thing that carries about a ton of freight, single engine, developed engine trouble, tried to go back to Boram, *couldn't make it. I was just taxiing out when I heard this May Day call, looked up and saw it coming down the strip straight at me, so I taxied out of the way quickly. He landed safely.*

PASSENGERS

Cardinal Gilroy of Sydney, Bishop Thomas (Ballarat), Cardinal Manning (Los Angeles). Famous among the local people was the sanguma man victim whom the DC, Mr. Elliot Smith and myself flew out to pick up one Sunday morning after Mass—got an SOS from Telefomin—they were bringing out this man on a stretcher, he was in very much pain. I asked the patrol officer what had happened. Evidently the sanguma man (the spirit killer) had attacked this man and then left him in a practically dying condition. What had happened, they follow a ritualistic killing in that they pound slivers of bamboo into the body in various places, near to vital organs but not into them. The victim therefore does not die. He crawls back to the village where he is shunned because they know he's been attacked by the spirit killer, and if they help him, they also may suffer. This man was the 'houseboy' (looking after the food, and so forth) and the reason for his being attacked was that he had been interfering with some of the girls of the village. The government clerk got to know of him and brought him in.

I went in with the doctor and told him about this spirit killing. He said "Well, if it's bamboo we won't be able to see it under X ray, but he took an X ray anyway and saw that instead of bamboo they'd used packing-case wire—could see them very clearly. The doctor began to pull them out one at a time. They were actually pounded in and the skin pulled over so you couldn't see where they'd gone in. He took out five metal ones, and we suspected there might be three more, because there had to be eight; did some exploratories and came across two bamboos; the third one he didn't find. Maybe they didn't use three, perhaps disturbed before finishing—that man is still alive.

The time the bishop brought in a man who was just skin and bone. There was so little flesh on his face that his eyes were almost falling out of his sockets, his cheekbones were in great relief. He could hardly walk. We finally found out that he was afraid to eat because the sanguma man had threatened his life, and he thought it would be by poisoning, so he just wouldn't eat. The bishop finally convinced him to come in. In the hospital by drip feeding and so on, finally got him back to reasonable health. And he's still alive today.

Another time I brought in a man afflicted with yaws—I'm not a very heroic person around disease, especially if it shows a great deal, and this man—most of the flesh of his face was almost gone, his eyes were in the sockets but that's all. I had to bring him in from Nuku, he was moaning and groaning. I'd look back to see if he was alright, he had a dirty rag in front of his face. I wasn't game to look at him because I was afraid I'd be sick. When he got to Wirui, I said to a couple of the native fellows "helpim dispela man," but they were frightened, too. But finally we got him into hospital, and he, too, was restored to health, but of course he was scarred and had a rather ugly face.

PILOTS

Over twenty-eight to twenty-nine years we had twenty-eight pilots, all characters, all different. Of course, everything my pilots did was blamed on me. Your pilot did this, your pilot did that. The operation of Wirui became my total responsibility. Some were very good pilots, but being young and daring and looking for a thrill, they did a lot of things that I would not have done or permitted but they were done without my knowledge. One of our pilots (who later became a pilot with TAA) under the influence of a few beers when challenged by the patrol officer at Amanab, a difficult type of strip, took off and landed at this most difficult place in moonlight with no experience in night flying. I didn't hear about this until after the pilot was gone. It was told me by Gus Bottrel, the superior of the P.O. about three years later.

Another of my pilots, a very good pilot but an extrovert and a fellow who liked to show off a bit, Bob Neale from Perth who now flies for MacRobertson Miller and who had a good job, still has the same temperament, but I'm sure is well watched by his airline! This fellow was out at a station, Taway, where Ed Fitzgerald and family (they ran a timber mill) were watching the takeoff. Bob decided to buzz the family, he headed right down towards them and just pulled up over the top of them. Of course, the whole family went to the ground. Bob thought it a great joke, but Ed was so angry and immediately wrote me a letter that under no conditions was Bob Neale ever to come to the strip again. I talked it over with Bob who still thought it a great joke.

But you have to be very careful with airplanes. A story on myself! Coming from Wirui to Chambri Lakes, I took a group of photographers working for the Department of the Interior. I was demonstrating a short takeoff, and I thought I'd make it much more exciting by coming as close as possible to the photographer and his tripod, which was right off the end of the strip. Having waited too long to apply full power, I just got my plane airborne before I got to him, and as I pulled it up sharp, the wheel hit the camera, knocked the man back, cut a deep wound in the flesh above his eye (where he had the eye on the eyepiece). He was not killed, but when I got in the air, I realized I'd hit something because it was like a gunshot when I hit that camera, which went into a thousand pieces. When I did a quick turnaround to come down again, I realized that I had no brake on one side. I was able, however, to effect a landing, and a very short landing because of the tense situation, I guess. I ran back. The man was holding a cloth over his eyes, and I thought I'd knocked his eye out. Afraid to move him around, I got back in the plane (with the one brake gone because the tire had hit the camera) and flew back to Wirui, then again made a landing without the brake, picked up another plane, and raced back out to bring this man back into the hospital. The doctor ascertained that the eye was not knocked out and it might be all right, but they would have to send him immediately down south. I can't blame the pilots too much for their indiscretions. I certainly made my own. I've learned through the years that this man's eye has never fully recovered, so I feel quite responsible. But he has been able to hold his job, and hasn't sued me as he might have done.

Heinz Heitfeld. His trick was to get himself over the mountains near Wewak, the 4,000-foot Mt. Turu, and shut down the engine. Of course all the passengers would be frightened and he who was a Silver C gliding pilot (which is the highest award in gliding) used to glide the Dornier on the winds that were on top of this mountain. He'd maintain altitude and fly around, the passengers livid with fear, then after a while he'd start the engine and fly back to Wewak. I didn't hear about this until it had happened a couple of times, when one of the passengers told me about it. Then I happened to be with him one day when he said, "Hey, did you ever see this?" and he shut off the engine. I realized he was a very capable gliding pilot, so I wasn't frightened, but I was a little amazed to be flying around the top of the mountain without any power.

This same pilot was doing airdrops to an oil company on a river. Normally a pilot will drop his load from twenty feet, but he would get right down on the river bank, his wheels practically touching, then he'd shove things down. Of course, this was a dangerous maneuver because the bouncing goods that came out could hit the tail. It was told to me shortly after it happened so I took him aside and said, "Why can't you do it the way everyone else does?" And he replied, "Oh, I love to fly . . . " in his German accent.

I've had all types of pilots, tall ones, skinny ones, fat ones. One fat one was fat because he loved his grog, he used to drink a lot of beer. On one occasion he drank 18 stubbies (half size) at one sitting, then he went out and drove a car, knocking over a native woman. Fortunately he didn't hurt her very badly, but he lost his license and when I heard this I also made sure he didn't fly unless he'd been off the grog for a longer time. Anyway you can't change people's characters, and pilots are particularly hard to change. They live in a different world much of the time and consequently their outlook is a bit different from other people's.

THE GROWTH OF OPERATIONS

The growth of our operations out of Wirui is to be attributed practically entirely to Bishop Arkfeld. Over the years, the bishop has continually moved into new areas, older priests into new areas, new priests into the established places; each place that was set up, there, immediately, the bishop would have work done on an airstrip. In fact, he would pick sites that were near to possible air strips. I must say that sometimes he was desperate and picked sites that very little imitated an airstrip. And this, of course, influenced our operations from Wirui. We began to look for planes that could land short and take off short because the people live in the mountainous areas, that's where the gardens grow best. On the plain in the kunai grass, the land is not very productive, so the people over the centuries have settled in the mountain areas, in the sharp new mountains, geographically new mountains with very little space for airstrips. Consequently, to be with the people, the missionaries had to establish stations in the hills. With the two things in view, the people and transport by air, we had to establish strips wherever we could. Consequently, we are still operating off very subnormal strips, subnormal in width, subnormal in length. Some are tilted, some are pitched to a high gradient, and surprisingly, over the years we have had very few accidents.

Wirui, of course, was the starting point for all things, sort of the mother strip of all these little strips around the mission. In fact, very few of our strips would come up to the standard required for normal charter operations. Although we operate only privately into all these places, still our loadings are very precious. Missionaries, the sick and the dying, the expectant mothers—this is a whole phase in itself. The times that Wirui has brought sick people, dying people!

One very striking one was Father Schwarzer at Turubu, only eight minutes away by plane, but he had his strip (no road then), and if he had not had it he would not be alive today. One Sunday a little note came to me, written by Father himself, which was almost entirely illegible. It was evident something was wrong with him, so I jumped in a plane immediately, landed, and went inside. He came staggering out the door, he could hardly recognize me, he was delirious. I practically carried him to the plane, got back to Wewak, called the ambulance, and got him out to the hospital. Next day, the doctor told me that if I hadn't brought him in then he would have died. So that's just one instance of where the airport here and the strips established by the bishop have saved lives. In saving the life of a missionary we've saved something precious in the eyes of the church, the eyes of the diocese, and, of course, we work equally for all. The bishop's principle has always been, the passengers come first, and especially the sick come before any other consideration. Often times we've had to offload our own people to bring in a sick person.

Another story on myself. I was changing the engine in one of our Cessnas. I had completed the installation, put the cowling on, and decided to go immediately to Maprik. So I said, "Put the cargo on and I'll make a test flight around about here, and then I'll shoot off to Maprik." In those days the law was stretched a little bit at times. The tower at the big airport at Boram was in control at the time but we only called after takeoff, so after takeoff I reached for the microphone. but, because the plane had been out of service, someone had removed the microphone, so I had to land without contacting the tower. So I landed and taxied back to the hangar, and as I came back, I saw one of the workers looking under the airplane. So I looked too, asking "What's the matter?" "Sampela wara i kam daun." ("There's water coming down.")

I said, "There's no water in the airplane, that must be fuel." And sure enough here was the fuel pouring out in a steady stream from a joint which had not been tightened, and why the airplane didn't catch fire in the air I don't know. It's just one of those things that by the grace of God and somebody's prayers looking after me. Fortunately, I had to come back for the microphone or I would have been on fire over Maprik. I then analyzed what had happened. One of the brothers from Marienberg had been helping me. He had to get into one area and I had to undo the hose to let him in, put the fuel hose back and just finger tightened it with a view to going back to it, but my attention was taken away by something and I never sufficiently tightened it. The vibration loosened it enough for the fuel to come pouring out.

POLITICS

Over the years Wirui strip has been a bone of contention. The Department of Civil Aviation said "we do not want to have two airstrips" (you see, Boram is within three miles of Wirui)—too hard to control. On the other hand, we had been operating out of here, considered it our own mission strip. It was right in the middle of the mission whereas the other is about six kilometers or four miles by road from the mission and inconvenient. Everything about Wirui: it had been the safe haven for that Dragon, the Norsman that was able to land and save the pilot's life, the DC3, we used all these arguments for years, and the airstrip being our own property (or so we thought). We continued to operate there with the blessing of the head of the DCA, who was a personal friend of the bishop. So each time there was a great clatter of tongues and letters about closing the strip at Wirui, the bishop would always flash his letter from the Director of Civil Aviation in Melbourne. So everyone else eventually moved off the strip except MAF and ourselves, and we justified ourselves because we were giving MAF a place to operate, also. So we kept on this way.

Then in about 1970, we all of a sudden discovered that the airstrip was not our property, but belonged to the administration, who was free to do what they wanted with that strip. So about 1970 the correspondence began with the Wewak-But council asking to attend a meeting with a view to closing Wirui airstrip. So over these last six years there's been this gradual working of the council and the administration to get us to move. We received requests, we received mandates . . . now is the time . . . we need this . . . and of course their need became greater as they saw the possibility of getting this area as a building area. So they said "Pick out a spot at Boram and we'll lease you an area."

So I began in good faith to seek out someone to design a hangar. I asked DCA who's the best man. They said that man there. So I went to that man there in Moresby. I gave him a rough sketch. Eight months later he still did not have a sketch. So that was eight months more operation out of Wirui. And finally, when this man produced a plan, DCA said this man is not an engineer, he is a plan drawer. We had to send it to an engineer in Brisbane and this man kept it for four to five months, charged me $1,500 for putting his name at the bottom and making a few changes, and then it was eventually approved by DCA. All this time I was satisfied I would move only when the hangar was ready. I would not have our planes out in the open.

So we gradually began to organize ourselves at Boram on a piece of ground 130 feet by 150 feet. Began building with the help of Brother Rudi but after a couple of months when only the uprights and the roofing were finished, he had to leave. The hangar was sort of stopped until I came back from leave in 1975. Of course, we were still operating from Wirui (MAF had long since left.)

Brother Xavier who is to be the engineer when he gets more experience is also a carpenter and agreed to finish the building. Happily, by June 30th he was ready to have us move in. So on July 1, 1976, we'd finished at Wewak; the instrument of authorization had been cancelled and there'd be no more operation off of Wirui. So Wirui airstrip ended on June 30. The last operation was the Dornier, which I flew myself over to the hangar at Boram.

We had thought Wirui Airstrip was our property, ours to do with as we wished so long as we didn't interfere with the safety of the operations of other airplanes. We needed to observe all the restrictions about when to take off and land, and we were happy to do this so long as we could remain there. I can remember the one and only DCA representative, Tony Miskell, here saying in 1954, "We're going to close this strip." It took twenty years to carry out this threat.

APPENDIX B

Recent Historical Emphases in Roman Catholic Theology

CONCEPT OF SALVATION

Ultra-Modern: "all religions are channels of God's saving grace for men;"

Post-Vatican II: "all Christian Churches are channels of God's saving grace for men;"

Vatican II: "God's grace of salvation is equally at work within each man;"

Pre-Vatican II: "the Catholic Church is *the* medium of God's saving grace for men;"

RELATIONSHIP OF MISSION TO DEVELOPMENT

Post-Vatican II: "development is an essential part of mission work;"

Vatican II: "development is useful to show people that the Church is relevant;"

Pre-Vatican II: "development work helps the missionary to make pastoral contact with people," or "it has no direct connection with missionary work, but it can be useful;"

Extremely Pre-Vatican II: "development work is dangerous, it distracts the missionary from his real work;"

CONCEPT OF CHURCH

Extreme Post-Vatican II: "the prophetic critic of society and culture;"

Post-Vatican II: "the pilgrim in this world, a servant of mankind's total needs;"

As defined by Arbuckle 1978:283–284.

Vatican II: "the people of God, intimately related with Christ; the Church is a sacrament or sign of man's union with God and with each other;"

Pre-Vatican II: "the Church, as mediator of God's grace and truth to men, is the *only* true way to salvation;"

More Traditional: "The Church is a perfect religious society organized under the Pope and Bishops;"

THEOLOGY OF MINISTRY

Post-Vatican II: "a Christian minister is someone who has been authorized by the people of God to build the Christian community, lead it to its celebration of the sacraments, and inspire it to share actively in the world's concerns;"

Vatican II: "the minister is someone whose fundamental obligation is to spread Christ's Gospel and to administer the sacraments to the faithful;"

Pre-Vatican II: "the Christian minister is someone ordained to the priesthood and thereby authorized to celebrate the Eucharist and administer the sacraments of Penance and anointing of the sick;"

PURPOSE OF MISSIONARY ACTIVITY

Post-Vatican II: "to help man develop his own resources to fulfill total human needs, i.e. religious, economic, educational, political;"

Vatican II: "to be witness of God's love, preach and form the Church among people who do not yet know about Christ;"

Pre-Vatican II: "to convert people to the Catholic Church through preaching, teaching, catechism, administering the sacraments."

Notes

I. INTRODUCTION

Ethnography in the Ironic Mode

1. As Petersen (1980:173) has pointed out, this picture may be not only dated but also stereotypical. In objecting to the views of Stipe (1980) on this matter, Petersen notes: "Among the anthropologists who currently work in the part of the Pacific I know, Micronesia, I have encountered no one without both negative and positive attitudes toward missionaries. We all rely upon their documents; we are all familiar with and lament the changes they have had a hand in; and we are all acquainted with one or another of the wise and humane men and women who serve in the missions there today. Fools and charlatans are there as well, but most of my colleagues manage to discriminate among them . . . . I am not at all sure to (or about) whom [Stipe] is speaking, for anthropologists are at least as heterogeneous a lot as missionaries." Still, however heterogeneous a lot anthropologists who work in Micronesia may be, and however complex their attitudes, Petersen claims that they "all . . . lament" the changes in which missionaries have been involved.

2. Louis J. Luzbetak, an anthropologist *and* a member of the Society of the Divine Word, considers this a problem of differing world views. "Absolute cultural relativists reject Christian missionary action outright. Their argument is simple enough: One culture is as good as another, and each culture must be judged by its own standards, within its own context and as an organic whole. Consequently, no society, Christian or otherwise, has the right to disturb this sacred wholeness . . . Missionaries 'impose' their 'unprovable' values on unwill-

ing, unwitting, and usually defenseless individuals and societies; missionaries 'destroy' cultures and 'deprive' societies of their self-respect" (1985:7). Luzbetak sees nothing but an impasse deriving from this position, but also sees possibilities for dialogue between anthropologists who take the less extreme position of "relative cultural relativism" (1985:7-12).

3. As Clifford points out, this move was accompanied by the emergence of "a subgenre of ethnographic writing . . . , the self-reflexive 'fieldwork account.' In this subgenre, the "ironic self-portrait" is used as the principal "textual strategy" through which to explore problems inherent in the "ethnographic experience and the participant-observation ideal" (1986:14).

4. In 1966, Wewak had a population of 7,967 indigenous people, some 76 percent of whom (6,148) claimed to be Catholic (Bureau of Statistics (1966:44). In that same year, the East Sepik Province as a whole had a population of 156,000, of whom 70 percent were reported by the Bureau of the Census to be Catholic.

2. THE FORMATION OF A COLONIAL FRONTIER

1. Laycock concludes his survey of Sepik languages by noting that "the area [bounded on the east and west by the Ramu River and the West Irian border and extending from the islands off the coast to the north and to the Highlands fringe in the south] must rank as one of the most linguistically complex in the world. A total of 214 languages are listed, out of an estimated total of 750 for the whole of Papua New Guinea—this is for a land area that is only about one-fifth of the whole, and containing only about one-seventh of the population. This means that the language/population ratio is around 2,000 speakers per language, or about half of the average for the rest of the Territory. In the heavily populated Lumi area, the language/population ratio drops to half that again, to around 1,000 speakers per language; while down the border area of West Irian, we reach the low figure of around 500 speakers per language. It is only the large languages of the Maprik area (Abelam approximately 40,000 speakers, Boiken approximately 31,000 speakers) that prevent the Sepik language figures from degenerating into complete incredibility" (1973:54).

2. Although no one has questioned the general significance of trade in the Sepik, ethnohistorical research has raised questions concerning the historical depth of the particular pattern sketched here. Allen, for example, argues that in the Dreikikir area, north-south trade followed rather than preceded colonial contact (1984:6; 1976); while Gewertz has argued that marketing arrangements among the Iatmul and Sawos, on the one hand, and among the Chambri and Hills people on the other, developed in relatively recent times from "more traditional trading partnerships" (1983:49).

3. See Höltker 1941:205, fn. 1, for discussion of the interest accorded to young *pinistaim* laborers in the 1930s in the hill region behind the coast in the neighboring district of Madang.

4. Sources are not entirely clear on the number of administrative field staff over the years. Lucy Mair cites Ainsworth's figures for 1924 of "sixteen district and twelve deputy district officers, with an unspecified number of patrol officers," and also states that the number "steadily expanded till in 1933 it numbered seventy-six. After that date figures were not published" (1970:35). Stephen Reed states that "the total number of European field-staff officers in 1922 was forty-

one. In 1937 the number had been increased to seventy-three." The information is attributed to personal communication from E.W.P. Chinnery, a former Director of District Services and Native Affairs (1943:166 and fn.28).

5. Sturgeon's estimate appears to refer exclusively to the Aitape District, a short-lived administrative jurisdiction created in 1924 and abolished in 1933. The Aitape District encompassed the area north of the Sepik river while the Sepik District, from which it was first separated and to which it was later rejoined, covered the Sepik River and the area to the south. It is probably not a coincidence that the separation of the Sepik and Aitape districts was made just as the Australian administration initiated its first serious attempt to pacify the river people and open the area to recruitment, and ended shortly after the administration's success was signaled by signs of overrecruitment in many river villages.

3. THE CATHOLIC MISSION AND ITS MATERIAL BASE

1. This opinion was shared by Townsend, but not by the thrifty administrators in Rabaul who refused to give Townsend funds for the purchase of his own horse (1968:114).

2. According to Fischer, "The economic establishments were to be only a means to an end, and the end was the salvation of pagan souls. The superior general frequently emphasized this point in his letters to the superior of the mission . . . ." (1925:397).

4. HIERARCHY AND THE MISSION STATION SYSTEM BETWEEN THE WARS

1. Sterr writes that during the war years "the mission made gratifying progress . . . . Ten new stations were built, even though the band of missionaries could not be reinforced . . . ." (Sterr 1950:183). My table shows seven new stations instead of ten. The difference may be owing to the fact that while Hagspiel visited the mission in 1922, Sterr appears to include stations founded up through 1925. It is also possible, of course, that Hagspiel simply did not mention some of the newer stations on his route.

2. According to Harris, Schmidt's degenerationism was a way of "reconciling the findings of anthropology with scriptural precedent . . . . His immense, twelve-volume *Der Ursprung der Gottesidee* (Origin of the Idea of God) was wholly given over to the proof that those cultures most nearly approximating the condition of the primitive hunting and gathering *Kreis* possessed a purer and more ethical understanding of the nature of God . . . . The most perfect phase of religion existed at the very outset of prehistory, for religion was given to man by God in a revelation, the memory of which became more and more distorted and confused as time wore on . . . ." (1968:391).

3. This idea has its roots in the social philosophy of medieval Catholicism, particularly as developed by Thomas Aquinas, the thirteenth century scholastic philosopher, and his followers. The heart of Thomist social philosophy was that "the individual parts [of the social system] are not independently related to the altruistic values and principles; they are related to them only through the medium of a whole, in which externally they are bound together . . . " (Troeltsch 1981:275). It was Troeltsch's opinion that "until the present day [c. 1908–1911] Thomism is the great fundamental form of Catholic social philosophy"

(1981:277). I am grateful to William Burrows for bringing this point to my attention.

4. A fuller account of Father Ross's activities in the highlands is available in Mennis (1982).

5. The Australians' confusion concerning Loerks' demeanor may have had a basis in fact: Townsend informs us that "Loerks had originally been a naval cadet in Germany before he decided to seek Holy Orders . . . " (1968:224).

6. There is some ambiguity about whether the name on this document, Father Angelus, refers to its author, or to the person who later donated the letter to the mission's files. For the purposes of this book, I have assumed the former.

5. MISSIONARIES IN BETWEEN
The Colonial "Triangle," Cargo Cults, and the War

1. According to Tiesler, who cites as his source an official report of 1900, there were twenty-four Europeans in the whole north coast region in 1899, eighteen of whom were in the Aitape region, one in Dallmanhafen (perhaps seeing to the business of the small plantation and trading post mentioned above), and five near the mouth of the Ramu River. This report noted ten stations in the same area: at Arop, Vokau, Paup, Suain, Jakamul, Forr (?), Dallmanhafen, Tarawai, Walis and Angel Island, the latter being a fishing station. These stations were reported to be manned by three Chinese, eleven Javanese, and 26 "Melanesians" (Tiesler 1969–70:118).

2. The earliest recruiting voyages that Tiesler found recorded for this area were in 1893, 1894, and 1895 (1969–70:116–117). A smallpox epidemic in 1895 is reported to have had severe effects on villages farther to the west. Tiesler suspects that the disease may have been carried there by one of the early recruiting vessels (1969-70:124, n.94).

3. In a court case of 1958, one native witness recalled that when the mission bought the land for its station in Wewak (probably referring to its first purchase in 1911), he had been a youngster of less than seven years, and his "elder brother" had been *luluai* (East Sepik Provincial Office, Land Files 1958).

4. According to Tiesler's reading of older studies and reports, the coastal villages of the Boiken-speaking people extended from the village of Kauwi in the west to the village of Brandi in the east—a distance of approximately fifty-five kilometers. The western part of this area was lightly settled (possibly only four villages) but east of Wom was a densely settled twenty-five kilometer strip, including the villages of Menga, Saure, Wewak, Kreer, Boram, Magon, Moem, Sauwaring, and Brandi. Tiesler says that most of these villages were "directly on the coast" (1969–70: 133).

5. A "slight outbreak of influenza" was reported for the Aitape area in January 1930 (Commonwealth of Australia 1931:47).

6. Father John Tschauder, SVD, tells me that three facts can help explain "why the missionaries, most of whom were German, were given such a bad treatment by the Japanese." First, "The Japanese Forces, when they occupied New Guinea . . . had come into contact with Missionaries in the Solomon Islands who did not observe strict neutrality. Hence the announcement by the Japanese Officer that they had strict 'orders to lock up all Europeans.' This was said to Bishop Wolf in December 1943." Second, "The Australian Government had interned and taken to

Australia all Lutheran Missionaries of German nationality at the very beginning of the war, while of all the Catholic German Missionaries in the whole of New Guinea only nine were removed to Australia, two of whom were not even Germans." Third, "The Japanese found this out, and from their military point of view the conclusion was obvious, and it was further confirmed by the pronounced uncooperative attitude of the German Catholic Missionaries whom the Japanese found in New Guinea . . . from Lae to Wewak when they landed there on December 18, 1942. The Japanese said that we had been deliberately left behind by the Australians so we could 'spy on them' " (personal communication, 25 May 1986).

7. Father Tschauder, who was one of the Alexishafen missionaries to survive the war, writes that "some now doubt the manner and circumstances" under which Bishop Loerks and his group of missionaries disappeared. Although the account that I present above has long been accepted, Father Tschauder states that "In the Australian Archives . . . there seems to be evidence that the Captain of the *Akikaze* never received from his Headquarters in Rabaul an order to 'rid the ship of all Europeans by killing them.' " Father Tschauder believes that the *Akikaze* may instead have "set out on westward course" (personal communication, 25 May 1986).

8. Concerning the Alexishafen missionaries, Father Tschauder notes that the Captain of the *Yorishime Maru* refused the missionaries' request to be allowed to take shelter in the hold, because if bombs were to hit the ship, the missionaries would not have had a chance to escape (personal communication, 25 May 1986). The name of this ship, by the way, is given as the *Dorish Maru* by Brother Gerhard in the article published in *Wantok* (1974).

6. THE FLYING BISHOP
Technical Ministries and the Cultural Frontier

1. Transcript of Father Ruiter's text contained in Appendix A.
2. According to Paul de Man, "Classical rhetoric generally classifies synecdoche as metonymy, which leads to difficulties characteristic of all attempts at establishing a taxonomy of tropes; tropes are transformational systems rather than grids. The relationship between part and whole can be understood metaphorically, as is the case, for example, in the organic metaphors dear to Goethe. Synecdoche is one of the borderline figures that create an ambivalent zone between metaphor and metonymy and that, by its spatial nature, creates the illusion of a synthesis by totalization" (1979:63, n.8).
3. In 1976 and 1977, Leo Arkfeld was officially the Archbishop of Madang, but was still serving as acting Bishop of Wewak until a successor could be appointed.
4. Although the first official trip in April 1955 had taken four days, by the fall of 1956 the *Pacific Islands Monthly* had been able to report a feat of driving in which the time of travel had been reduced to ten hours (1956a).
5. Gesch reports that a branch of Yauiga's movement had been "under the inspiration" of an ex-police sergeant of the same name (Beibi) as the founder of Peligo settlement (1985:24).
6. Gesch notes that Leo Arkfeld's thinking on cargo cults changed during the course of the Peli Movement, the most widely studied and most highly publicized cult that had taken place during his tenure as bishop. Arkfeld's first pastoral letter

on the matter, written for distribution within the diocese on 15 May 1971, included the following passage:

> It seems we should try to explain the matter as best we can to the people. We must, however, be careful not to hurt the peoples' sensibilities and their national pride, but it seems we should remind them again and again of the serious consequences of the situation when all fails . . .
> May I close by asking all to pray earnestly that this latest move of the Devil in our Mission be broken . . . If the whole Wewak Mission seriously starts praying and sacrificing against this evil power . . . then the power of God would come into operation [Gesch 1985:66].

Gesch reports that in a second pastoral letter, written two weeks later, the Bishop quoted an anthropologist, Hermann Janssen, who warned missionaries against seeing in cargo cults a "direct evil influence" (1985:66). Gesch also notes that in an interview with Arkfeld in 1981, in which he asked directly about "the matter of Satan's control," Arkfeld replied:

> I wouldn't say that now. Satan might have used the thing of course, but I would keep clear of that now. Because it's just a natural phenomenon based on a human being. Apparently it comes up in all kinds of forms all over the world. It comes up in our society in different forms [Gesch 1985:66–67].

7. Father John Tschauder writes that "The sudden American invasion after World War II, was indeed what we call in German a Zasur, it was the end of one essential aspect of Church History: TRADITION" (personal communication, March 12, 1986). The New Cassels German dictionary defines "zasur" as "caesura," which is, literally, a break in rhythm in music or in verse.

8. In the preface to a book published in 1950 about the SVD's New Guinea field, the editor notes that "It was not easy to find pictures . . . . Current photographs of the destroyed mission are scarce. To my request for pictures of the mission, one missionary replied 'Where nothing exists, it cannot be photographed!'" (Sterr 1950:6).

9. Gesch notes that in January 1977 villagers in the Negrie area, where the Morman-Godfrey movement took place in the early 1960s, "became excited once again by Godfrey's 'work' . . . . There was a minor religious revival at Negrie to help people get in a holy state . . . . For a while Godfrey insisted on a rather startling discovery, despite his many years of service to the Church. His insight was presented to me one day in his home village of Parina: 'This nun coming towards us now is Maria. Bishop Leo is Jesus; the Pope is God; and the priests are the angels of God.' This theory was often propounded despite strong renunciations by the bishop and the priests" (1985:125).

10. I do not know whether or not the situation with Father Morman had contributed to this policy. It is nonetheless worth mentioning that Father Morman remained a figure of note in the Negrie area even after his departure for the coast. According to Gesch, enthusiasts from Negrie intended to gather at Hawain, where both Morman and Godfrey were stationed in 1977, "to revive the previous hope in the good times" (1985:125). Godfrey died in October 1977, and "in a tribute to his long-time close friend, Willie Morman proposed that the revival . . .

take place at Negrie . . . . [He] addressed the elders privately and said, 'If you drop sorcery and cease disputing, then the good times will surely come.' I suspect that the orthodox church teaching had definite eschatological significance for those who heard it" (Gesch 1985:124–125).

7. THE CATHOLIC MISSION AND THE LOCAL CHURCH

1. The positions defined by Arbuckle (1978) are listed in Appendix B.
2. Judging by names and by status and affiliation, it is unlikely that more than three or four of the thirty members of the mission staff whose nationality I did not obtain, were Papua New Guineans. One of the Marist Brothers and three of the Christian Brothers were Papua New Guineans in 1975. The four seminarians whose nationalities are unknown to me are probably from overseas, judging by their names.
3. Father Dambui's position, it should be made clear, was itself somewhat ambiguous. Originally from one of the Iatmul villages on the middle Sepik River, Father Dambui was ordained in 1975; when I first arrived in Wewak in June 1976, Father Dambui was the diocese's first, and only, native priest. As a diocesan priest (as opposed to being a member of the SVD), and as a Papua New Guinean priest (as opposed to being one from overseas), Father Dambui could be considered an insider with an outsider's credentials. For practical purposes, however, the balance tips towards the outsider direction, for when I met Father Dambui, he was on temporary leave from church duties to serve as the Acting Premier of the East Sepik Province, an office created (and only temporary until elections could be held) by the new national government's decentralization plan.
4. I was told by another priest that the Mass was changed to New Guinea Pidgin in 1967 or 1968, and that hymns based on indigenous songs and chants had made their first appearance in 1962. This priest thought resistance to the change in communion, which had previously been offered on the tongue, but was now offered in the hand, came from indigenous conceptions of purity and pollution. The priest, because he was unmarried, was categorized as pure, and people could participate in his purity by receiving communion on the tongue. This benefit was lost, however, when people had to receive the communion wafers in their own "impure" hands.
5. Smith notes that recent changes in mission Catholicism have been seen by some village Catholics as an attempt to prevent them from access to "the truth." In the village of Koragur on Kairiru Island, in the mid-1970s, one "member of the village Legion of Mary tells how in the past villagers were told that if they prayed with sufficient diligence they would be able actually to see Jesus and the Virgin but that now thay are told that the best they can hope for is an indirect manifestation of their power. This village Legion member sees the Mission as abandoning the work of God and of the Legion—that is, the work of diligent prayer and religious observance . . . . Certain individuals, more extreme, interpret these trends as evidence of conscious deception on the part of the Mission in order to maintain its monopoly of the true power and knowledge of Catholicism. As one such villager says, 'They want to deceive us . . . they don't want us to gain knowledge . . . They think that we've come too close to God and its better that they misdirect us now . . . Before, the fathers were more truthful' " (1980:44).
6. It must be noted that one of the leaders of the Peli Association ran for national

office in the critical elections of 1972 and won an impressive victory over the father of the Provincial Commissioner himself (May 1982:49–53).

7. This idea is evident in what the diocese's director of catechetical training described to me as the mission's new "ideal of recruitment:" catechists should come from, and be chosen by, local village communities themselves. Although he noted that this would lead to variation in the educational backgrounds of the catechists thus selected, he considered the gain greater than the loss. Although the diocese's new catechetical program was not universally approved by all the priests, acceptance had been facilitated by the fact that it was based on recommendations from Rome. Indeed, I was told that some elements of the new program in the Diocese of Wewak had already been adopted by the SVD dioceses of Madang and Goroka as well.

8. Parratt has argued that "the decline in formal religion in the town . . . may be attributable to the village orientation of the average migrant and to his feeling that he still belongs to his village church even while living in the town" (1975:183).

9. It should be noted that one attempt to do so through the development of the deaconate had come to grief, so I was told, when Rome disapproved the plan.

10. Michael Smith's observations on Catholicism in Kragur village on Kairiru Island are relevant to this point. Villagers here contrast gift-giving relationships (morally good) with money transactions, noting that "missionaries had preached to them that excesive concern with money was sinful—and that to give things away without thought of reward, to *givim nating* in Pidgin, was also a custom with deep indigenous roots" (1987:11). Yet Smith also notes that "Villagers seem to be untroubled by the fact that delayed reciprocity is not exactly the same as ideal Christian charity, which expects no return. While it is clear that it is delayed reciprocity, not bottomless charity, that rules in practice, villagers often speak of the indigenous norm as though it were actually analogous to the Christian ideal" (1987:25, fn.4).

8. THE BISHOPS' PROGRESS
Summary and Conclusions

1. Among the definitions for "connivance" listed in the Oxford English Dictionary, those closest to the meaning I suggest here are "to dispense covertly *with;*" and "to wink at, overlook, tacitly permit, pass over (a fault or offense)." The OED lists both meanings as obsolete: I have borrowed the term from an historian, Sidney Mead (1956), who in turn, borrowed it from 17th century churchmen in America.

2. Michael Smith (1987:14) reports that "failure to pray regularly" is listed as a sin "one should reveal to the confessor" in a 1968 New Guinea Pidgin version of the Prayer Book and Hymnal for Catholic Natives of New Guinea.

3. I am indebted to Fernandez (1986) for the phrase, and concept, of an "argument of images."

4. A fine example of the way in which "concealed" processes might have affected the history (that is, "evolution") of Christianity in the Sepik can be found in a recent study of the history of initiation in the southern foothills of the coastal range. Roscoe and Scaglion (1984) have argued that those communities that gave up initiation rites in the colonial period (for whatever combination of reasons, including the press of labor migration), tend to be those among whom the rites were arranged so as not to require the reciprocation of initiation services at a later

date. Structural features like these may have influenced the kind of impact missionary teaching has had, quite apart from missionaries' knowledge of the intricacies of initiation sequences in the villages, or their attitudes towards initiation at all.

Appendixes

1. Father Ivo Ruiter has graciously permitted me to include this transcript as an appendix to this work (personal communication, 25 Feb. 1986).
2. Arbuckle acknowledges "the assistance provided by the Society of the Divine Word Self-Study Survey, Rome" in formulating the emphases listed here (1978:298, n.2).

Bibliography

Allen, Bryant J.

1976   Information Flow and Innovation Diffusion in the East Sepik District, Papua New Guinea. Ph.D. diss., Australian National University, Canberra.

1984   The Importance of Being Equal: The Colonial and Post-Colonial Experience in the Torricelli Foothills. Paper prepared for Wenner Gren Symposium no. 95, "Sepik Research Today." (In Press)

Andriolo, Karin R.

1979   *Kulturkreislehre* and the Austrian Mind. *Man* 14:133–144.

Angelus, Fr.

1936   Unpublished letter from Tumleo Island, Feb. 20, 1936. Bishop's Office, Diocese of Wewak. Mimeo.

Anonymous

1980   An Official Journey to the Eastern Part of the Aitape District in 1907. *Oral History* 8 (2):109–120.

Anonymous Missionary

1932–33   Die Ernte am Sepik reift. *Steyler Missionsbote* 60:11–12. (Summarized in Höltker 1940–41:40)

APR

    1943–44 *Aitape Patrol Report No. 4, 1943–44.* District Office, Wewak.

Arbuckle, Gerald A.

    1978   The Impact of Vatican II on Marists in Oceania. In *Mission, Church, and Sect in Oceania,* edited by J. A. Boutilier, D. T. Hughes, and S. W. Tiffany, 275–99. Ann Arbor: University of Michigan Press.

Arkfeld, Leo

    n.d.   Letter to "Dear friends of Wewak." Bishop's Office, Diocese of Wewak. Mimeo.

Asad, Talal, ed.

    1973   *Anthropology and the Colonial Encounter.* New York: Humanities Press.

Baar, Wilhelm van

    1931–32 Ein ganz eigentümlicher Vorgang. *Steyler Missionsbote* 59:127–128. (Summarized in Höltker 1940–41:58)

Bader, Otto

    1935–36 Im Dunkel des Heidentums. *Steyler Missionsbote* 63:287–288. (Summarized in Höltker 1940–41:57)

Ballard, J. A.

    1972   The Politics of Localization in Papua New Guinea. Paper presented at the seminar on the politics of bureaucracy, Dept. of Political Science, RSSS, Australian National University, Canberra, 1 Nov. 1972.

Barnett, Steve and Martin G. Silverman

    1979   *Ideology and Everyday Life: Anthropology, Neomarxist Thought, and the Problem of Ideology and the Social Whole.* Ann Arbor: University of Michigan Press.

Barrett, Don

    1969   The Pacific Islands Regiment. In *History of Melanesia.* Second Waigani Seminar, Port Moresby, 493-502. Canberra: Australian National University Press.

Barthes, Roland

    1972   *Mythologies.* New York: Hill and Wang.

Bartholomaus, Br.

    1932–33 (Notice.) *Steyler Missionsbote* 60:107-108. (Summarized in Höltker 1940–41: 23, 36-37), translated by John Tschauder in

"Cargo Cult Activities at Kaiep in the 1930's," *Oral History* 8 (1980):88–89.

Basso, Keith H.
  1979   *Portraits of 'the Whiteman': Linguistic Play and Cultural Symbols among the Western Apache.* Cambridge: Cambridge University Press.

Beidelman, T. O.
  1971   *The Kaguru: A Matrilineal People of East Africa.* New York: Holt, Rinehart and Winston, Inc.

  1974   Social Theory and the Study of Christian Missions in Africa. *Africa* 44 (3):235–249.

  1981   Contradictions between the Sacret and the Secular Life: The Church Missionary Society in Ukaguru, Tanzania, East Africa, 1876–1914. *Comparative Studies in Society and History* 23 (1):73–95.

  1982a   *Colonial Evangelism: A Socio-Historical Study of an East African Mission at the Grassroots.* Bloomington: Indiana University Press.

  1982b   The Organization and Maintenance of Caravans by the Church Missionary Society in Tanzania in the Nineteenth Century. *The International Journal of African Historical Studies* 15:601–623.

  n.d.   Early Women Missionaries in the Church Missionary Society in Ukaguru, German East Africa. Manuscript.

Booth, Wayne C.
  1974   *A Rhetoric of Irony.* Chicago: The University of Chicago Press.

Bornemann, Fritz.
  1975   *Arnold Janssen: Founder of Three Missionary Congregations, 1837–1909: A Biography.* Manila: Arnoldus Press.

Brandewie, Ernest
  1985   Ethnology and Missionaries: The Case of the Anthropos Institute and Wilhelm Schmidt. In *Missionaries, Anthropologists, and Cultural Change,* edited by Darrell L Whiteman, 369–86. Studies in Third World Societies, Publication Number 25. Williamsburg, Va.: Department of Anthropology, College of William and Mary.

Braukaemper, Ulrich
  1979   The Enigma of the Austrian Mind. *Man* 14:560–561.

Brookfield, H. C.
  1972   *Colonialism, Development and Independence: The Case of the Melanesian Islands in the South Pacific.* Cambridge: The University Press.

Brouwer, Leo
1969   Catechists for New Guinea. *The Word in the World, 1969. New Guinea: A Report on the Missionary Apostolate*, 119–123. Techny, Ill.: Divine Word Publications.

Bureau of Statistics
1966   *Territory of Papua and New Guinea, Population Census 1966.* Preliminary Bulletin No. 31: East Sepik District and Wewak Urban Area. Konedobu, Papua: Bureau of Statistics.

1971   *Papua New Guinea, Population Census 1971.* Population Characteristics. Bulletin No. 13: East Sepik District. Port Moresby: Bureau of Statistics.

1976   Papua New Guinea National Population Projections by Provinces, and National Population Projections by 8 Major Urban Centres. Port Moresby: Population Section of the PNG Bureau of Statistics. Mimeo.

Burke, Kenneth
1965   *Permanence and Change: An Anatomy of Purpose.* Indianapolis: The Bobbs-Merrill Company, Inc.

1969   *A Grammar of Motives.* Berkeley: University of California Press.

Burridge, Kenelm O. L.
1960   *Mambu: A Melanesian Millennium.* London: Methuen & Co. Ltd.

1969   *New Heaven, New Earth.* Oxford: Basil Blackwell.

1978   Missionary Occasions. In *Mission, Church, and Sect in Oceania*, edited by J. A. Boutilier, D. T. Hughes, and S. W. Tiffany, 1–30. Ann Arbor: University of Michigan Press.

Burrows, William R.
1980   *New Ministries: The Global Context.* Maryknoll, N.Y.: Orbis Books.

1985   Tensions in the Catholic Magesterium about Mission and Other Religions. *International Bulletin of Missionary Research* 9:2–4.

Clifford, James
1982   *Person and Myth: Maurice Leenhardt in the Melanesian World.* Berkeley: University of California Press.

1984   Encounters with the Exotic. *The Times Literary Supplement*, June 22, 1984, pp. 683–684.

1986   Introduction: Partial Truths. In *Writing Cultures: The Poetics and Politics of Ethnography*, edited by James Clifford and George E. Marcus, 1–26. Berkeley: University of California Press.

Clifford, James and George E. Marcus, eds.

1986   *Writing Culture: The Poetics and Politics of Ethnography.* Berkeley: University of California Press.

Commonwealth of Australia

1923   *Report ot the League of Nations on the Administration of the Territory of New Guinea from 1st July 1921, to 30th June, 1922.* Victoria: Government of the Commonwealth of Australia.

1925   *Report to the League of Nations on the Administration of the Territory of New Guinea from July 1st, 1923, June 30th, 1924.* Geneva: League of Nations.

1926   *Report to the League of Nations on the Administration of the Territory of New Guinea from 1st July, 1924, to 30th June, 1925.* Victoria: Government of the Commonwealth of Australia.

1931   *Report to the Council of the League of Nations on the Administration of the Territory of New Guinea from 1st July, 1929, to 30th June, 1930.* Canberra: Government of the Commonwealth of Australia.

1932   *Report to the Council of the League of Nations on the Administration of the Territory of New Guinea from 1st July 1930, to 30th June, 1931.* Canberra: Government of the Commonwealth of Australia.

Coser, L. A.

1974   *Greedy Institutions.* New York: Free Press.

Curtain, Richard

1977   The Structure of Internal Migration in Papua New Guinea. Paper presented at A.N.Z.A.A.S., September 1, 1977.

1980   Dual Dependence and Sepik Labour Migration. Ph.D. diss., Australian National University.

Curtain, Richard and May, Ron

1979   Wewak. In *The Urban Household Survey: Town Profiles,* edited by R. J. May, 52-67. IASER Monograph 12. Boroko, PNG: Institute of Applied Social and Economic Research.

De Man, Paul

1979   *Allegories of Reading: Figural Language in Rousseau, Nietzche, Rilke, and Proust.* New Haven: Yale University Press.

Diocese of Wewak

1975   Response to Questionnaire from the National Missionary Council Resource Center. Bishop's Office, Diocese of Wewak. Mimeo.

1976   Mission Directory (May 1976). Bishop's Office: Diocese of Wewak.
        Mimeo.

Divine Word Missionaries
    1969   Divine Word Missionaries in New Guinea. *The Word in the World
            1969, Divine Word Missionaries: New Guinea: A Report on the
            Missionary Apostolate*. Techny, Ill.: Divine Word Publications.

Downs, Ian
    1980   *The Australian Trusteeship of Papua New Guinea: 1945–1975*.
            Canberra: Australian Government Publishing Service.

East Sepik District
    1966–67 *Annual Report 1966–67*. District Office, Wewak.

East Sepik Provincial Office, Land Files
    1958   Hearing of Claims by the Mission of the Holy Ghost (New Guinea)
            Property Trust and the Mission of the Divine Word (Central New
            Guinea) Property Trust to Freehold of Birue, Portion 16. 23 June
            1958.

Eckert, Georg
    1940   Prophetentum und Kulturwandel in Melanesien. *Baessler Archiv*
            23:26–41.

Erdweg, Josef
    1919–20 (Notice). *Steyler Missionsbote* 47:61. (Summarized in Höltker
            1940–41:9)

Falding, Harold
    1968   *The Sociological Task*. Englewood Cliffs, N.J.: Prentice-Hall.

Faulkner, T. A.
    1967   Bishop (Canon Law). *New Catholic Encyclopedia*. Vol. 2:586–588.
            New York: McGraw Hill Book Co.

Ferguson, James J.
    1984   A Paradigm Shift in the Theology of Mission: Two Roman Catho-
            lic Perspectives. *International Bulletin of Missionary Research*
            8:117–119.

Fernandez, James W.
    1964   The Sound of Bells in a Christian Country–in Quest of the Histori-
            cal Schweitzer. *The Massachusetts Review*, Spring 1964, pp. 537–
            562.

    1986   The Argument of Images and the Experience of Returning to the
            Whole. In *The Anthropology of Experience*, edited by Victor W.

Turner and Edward M. Bruner, 159–187. Urbana, Ill.: University of Illinois Press.

Firth, Stewart G.
1972   The New Guinea Company, 1885–1899: A Case of Unprofitable Imperialism. *Historical Studies* 15:361–377.

1976   The Transformation of the Labour Trade in German New Guinea, 1899–1914. *Journal of Pacific History* 11:51–65.

1977   Review Article: German Rule: Ideology and Practice. *Journal of Pacific History* 12:238–241.

1982   *New Guinea under the Germans.* Melbourne: Melbourne University Press.

Fischer, Herman
1925   *Life of Arnold Janssen: Founder of the Society of the Divine Word and of the Missionary Congregation of the Servants of the Holy Ghost.* Techny, Ill.: Mission Press S.V.D.

Foucault, Michel
1973   *The Order of Things: An Archaeology of the Human Sciences.* New York: Vintage Books.

Francis, E. K.
1950   Toward a Typology of Religious Orders. *American Journal of Sociology* 55:437–49.

Franks, James
1969   Threshold of Self-Government. *The Word in the World, 1969. New Guinea: A Report on the Missionary Apostolate,* 25–28. Techny, Ill.: Divine Word Publications.

Frerichs, A. C.
1957   *Anutu Conquers in New Guinea: A Story of Seventy Years of Mission Work in New Guinea.* Columbus, Ohio: The Wartburg Press.

Fussell, Paul
1975   *The Great War and Modern Memory.* London: Oxford University Press.

Geertz, Clifford
1968   Thinking as a Moral Act: Ethical Dimensions of Anthropological Fieldwork in the New States. *The Antioch Review* 28:139–158.

Gerstner, Andreas
1951   Die Handflügler in Glauben und Brauch der Wewäk-Boiken-Leute Neuguineas. *Anthropos* 46:418–30.

1952a   Der Geisterglaube im Wewäk-Boiken-Gebiet Nordost-Neuguineas. *Anthropos* 47:795–821.

1952b   Jagdgebräuche der Wewäk-Boiken Leute in Nordost-Neuguinea. *Anthropos* 47:177–192.

1953   Aus dem Gemeinschaftsleben der Wewäk-Boiken-Leute, Nordost Neuguinea. *Anthropos* 48:413–57, 795–808.

1954–55   Die glaubensmässige Einstellung der Wewäk-Boiken Leute zu den Krankheiten und deren Heilung (Nordost-Neuguinea). *Anthropos* 49 (1954):460–480; 50 (1955): 319–336.

1958   Jagdgebräuche der Wewäk-Boikin-Leute in Nordost-Neuguinea (Nachtrag zu Anthropos 46, 1951:418–430). Einladung von Fliegenden Hunden. *Anthropos* 53:268–269.

1963   Der Magische Meuchelmord im Wewäk-Boikin-Gebiet (Nordost-Neuguinea). *Anthropos* 58:719–736.

Gerth, H. H. and C. Wright Mills
1958   *From Max Weber: Essays in Sociology.* New York: Oxford University Press.

Gesch, Patrick F.
1985   *Initiative and Initiation: A Cargo Cult-Type Movement in the Sepik Against its Background in Traditional Village Religion.* Studia Instituti Anthropos, 33. St. Augustin: Anthropos-Institut.

Gewertz, Deborah B.
1983   *Sepik River Societies: A Historical Ethnography of the Chambri and their Neighbors.* New Haven: Yale University Press.

Gordon, Robert J.
1983   The Decline of the Kiapdom and the Resurgence of 'Tribal Fighting' in Enga. *Oceania* 53:205–223.

Gordon, Robert J. and Mervyn J. Meggitt
1985   *Law and Order in the New Guinea Highlands: Encounters with Enga.* Hanover, N.H.: University Press of New England.

Guiart, Jean
1970   The Millenarian Aspect of Conversion to Christianity in the South Pacific. In *Millennial Dreams in Action,* edited by Sylvia L. Thrupp, 122–138. New York: Schocken Books.

Hagspiel, Bruno
1926   *Along the Mission Trail.* Vol. 3, *In New Guinea.* Techny: Mission Press, S.V.D.

Harris, Marvin
1968   *The Rise of Anthropological Theory: A History of Theories of Culture.* New York: Thomas Y. Crowell Company.

Hezel, Francis X.
1978   Indigenization as a Missionary Goal in the Caroline and Marshall Islands. In *Mission, Church, and Sect in Oceania,* edited by J. A. Boutilier, D. T. Hughes, and S. W. Tiffany, 251–73. Ann Arbor: University of Michigan Press.

Hogbin, H. Ian
1935   Trading Expeditions in Northern New Guinea. *Oceania* 5:375–407.

1978   *The Leaders and the Led: Social Control in Wogeo, New Guinea.* Carlton, Victoria: Melbourne University Press.

Höltker, Georg
1940–41 Verstreute ethnographische Notizen Über Neuguinea: Eine Art Regestensammlung aus dem 'Steyler Missionsbote' 1895–1941. *Anthropos* 35–36:1–67.

1941   Die Mambu-Bewegung in Neuguinea: Ein Beitrag Zum Prophetentum in Melanesien. *Annali Lateranensi* 5:181–219.

Huber, Mary Taylor
1979a   Big Men and Partners: The Development of Urban Migrant Communities at Kreer Beach, Wewak. *Yagl-Ambu: Papua New Guinea Journal of the Social Sciences and Humanities* 6:39–49.

1979b   Placing the Priest: A Problem for Catholic Missionaries in the East Sepik Province, Papua New Guinea. Paper presented at the 1979 meeting of the American Anthropological Association, Cincinnati, Ohio.

1983   Trade and the Articulation of an Interethnic Community in Wewak. Paper presented at the 1983 meeting of the American Anthropological Association, Chicago, Illinois.

1984   War and *Bisnis* in the History of Settlement in Wewak. Paper presented at the 1984 meeting of the American Anthropological Association, Denver, Colorado.

1987   Constituting the Church: Catholic Missionaries on the Sepik Frontier. *American Ethnologist* 14:107–125.

Hudson, W. J.
1974   *New Guinea Empire.* Melbourne: Cassell Australia, Ltd.

Hymes, Dell, ed.
1969   *Reinventing Anthropology.* New York: Pantheon Books.

Jameson, Fredric R.
  1982   The Symbolic Inference; or, Kenneth Burke and Ideological Analy-
          sis. In *Representing Kenneth Burke,* edited by Hayden White and
          Margaret Brose, 68–91. Selected Papers from the English Institute,
          New Series, no. 6. Baltimore: The Johns Hopkins University Press.

Karp, Ivan
  1984   Review of Colonial Evangelism, by T. O. Beidelman. *American
          Ethnologist* 4:215–216.

Kluckhohn, Clyde
  1936   Some Reflections on the Method and Theory of the
          Kulturkreislehre. *American Anthropologist* 38:157–196.

Knight, James J.
  1982   Melanesia. In *Mission in Dialogue: The Sedos Research Seminar
          on the Future of Mission, March 8-19, 1981, Rome, Italy,* edited by
          M. Motte and J. R. Lang, 392–412. Maryknoll, N.Y.: Orbis
          Books.

Knight, Michael
  1975   The Peli Ideal: An Evaluation of the Ideology of the Peli Associa-
          tion. *Catalyst* 5:3–22.

Kunisch, Edmund
  1930–31 (Notice.) *Steyler Missionsbote* 58:68–69. (Summarized in Höltker
          1940–41: 24,25).

Laracy, Hugh
  1976   *Marists and Melanesians.* Canberra: Australian National Univer-
          sity Press.

Laumann, Karl
  1939–40 Eine Firmungsreise in den Busch. *Steyler Missionsbote* 68:120–123.

Lawrence, Peter
  1964   *Road Belong Cargo: A Study of the Cargo Movements in the
          Southern Madang District, New Guinea.* Manchester: Manchester
          University Press.

Laycock, Donald C.
  1973   *Sepik Languages: Checklist and Preliminary Classification.* Pacific
          Linguistics, Series B–No. 25. Canberra: Department of Linguistics,
          Research School of Pacific Studies, Australian National University.

Lea, D. A. M.
  1972   Sepik Districts, East and West. In *Encyclopedia of Papua New
          Guinea,* Vol. 2:1030–1036. Melbourne University Press, in associa-
          tion with the University of Papua and New Guinea.

Levine, Hal B. and Marlene Wolfzahn Levine

    1979   *Urbanization in Papua New Guinea: A Study of Ambivalent Townsmen.* Cambridge: Cambridge University Press.

Liebert, William

    1969   Launch Out into the Deep. *The Word in the World, 1969. New Guinea: A Report on the Missionary Apostolate,* 113–116. Techny, Ill.: Divine Word Publications.

Limbrock, Eberhard

    1909–10 Übersicht uber die Tätigkeit in unserer Mission von Deutsch-Neuguinea. *Steyler Missionsbote* 37: 136–138, 153–154. (Summarized in Höltker 1940–41:10).

Lommel, Andreas

    1953   'Der Cargo-Kult' in Melanesien: Ein Beitrag zum Problem der Europaisierung der Primitiven. *Zeitschrift für Ethnologie* 78:2–63.

Long, Gavin

    1963   *Australia in the War of 1939–1945.* Series 1, *Army,* Vol. 7, *The Final Campaigns.* Canberra: Australian War Memorial.

Louisson, Alma

  c. 1963 Father Andreas Gerstner, S.V.D (R.I.P.). *Wewak* (Missionary Newsletter) 1 (1):2–3.

Lutkehaus, Nancy

    1983   Introduction. In *The Life of Some Islanders of New Guinea,* by Karl Bohm, 12–70. Berlin: Deitrich Reimer Verlag.

Luzbetak, Louis J.

    1985   Prospects for a Better Understanding and Closer Cooperation Between Anthropologists and Missionaries. In *Missionaries, Anthropologists, and Cultural Change,* edited by Darrell L. Whiteman, 1–53. Studies in Third World Societies, No. 25. Williamsburg, Va.: Department of Anthropology, College of William and Mary.

McCarthy, J. K.

    1963   *Patrol into Yesterday: My New Guinea Years.* Melbourne: Cheshire Publishing Pty. Ltd.

McSwain, Romola

    1977   *The Past and Future People: Tradition and Change on a New Guinea Island.* Melbourne: Oxford University Press.

McSweeney, Bill

    1974   The Priesthood in Sociological Theory. *Social Compass* 21:5–23.

Mair, Lucy P.
　1970　*Australia in New Guinea.* Carlton, Victoria: Melbourne University
　　　　Press.

Marcus, George E.
　1980　Rhetoric and the Ethnographic Genre in Anthropological Re-
　　　　search. *Current Anthropology* 21 (4): 507–510.

Marcus, George E. and Michael M. J. Fischer, eds.
　1986　*Anthropology as Cultural Critique: An Experimental Moment in
　　　　the Human Sciences.* Chicago: University of Chicago Press.

Marshall, A. J.
　1938　*The Men and Birds of Paradise: Journeys through Equatorial New
　　　　Guinea.* London: William Heinemann Ltd.

Maude, H. E.
　1968　*Of Islands and Men: Studies in Pacific History.* Melbourne: Ox-
　　　　ford University Press.

May, Ron
　1982　The View from Hurun: The Peli Association. In *Micronationalist
　　　　Movements in Papua New Guinea,* edited by Ron May, 31–62.
　　　　Canberra: Department of Political and Social Change, Research
　　　　School of Pacific Studies, Australian National University.

Mead, Margaret
　1970　*The Mountain Arapesh,* Vol. 2: *Arts and Supernaturalism.* Garden
　　　　City, N.Y.: The Natural History Press.

　1977　*Letters from the Field 1925–1975.* New York: Harper & Row.

Mead, Sidney E.
　1956　The Rise of the Evangelical Conception of the Ministry in America
　　　　(1607–1850). In *The Ministry in Historical Perspectives,* edited by
　　　　H. R. Niebuhr and D. D. Williams, 207–249. New York: Harper
　　　　and Brothers.

Mennis, Mary T.
　1982　*Hagen Saga: The Story of Father William Ross, First American
　　　　Missionary to Papua New Guinea,* with notes and articles by Fa-
　　　　ther Ross. Boroko, PNG: Institute of Papua New Guinea Studies.

Merton, Robert K.
　1976　*Sociological Ambivalence and Other Essays.* New York: The Free
　　　　Press.

Mihalic, Francis
   1977a   On a Wing and a Prayer: Papua New Guinea's Flying Bishop. *Paradise* (In-flight magazine of Air Niugini), No. 3 (January 1977):29–30.

   1977b   Biography of Br. Joseph Czubek, SVD. Bishop's Office, Diocese of Wewak. Mimeo.

Moses, J. A.
   1969   The German Empire in Melanesia, 1884–1914: A German Self-Analysis. In *The History of Melanesia*. Second Waigani Seminar, Port Moresby, 45–76. Canberra: Australian National University.

Murphy, Patrick
   1969   Holy Spirit Regional Seminary. *The Word in the World, 1969. New Guinea: A Report on the Missionary Apostolate*, 86–91. Techny, Ill.: Divine Word Publications.

   1970   From Mission in New Guinea to Church of New Guinea. In *The Politics of Melanesia*. Fourth Waigani Seminar, Port Moresby, 681–705. Canberra: The Australian National University.

Nemer, Lawrence
   1981   *Anglican and Roman Catholic Attitudes on Missions: An Historical Study of Two English Missionary Societies in the Late Nineteenth Century (1865–1885)*. Studia Instituti Missiologici Societatis Verbi Divini, No. 29. St Augustin: Steyler Verlag.

National Statistical Office
   1982   *1980 National Population Census. Final Figures: Census Division Populations*. Port Moresby: National Statistical Office.

Noser, Adoph
   1969   Yesterday, Today and Tomorrow. *The Word in the World, 1969. New Guinea: A Report on the Missionary Apostolate*, 58–63. Techny, Ill.: Divine Word Publications.

Pacific Islands Monthly
   1932   Outbreak of Religious Mania in New Guinea. *Pacific Islands Monthly* Dec. 20, 1932: 46.

   1948   Notes from Wewak. *Pacific Islands Monthly* 18 (May): 78.

   1955a   Wewak-Maprik Road. *Pacific Islands Monthly* 25 (May):39.

   1955b   Opening Up NG's Sepik District. *Pacific Islands Monthly* 25 (June):141.

   1956a   Trucked Across. *Pacific Islands Monthly* 27 (Sept):53.

   1956b   Economic Strength of Papua and New Guinea. *Pacific Islands Monthly* 27 (Nov):49-51.

Parratt, J. K.
1975   Religion and the Migrant to Port Moresby. *Missiology* 3:177–189.

Paul VI
1967   *Populorum Progressio.* In *The Gospel of Peace and Justice: Catholic Social Teaching since Pope John,* edited by Joseph Gremillion, 387-415. Maryknoll, N.Y.: Orbis Books, 1976.

Petersen, Glenn T.
1980   Comment on "Anthropologists versus Missionaries: The Influence of Presuppositions," by Claude E. Stipe. *Current Anthropology* 21: 173.

Pöhl, Rudolph
1977   *Der Missionar zwischen Ordensleben und Missionarischen Auftrag.* Studia Instituti Missiologici Societatis Verbi Divini, No. 18. St. Augustin: Steyler Verlag.

Puff, Andreas
1912–13 Der Tapelzauber. *Steyler Missionsbote* 40:186–188. (Summarized in Höltker 1940–41:15).

Pung, Robert
1968   A Fitting Anniversary. *The Word in the World, 1968,* 177–180. Techny, Ill.: Divine Word Publications.

Ranger, Terence
1987   An Africanist Comment. *American Ethnologist* 14:182–185.

Reed, Stephen Winsor
1943   *The Making of Modern New Guinea.* Philadelphia: The American Philosophical Society.

Rosaldo, Renato I.
1978   The Rhetoric of Control: Ilongots Viewed as Natural Bandits and Wild Indians. In *The Reversible World: Symbolic Inversion in Art and Society,* edited by Barbara Babcock, 240–57. Ithaca: Cornell University Press.

Roscoe, Paul B.
1981–82 The Path to Hurun: A History of the Yangoru Subdistrict. Typescript.

1983   The Ethnohistories of Business in the Yangoru Subdistrict, East Sepik Province, Papua New Guinea. Paper prepared for the 1983 ASAO Working Session, "Ethnohistory in Oceania."

Roscoe, Paul B. and Richard Scaglion
 1984   Male Initiation and European Intrusion in the Sepik. Paper pre-
        pared for Wenner-Gren symposium no. 95. "Sepik Research Today."
        (In press)

Ross, William A.
 1969   The Catholic Mission in the Western Highlands. In *History of
        Melanesia*. Second Waigani Seminar, Port Moresby, 319–327. Can-
        berra: Australian National University Press.

Rowley, C. D.
 1958   *The Australians in German New Guinea, 1914–1921*. Melbourne:
        Melbourne University Press.

 1965   *The New Guinea Villager: The Impact of Colonial Rule on Primi-
        tive Society and Economy*. New York: Frederick A. Praeger.

Ruiter, Ivo J.
 1969   Airborne Apostles. *The Word in the World, 1969. New Guinea: A
        Report on the Missionary Apostolate*, 117–118. Techny, Ill.: Divine
        Word Publications.

 1976   Wirui Services Story. Unpublished transcript. Bishop's Office, Dio-
        cese of Wewak. Mimeo. (Reproduced in Appendix A)

Sack, Peter G.
 1973   *Land Between Two Laws: Early European Land Acquisitions in
        New Guinea*. Canberra: Australian National University Press.

Sack, P. and Clark, D.
 1979   *German New Guinea: The Annual Reports*. Canberra: Australian
        National University Press.

Sahlins, Marshall
 1972   *Stone Age Economics*. Chicago: Aldine Publishing Company.

 1981   *Historical Metaphors and Mythical Realities: Structure in the
        Early History of Sandwich Island Kingdoms*. Ann Arbor: Univer-
        sity of Michigan Press.

 1983   Other Times, Other Customs: The Anthropology of History.
        American Anthropologist 85: 517–44.

 1985   *Islands of History*. Chicago: University of Chicago Press.

Salamone, Frank A.
 1977   Anthropologists and Missionaries: Competition or Reciprocity?
        Human Organization 36: 407–412.

Scaglion, Richard
1983   The 'Coming' of Independence in Papua New Guinea: An Abelam
        View. *The Journal of the Polynesian Society* 92: 463–486.

Schmidlin, Joseph
1913   *Die katholischen Missionen in den deutschen Schutzgebieten.*
        Munster in Westfalen: Aschendorffsche Verlagsbuchhandlung.

1931   *Catholic Mission Theory.* Techny, Ill.: Mission Press, SVD.

1933   *Catholic Mission History.* Techny, Ill.: Mission Press, SVD.

Schneider, Jane and Shirley Lindenbaum
1987   Frontiers of Christian Evangelism: Essays in Honor of Joyce
        Riegelhaupt. *American Ethnologist* 14:1–8.

Schwab, Ignaz
1935–36 Ein 'Versehgang.' *Steyler Missionsbote* 63:320–321. (Summarized in
        Höltker 1940–41:42).

1937–38 Die Koch des Teufels. *Steyler Missionsbote* 65:236–237. (Summa-
        rized in Höltker 1940–41:42–43).

Siefert, William
1978   Can we enter the urban church through a different door? *Catalyst*
        8:23–32.

Simmel, Georg
1950   The Stranger. In *The Sociology of Georg Simmel,* edited by Kurt
        H. Wolff, 402–408. New York: The Free Press.

Smart, John
1967   Christian Missions in Many Lands, Ltd. In *The Encyclopedia of
        Modern Christian Missions: The Agencies,* 140–154. Camden,
        New Jersey: Thomas Nelson & Sons.

Smith, Michael French
1978   Good Men Face Hard Times in Koragur: Ideology and Social
        Change in a New Guinea Village. Ph.D. diss., University of Cali-
        fornia, San Diego.

1980   From Heathen to Atheist: Changing Views of Catholicism in a
        New Guinea Village. *Oceania* 51: 40–52.

1982a   Bloody Time and Bloody Scarcity: Capitalism, Authority, and the
        Transformation of Temporal Experience in a Papua New Guinea
        Village. *American Ethnologist* 9:503–518.

1982b   The Catholic Ethnic and the Spirit of Alcohol Use in an East Sepik
        Province Village. In *Through a Glass Darkly: Beer and Moderniza-*

tion in Papua New Guinea, edited by Mac Marshall, 271–288. IASER Monograph 18. Boroko, PNG: Institute of Applied Social and Economic Research.

1987   Catholicism, Capitalist Incorporation, and Resistance in Kragur Village. Paper prepared for Annual Meeting of Association for Social Anthropology in Oceania, Monterey, California, February 18–22, 1987.

Somare, Michael
1975a   *Sana: An Autobiography of Michael Somare.* Port Moresby: Niugini Press Pty., Ltd.

1975b   Address to the Graduating Class of St. Benedict's Teachers College, Wewak 1975. Tape Recording. Diocese of Wewak: Radio Broadcasting Office.

Sperber, Dan and Dierdre Wilson
1981   Irony and the Use-Mention Distinction. In *Radical Pragmatics,* edited by Peter Cole. New York: Academic Press.

Sperber, Jonathan
1984   *Popular Catholicism in Nineteenth-Century Germany.* Princeton, N.J.: Princeton University Press.

Sterr, Josef
1950   *Zwischen Geisterhaus und Kathedrale: Unter Steinzeit-Menschender Südsee.* Modling bei Wien: St. Gabriel Verlag.

Steinbauer, Friedrich
1971   *Melanesische Cargo-Kulte: Neureligiöse Heilsbewegungen in der Südsee.* München: Delp.

Stipe, Claude E.
1980   Anthropologists versus Missionaries: The Influence of Presuppositions. *Current Anthropology* 21: 165–179.

Strayer, Robert W.
1978   *The Making of Mission Communities in East Africa: Anglicans and Africans in Colonial Kenya, 1875–1935.* Albany, N.Y.: State University of New York Press.

Sturgeon, Charles H.
1942   Aitape and its Hinterland. In *The Pacific Islands Yearbook, 1942,* edited by R. W. Robson, 309–310. Sydney: Pacific Publications Pty. Ltd.

Tangugo Pastoral Center
1976   The Opening of Tangugo Pastoral Center, Wewak 1976. Tape Recording. Diocese of Wewak: Radio Broadcasting Office.

Taylor, Lawrence J.
   1985   The Priest and the Agent: Social Drama and Class Consciousness
            in the West of Ireland. *Comparative Studies in Society and History*
            27:696–712.

Thomas, Gordon
   1935   A Plea for Better Regulation of Mission Activities in New Guinea.
            Pacific Islands Monthly, Nov. 20, 1935:25–26.

Thurnwald, R.
   1914   Vom Mittleren Sepik zur Nordwestküste von Kaiser Wilhelmsland.
            Mitteilungen aus den Deutshen Schutzgebieten 27: 81–84. Berlin.

Tiesler, Frank
   1969–70 *Die intertribalen Beziehungen an der Nordküste Neuguineas im
            Gebiet der Kleinen Schouten-Inseln.* Abhandlungen und Berichte
            des Staatlichen Museums für Völkerkunde Dresden, Vols. 30, 31.
            Berlin: Akademie-Verlag.

Tonkinson, Robert
   1974   *The Jigalong Mob: Aboriginal Victors of the Desert Crusade.*
            Menlo Park, Calif.: Cummings Publishing Co.

Townsend, G. W. L.
   1968   *District Officer: From Untamed New Guinea to Lake Success,
            1921–46.* Sydney: Pacific Publications.

Troeltsch, Ernst
   1981   *The Social Teaching of the Christian Churches.* Vol. 1 Chicago:
            The University of Chicago Press.

Tuzin, Donald F.
   1976   *The Ilahita Arapesh: Dimensions of Unity.* Berkeley: University of
            California Press.

Wagner, Roy
   1981   *The Invention of Culture.* Chicago: University of Chicago Press.

Wantok (Newspaper)
   1974   Ting Ting Bek (Four stories). Ami bilong Japan i kam long Wewak,
            No. 100 (18 Sept. 1974):16, Soldia Kilim ol Misinari, No. 101 (2
            Oct. 1974):12; Stori namba tri, No. 102 (16 Oct. 1974):16 Mipela i
            Fri, No. 103 (6 Nov. 1974):13.

Ward, R. Gerard and J. A. Ballard
   1976   In Their Own Image: Australia's Impact on Papua New Guinea
            and Lessons for Future Aid. *Australian Outlook* 30:439–458.

Weber, Max
  1963   *The Sociology of Religion.* Boston: Beacon Press.

White, Hayden.
  1973   *Metahistory: The Historical Imagination in Nineteenth Century Europe.* Baltimore: The Johns Hopkins University Press.

Wiltgen, Ralph M.
  1969a   Catholic Mission Plantations in Mainland New Guinea: Their Origin and Purpose. In *History of Melanesia.* Second Waigani Seminar, Port Moresby, 329–362. Canberra: Australian National University Press.

  1969b   A Difficult Mission. *The Word in the World. 1969. New Guinea: A Report on the Missionary Apostolate,* 9–24. Techny, Ill.: Divine Word Publications.

Winslow, F. J.
  1967a   Prefect Apostolic. *New Catholic Encyclopedia.* Vol. 11: 727. New York: McGraw Hill Book Co.

  1967b   Vicar Apostolic. *New Catholic Encyclopedia* Vol. 14: 638–639. New York: McGraw Hill Book Co.

Wolf, Eric R.
  1982   *Europe and the People Without History.* Berkeley: University of California Press.

Worsley, Peter
  1957   *The Trumpet Shall Sound: A Study of "Cargo" Cults in Melanesia.* London: MacGibbon & Kee.

WPR
  1945–46 *Wewak Patrol Report No. 1, 1945–46.* District Office, Wewak.

  1949–50 *Wewak Patrol Report No. 1, 1949–50.* District Office, Wewak.

  1952–53 *Wewak Patrol Report No. 2, 1952–53.* District Office, Wewak.

  1958–59 *Wewak Patrol Report No. 1, 1958–59.* District Office, Wewak.

Index

Ethnography, 4–9, 85
Ethnology, 3, 86, 126
Evangelism, 8, 20, 48, 71, 84, 210
Expatriates, 12, 13, 21, 27, 145, 172, 186, 211

Falding, Harold, 6–7
Farming, 28, 54, 70, 77
Fasting, 57
Fathers. *See* Priests
Feathered bishop, 166, 208. *See also* Arkfeld, Leo
Feinberg, Captain D.M., 134–35
Fellowship structures, 15, 173
Fernandez, James W., 5, 8
Fieldwork. *See* Anthropology
Fighting bishop, 1, 100–102, 131. *See also* Loerks, Joseph
Finsch, Otto, 35, 108
Finschhafen, 28, 29, 30
Firth, Stewart, 39, 40, 110
Fischer, Michael, 8
Fishing, 33
Flierl, Johann, 17
Flying bishop, 1, 14, 22, 138, 143, 164, 165, 207. *See also* Arkfeld, Leo; Imagery, *s.v.* episcopal
Fortune, Reo, 50
Four Black Kings, 120, 121, 122, 123, 127–30
Francis, E.K., 56
Franciscans, 158, 161, 213–14; Australian, 147; Dutch, 140
Friedrich Wilhelmshafen (Madang), 36, 37, 45, 62, 64, 65, 68, 77, 93, 110
Friends of Wewak, 141
Frontier: colonial, 25–74, 47; cultural, 144, 170; ecclesiastical, 21, 168, 203; economic, 66; labor, 146; life, 50–51; mission, 138, 199; society, 48–54
Fussell, Paul, 205

Gabriel, 76–77, 77, 100, 101, 114, 117, 138, 144, 190
Garankom, 121
Gazelle Peninsula, 27
Geertz, Clifford, 5, 8–9
Gemeinshaft, 56
German: colonial administration,

27–31, 35, 37–38, 38–42, 45, 108; colonists under Australian rule, 43–44; culture, 110; business firms, 27; language, 15, 84, 87, 103, 110; New Guinea, 26 (fig. 3)
Gerstner, Andreas, 112, 114, 151–152, 153, 190
Gesch, Patrick, 118, 120, 154, 155
Gesellschaft, 56
Gibbes Sepik Airways, 141
Gier, William, 76, 114
Gilroy, Cardinal, 143
God Father Movement, 128
Godeffroys, 27
Gold, 25, 35, 44, 45, 130, 146, 152; prospectors, 45
Gonzaga (Brother Gonzaga Schneidengers), 160
Gordon, Robert, 188, 211
Goroka, diocese of, 19, 161
Government officers (*kiaps*), 44, 45, 48, 51, 53, 101, 118, 124, 157
Graebner, Fritz, 86
Groton, John C., 171

Hagspiel, Bruno, 22, 70, 76–103 *passim,* 114, 143, 147, 201
Hahl, Albert, 39, 40, 41, 65, 70, 73, 110
Hansemann, Adolph von, 28, 29
Hasluck, Paul, 162, 165, 170, 171, 172
Hatzfeldhafen, 29
Head tax. *See* taxation
Headhunting, 84, 88–89, 122
Health, 21, 146, 164. *See also* Medical care
Hemel, Constantine van den, 112
Herbertshohe, 30, 45
Hernsheims, 27
Hesse (Father), 115
Hezel, Francis X., 169, 170
Hierarchy. *See* Church organization
Hirohito, Emperor of Japan, 133
Historiography, 4, 16–20, 25, 35; mission, 95, 97, 100
History, views of, 5, 16–20, 86
Hitler, Adolph, 130
Hogbin, Ian, 11
Hollandia, 131

Limbrock, Eberhard: death of, 98; farming system of, 54; and the frontier, 66; and the material base, 54–72; and mission's plantation system, 14; report on mission, 100; resignation of, 71; *mentioned*, 1, 47–48, 62, 73, 76, 77, 78, 92, 99, 110, 147, 168, 201, 208, 209
Linguistic diversity, 67
Livestock, 28, 67, 70, 88, 124, 163, 165
Local efficacy, 144, 189
Localism, 163. *See also* Catholic mission (Sepik region): services of
Localization, 22, 165–66, 167–68, 171, 172, 202
Loerks, Joseph, 1, 14, 100–102, 138, 145, 159, 206; death of, 131
Lommel, Andreas, 120
London Missionary Society, 201
Luecker, P., 64
Luluais, 40, 111, 117, 118, 152, 153
Lutheran mission: 16–17, 66, 68, 77, 131, 202; American Lutheran Church, 17; Evangelical Lutheran Church of New Guinea (ELCONG), 16, 201; Lutheran World Federation, 17; Neuendettelsau, 17; Rheinische Mission Society, 66
Lutkehaus, Nancy, 99

McCarthy, J.K., 49–50
Macgregor, William, 93
McSwain, Romola, 47
McSweeney, Bill, 194
Madang: area, 31, 143; district, 15, 19, 47, 128, 161; province, 23, 149; town, 32, 36, 39, 42, 45, 50, 69, 99, 125, 135
Magic, 89, 126. *See also* Sorcery
Mair, Lucy, 45
MAL (Mandated Airlines), 141
Malays, 35, 38
Malinowski, Bronislaw, 3
Malol, 81
Mambu: movement, 23, 108, 120, 123, 129, 152; prophet, 123–7, 128
"Man of Providence," 1, 74, 100, 208. *See also* Limbrock, Eberhard

Manam Island, 31, 78, 211
Manning, Cardinal, 143
Manus Island, 40, 131
Maprik, 45, 147, 162, 195
Marcus, George, 4, 8
Marienberg, 32, 43, 88, 157, 160, 175
Marists, 61, 169–70, 181–84
Markets, 52, 152. *See also* Development, economic; Plantation economy; Trade
Marshall, A.J., 53, 102
Mass, 185
Matapau, 117
Material base. *See* Limbrock, Eberhard: and the material base; Catholic mission (Sepik region), *s.v.* material base of
Material work, 22, 54–56, 59, 67–68, 70, 75, 86, 103, 104, 156, 201, 207
Matupi, 27
Maude, H.E., 49
Mead, Margaret, 50–51, 53, 113, 120, 122
Mead, Sidney, 201, 202, 206
Medical care 5, 66, 125, 142, 164, 181, 187. *See also* Health; Hospitals
Melanesian Institute, 193
Metaphor, 4, 142, 212
Methodists, 27, 201
Metonymy, 4, 142, 212
Michaelius, Jonas, 201
Migrant settlements, 11, 152
Migration, urban, 163
Mihalic, Francis, 138–143 *passim,* 156, 159, 164, 208, 209
Mill Hill Society, 57, 58
Mingende, 98
Ministry, 87, 137, 196. *See also* Catholic mission (Sepik region); Spiritual work
Missiology, 15, 55, 126, 169
Missionaries: anthropologists' view of, 2–9 *passim;* goals of, 15–21; moral stance of, 3, 4, 6, 84; relations with native people, 3, 10, 11, 108; stories about, 2, 10; *mentioned*, 4, 6, 16, 48, 55
Missionary means, hierarchy of, 55–56, 68

Mission: churches, 10, 16, 78; development, models of, 16–19; publishing, 60, 61, 85; -sending societies, 56, 58, 95. *See also* Religious orders
Mission Hill, 157
Moagende, 121
Moem, 112, 152
Moities, 112, 115
Montoro, 50, 51
Monumbo, 78, 80
Mormon, Wilbert, 154–55
Mormon-Godfrey movement, 154–55
Morobe, 40, 42, 44, 45, 130
Mountains: Bewani, 32; Bismarck, 99; Mt. Hagen, 98; Mt. Turu, 32, 140; Prince Alexander, 32, 41, 112; Torricelli, 32, 33, 38, 41, 90
Mt. Hagen, diocese of, 161
Mugil, 121
Mundugumor, 50
Murik: area, 151, 157; Lakes, 31, 117, 151
Murphy, Patrick, 176–79
Museums, 85, 86
Mushu Island, 65, 109, 111

Nationalism, 170–71
Native policy, Hahl's, 40
Negrie, 120
Nemer, Lawrence, 57, 58
Neu Guinea Compagnie, 26–30, 36–40 *passim*, 48, 62, 64, 66, 68, 72, 109; settlement scheme of, 28–29, 35
New Britain, 27, 62, 171
New Caledonia, 9
New Ireland, 27, 40
Norddeutscher Lloyd, 37, 38, 45, 68, 69
Noser, Adolph, 19, 158–59, 161
Nuigo, 193, 194

Occupational code, 48–54, 73
Oil, 45, 46
Oneputa, 88
Organic solidarity, model of, 48

Pacification, 45, 110
Pacific model, 26, 27, 30
Papua, 44, 50, 93, 140, 145

Papua New Guinea, 150, 165, 168, 170, 193
Pastoral Training Center, 191, 197–98
Paternalism, 187
Patrols, 52–53, 118, 124, 150
Pawa, 164, 197
Peanuts, 150, 163, 193
Peligo, 152
Peli Movement, 155, 156, 164
Pidgin, New Guinea, 11, 84, 103, 118, 126, 161, 185, 205
Pigs, 124, 196
Pioneer period, 14, 199
Pious Work for the Propagation of the Faith, 62
Pius XII, Pope, 173
Plantation economy, 26–31, 34–35, 37, 40, 109
Plantations, 25, 45, 52, 62, 64, 77, 80, 90, 110, 144; indigenous, 150, 152; Limbrock's system of, 1, 14, 55, 56, 65, 68, 76, 88
Planters, colonial, 26, 45, 48, 52, 59, 108
Pöhl, Rudolph, 57
Police, 110, 116, 118, 150, 151, 152
Polygamy, 154, 155, 156
Port Moresby, 140, 164, 171
Poverty, vow of, 174, 196, 212
Power, 176; pastoral, 194–98, 203; political, 172. *See also Pawa*
Prayers, 55, 175
Prefecture apostolic, 18, 19, 92, 94
Prefiguration, 4
Priests, 12, 13, 22, 27, 53, 56, 57, 59, 61, 62, 72, 73, 76, 78, 80, 84, 90, 105, 132, 156, 160, 182, 184, 186, 203. *See also* Clergy
Procurator, 71, 130
Progress, ecclesiastical: 16, 18, 97, 99, 158, 199. *See also* History, views of
Propaganda Fide, 20, 58, 73, 97
Prophets, 121, 127, 128, 129, 130, 203
Puff, Andreas, 72–73

Rabaul, 37, 49–52 *passim*, 72, 94, 123, 130, 131
Rabisman, 174
Racism, 187

Shells, 27, 109
Shipping, 45, 52, 100, 145
Ships, 21, 39, 50, 66, 68, 76, 131, 147
Siefert, William, 193
Silverman, Martin, 54
Simogun, Pita, 149–153 *passim*
Sissano, 51, 76
Sisters, 12, 13, 57, 59, 62, 73, 78, 80, 90, 115, 116, 131, 132, 173. *See also* Religious orders
Slit-gongs, 88, 113
Smith, Michael, 191
Social: distance, 6, 202, 203–204; ideology, 47
Society of the Divine Word (SVD): and anthropology, 13; expansion of, 36, 60, 61–72; founding of, 63; organization of, 56–61
Somare, Michael, 150, 167, 168, 172, 209
Sorcery, 33, 84, 89, 118, 122, 143, 151, 155, 156
Spellman, Cardinal Francis, 135
Spirit cult, 89, 112, 113, 121, 151. *See also* Religion, indigenous; Tambaran cult
Spiritual work, 22, 54, 55, 56, 59, 62, 63, 67–68, 70, 75, 82, 84, 86, 90, 92, 93, 103, 104, 138, 156, 157, 194, 201, 207
Sports clubs, 163, 165
Steinbauer, Friedrich, 120
Stella Maris, 121
Steyl, 63, 70
Steyler Missionsbote, 99, 102, 120, 122, 127, 128
Stories: aviation, 139–141; missionary, 2–4, 10, 200, 205; *mentioned,* 14, 115, 126
Strayer, Robert, 21
Sturgeon, Charles H. 45, 46
Suain, 121, 128
Summer Institute of Linguistics, 9
Superior General, 36, 37, 57, 58, 65, 71, 76, 80, 92, 96, 114
Supernatural, 84, 87, 130
Surveying, 61
Syncretism, 186
Synechdoche, 4, 142

Tambaran cult, 91, 167. *See also* Religion, indigenous; Spirit cult
Tambari, 121
Tangu, 123, 125, 211
Taxation, 40, 118, 121, 124, 127, 129
Taylor, Lawrence, 195
Technical ministries, 156–65, 207
Technology, 56, 60–61, 70, 77, 147, 157, 163. *See also* Science
Telefomin, 143
Theology, mission, 169. *See also* Missiology
Thomas (Bishop), 143
Thurnwald, Richard, 41–42
Tiesler, Frank, 85
Timbunke, 99
Time. *See* History, views of
Tobacco, 26, 29, 30
Tonkinson, Robert, 6
Townsend, G.W.L., 45, 51–52, 101–102, 116, 130, 206
Trade: colonial, 27, 36, 38, 145; indigenous, 27, 33–34, 38, 113; stores, 10, 109, 162. *See also* Development, economic; Markets; Plantation economy
Tradition, 21, 74, 140, 156, 185. *See also* Kastam
Tranell, Wilhelm, 123
Transcendence, 5
Transportation, 164, 187
Trepang, 27, 109
Triangle: colonial, 22, 108, 114, 119, 126, 128, 130, 132, 211; postwar, 135, 138, 148, 163
Troeltsch, Ernst, 20
Truman, Harry S, 135
Tsepa, 88
Tultuls, 40, 111, 117, 153
Tumleo Island, 36, 37, 50, 64, 68, 69, 80, 81, 84, 89, 100, 168
Turner, Frederick Jackson, 48
Turubu, 99
Tuzin, Donald, 41

Ulau, 90
Uligan, 122, 123
Umboi Island, 62